Marginalized Masc

Across Europe we are witnessing a series of events that are drawing upon representations of men and masculinity that are rupturing the social fabric of everyday life. For example, media reports of social unrest, misogynous hate crime, religious extremism, drug trafficking and political Far Right mobilization have often been at the centre of the discussion the figure of the apathetic, disenchanted, socially excluded young man.

Marginalized Masculinities explores how men in precarious positions in different countries and social contexts understand and experience their masculinities, focusing on men who are viewed as being marginal in a range of fields in society including the family, work, the media and school. By focusing on atypical or marginal masculinities in each subfield, Haywood and Johansson provide an informed understanding of what it means to experience marginalization. Indeed, within this enlightening volume the chapters engage with the issue of whether it is necessary to name 'a' dominant masculinity in order to make sense of and understand the nature of marginalized masculinity.

This insightful title will be of interest to researchers, undergraduates and postgraduates interested in fields such as Gender Studies, International Studies, Comparative Studies and Men Studies.

Chris Haywood, PhD, is a Senior Lecturer in Media and Cultural Studies at Newcastle University, UK.

Professor Thomas Johansson is a Professor of Pedagogy specializing in Child and Youth Studies at the University of Gothenburg, Sweden.

Routledge Research in Gender and Society

46 **Masculinities and Femininities in Latin America's Uneven Development**
Susan Paulson

47 **Gender, Nutrition, and the Human Right to Adequate Food**
Toward an Inclusive Framework
Edited by Anne C. Bellows, Flavio L.S. Valente, Stefanie Lemke, and María Daniela Núñez Burbano de Lara

48 **Teaching Women's Studies in Conservative Contexts**
Considering Perspectives for an Inclusive Dialogue
Edited by Cantice Greene

49 **Ageing, Gender and Sexuality**
Equality in Later Life
Sue Westwood

50 **Gendering the Memory of Work**
Women Workers' Narratives
Maria Tamboukou

51 **Men's Intrusion, Women's Embodiment**
A Critical Analysis of Street Harassment
Fiona Vera Gray

52 **Neoliberal Bodies and the Gendered Fat Body**
Hannele S. Harjunen

53 **Women's Magazines in Print and New Media**
Edited by Noliwe Rooks, Victoria Rose Pass and Ayana K. Weekley

54 **Changing Names and Gendering Identity**
Social Organisation in Contemporary Britain
Rachel Thwaites

55 **Genealogies and Conceptual Belonging**
Zones of Interference between Gender and Diversity
Eike Marten

56 **Black Women, Agency, and the New Black Feminism**
Maria del Guadalupe Davidson

57 **Marginalized Masculinities**
Contexts, Continuities and Change
Edited by Chris Haywood and Thomas Johansson

Marginalized Masculinities
Contexts, Continuities and Change

Edited by Chris Haywood and
Thomas Johansson

LONDON AND NEW YORK

First published 2017
by Routledge

2 Park Square, Milton Park, Abingdon, Oxfordshire OX14 4RN
52 Vanderbilt Avenue, New York, NY 10017

Routledge is an imprint of the Taylor & Francis Group, an informa business

First issued in paperback 2019

Copyright © 2017 selection and editorial matter, Chris Haywood and Thomas Johansson; individual chapters, the contributors

The right of Chris Haywood and Thomas Johansson to be identified as the authors of the editorial matter, and of the authors for their individual chapters, has been asserted in accordance with sections 77 and 78 of the Copyright, Designs and Patents Act 1988.

All rights reserved. No part of this book may be reprinted or reproduced or utilised in any form or by any electronic, mechanical, or other means, now known or hereafter invented, including photocopying and recording, or in any information storage or retrieval system, without permission in writing from the publishers.

Notice:
Product or corporate names may be trademarks or registered trademarks, and are used only for identification and explanation without intent to infringe.

Library of Congress Cataloging in Publication Data
Names: Haywood, Chris (Christian), 1970– editor. | Johansson, Thomas, 1959– editor.
Title: Marginalized masculinities : contexts, continuities and change / [edited by] Chris Haywood and Thomas Johansson.
Description: Abingdon, Oxon ; New York, NY : Routledge, 2017. | Series: Routledge research in gender and society ; 57 | Includes bibliographical references and index.
Identifiers: LCCN 2016046346 | ISBN 9780415347570 (hardback)
Subjects: LCSH: Masculinity–Europe. | Men–Europe–Social conditions.
Classification: LCC HQ1090.7.E85 M36 2017 | DDC 305.31094–dc23
LC record available at https://lccn.loc.gov/2016046346

ISBN: 978-0-415-34757-0 (hbk)
ISBN: 978-0-367-45979-6 (pbk)

Typeset in Times New Roman
by Wearset Ltd, Boldon, Tyne and Wear

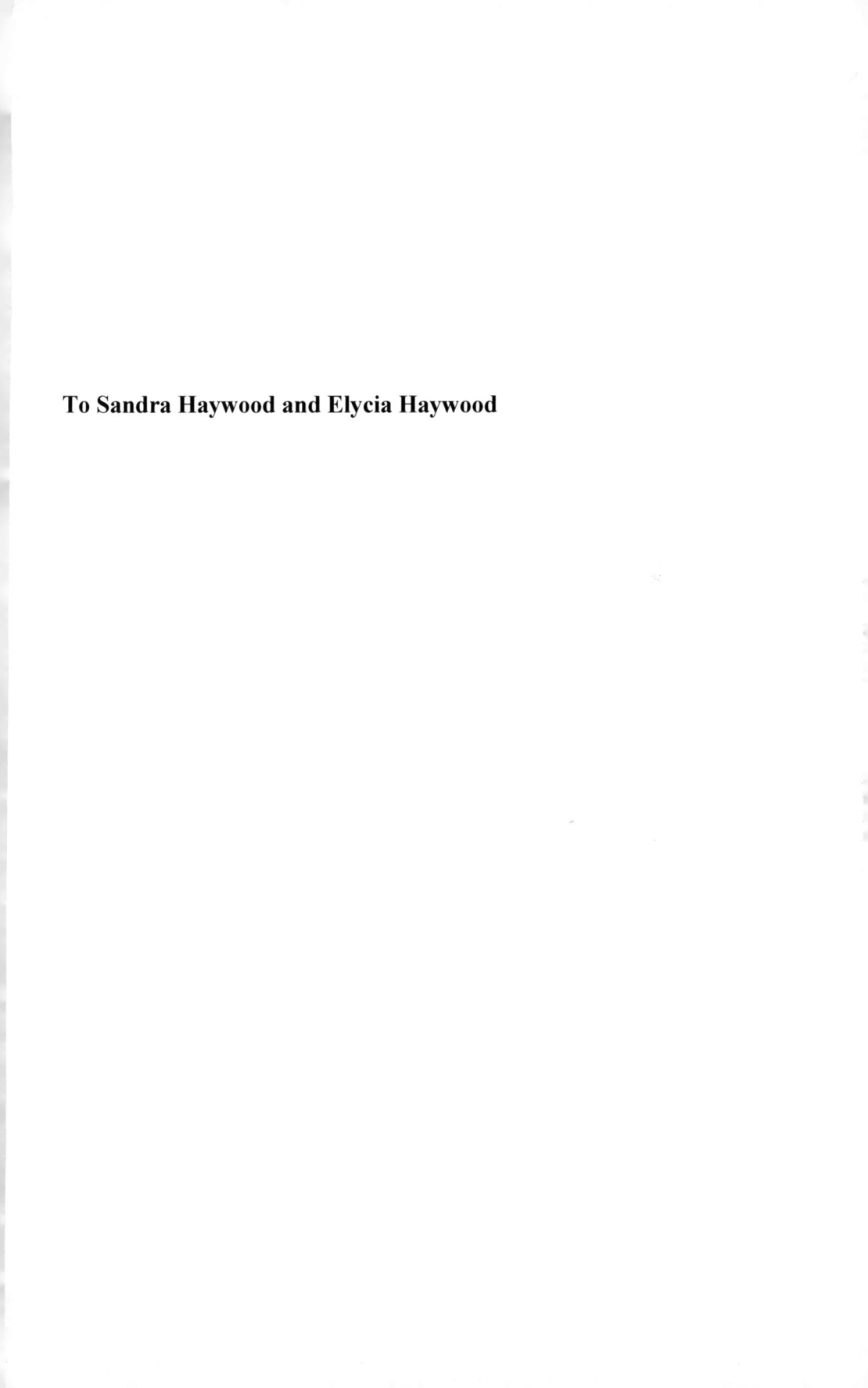

To Sandra Haywood and Elycia Haywood

Contents

List of Illustrations ix
Notes on Contributors x

Introduction 1
CHRIS HAYWOOD AND THOMAS JOHANSSON

PART I
Crisis, Risk and Socialization 19

1 Becoming a "Real Boy": Constructions of Boyness in Early Childhood Education 21
ANETTE HELLMAN AND YLVA ODENBRING

2 Being at Risk or Being a Risk? Marginalized Masculinity in Contemporary Social Work 34
MARCUS HERZ

PART II
Transformations of Work and Unemployment 49

3 'Crack in the Ice': Marginalization of Young Men in Contemporary Urban Greenland 51
FIROUZ GAINI

4 Marginalized Masculinities and Exclusion in the New Low-Skill Service Sector in Sweden 67
PETER HÅKANSSON

viii Contents

5 Masculinity, Socio-emotional Skills and Marginalization
   Amongst Emergency Medical Technicians   83
   MORTEN KYED

6 Male Migrant Workers and the Negotiation of
   'Marginalized' Masculinities in Urban China   103
   XIAODONG LIN

PART III
Marginalization, Bodies and Identity   115

7 Derailed Self-constructions: Marginalization and
   Self-construction in Young Boys' Accounts of Well-being   117
   NIELS ULRIK SØRENSEN AND JENS CHRISTIAN NIELSEN

8 Doped Manhood: Negotiating Fitness Doping and
   Masculinity in an Online Community   139
   JESPER ANDREASSON AND THOMAS JOHANSSON

PART IV
Rethinking Marginalization   155

9 Epistemologies of Difference: Masculinity, Marginalisation
   and Young British Muslim Men   157
   MAIRTIN MAC AN GHAILL AND CHRIS HAYWOOD

10 Marginalized Adult Ethnic Minority Men in Denmark:
    The Case of Aalborg East   170
    ANN-DORTE CHRISTENSEN, JEPPE FUGLSANG LARSEN AND
    SUNE QVOTRUP JENSEN

    Conclusion   188
    THOMAS JOHANSSON AND CHRIS HAYWOOD

    Index   195

Illustrations

Figures

2.1	Over-mortality among men in Sweden, 2014 per year at time of death	37
4.1	Number of men and women employed within metal, machinery and related trades work in Sweden. Year 2001–2013	69
4.2	Men in low-skill occupations within retail, hotel/restaurants and care in relation to women. Year 2005–2013	73
4.3	Significant differences in probability between women with secondary resp. tertiary education working in hotel/restaurants resp. care *compared to women with primary education*	76
4.4	Significant differences in probability between men with secondary resp. tertiary education working in hotel/restaurants resp. care *compared to men with primary education*	76
4.5	Significant differences in probability between men/women with *both* parents brought up outside of the Nordic countries working in hotel/restaurants resp. care *compared to men/women with at least one parent brought up in the Nordic countries*	77
4.6	Significant differences in probability between women in urban locations working in hotel/restaurants resp. care *compared to women in rural location*	78
4.7	Significant differences in probability between men in urban locations working in hotel/restaurants resp. care *compared to men in rural locations*	78

Table

4.1	High-touch jobs (retail, hotel/restaurant, care) and other jobs in Sweden 2007–2013 in the sample Riks-SOM 2007–2013	75

Contributors

Jesper Andreasson has a PhD in Sociology and is Associate Professor of Sport Science at the Department of Sport Science, Linnaeus University, Sweden. He has written mainly in the fields of Gender Studies, Cultural Sociology, and gym/fitness culture. Recently he published *The Global Gym: Gender, Health and Pedagogies* with Thomas Johansson (Palgrave Macmillan, 2014).

Ann-Dorte Christensen is a professor of Sociology and Director of CeMAS, Centre for Masculinity Studies, Department for Sociology and Social Work, Aalborg University, Denmark. She also holds the position of Director of Doctoral School of Social Sciences, Aalborg University. Her field of research is focused on gender, intersectionality, masculinity, everyday life and belonging. Within masculinity studies she has been writing on hegemonic masculinity and intersectionality; masculinity ideals; masculinity risk and safety; war and masculinity; violence in left wing movements; marginalized masculinities, and the intersections on class, ethnicity and gender. She is co-editor of *NORMA, International Journal for Masculinity Studies*.

Firouz Gaini is Associate Professor of Social Anthropology at the University of the Faroe Islands. He has written on young people's cultural identities and education, and other subjects relating to children and young people's everyday lives. He has conducted fieldwork in the Faroe Islands, Greenland, Southern France and Japan. Among his books are *Lessons of Islands* (2013) and *Among the Islanders of the North* (Editor, 2011).

Peter Håkansson has a PhD in Economic History and works at the Centre for Work Life Studies (CTA), Malmö University and at the Department of Education, Communication and Learning, University of Gothenburg, Sweden. In Håkansson's dissertation from 2011, 'Youth unemployment – transition regimes, institutional change and social capital', he analysed the relationship between youth unemployment and social capital using quantitative methods. Håkansson has also studied trust in different contexts (Håkansson and Sjöholm, 2007; Håkansson, 2015; Håkansson and Witmer, 2015). In his recent research, he studies network recruitment from both long- and short-term perspectives.

Chris Haywood is a senior lecturer at Newcastle University with a main focus on men and masculinities. He is currently exploring the emergence of new sexual cultures with a particular focus on anonymous sex with strangers. This is part of a broader study on men's dating practices with a particular focus on mobile dating, online dating and speed dating. Overall, he is interested in pushing the conceptual limits of masculinity models to consider ways of gendering that are not reducible to masculinity or femininity.

Anette Hellman, PhD, is Assistant Professor of Education, Department of Education, Communication and Learning at the University of Gothenburg, Sweden. Her research interests include issues related to critical childhood studies, such as norm and normality constructions in children's everyday lives and masculinity and care in preschool.

Marcus Herz, PhD, is Senior Lecturer and researcher in Social Work at Malmö University, Sweden. His research interests and publications include studies on social work, gender, masculinities, ethnicity, race and youth studies.

Sune Qvotrup Jensen is an associate professor and member of CeMAS, Centre for Masculinity Studies, Department for Sociology and Social Work, Aalborg University, Denmark. He also holds the position of Head of the School of Sociology and Social Work. His research interests include masculinity, class, ethnicity and intersectionality, street culture, subculture and marginalized masculinities, urban sociology, masculinity risk and safety, social work, ethnography and methodology as well as analysis of labour market relations in neo-liberal and post-industrial societies.

Thomas Johansson is Professor of Education at the University of Gothenburg, Sweden. He has published extensively in the areas of family studies, urban studies, youth studies and cultural studies. Recently he published *The Global Gym: Gender, Health and Pedagogies* with Jesper Andreasson (Palgrave Macmillan, 2014) and *Leadership Varieties: The Role of Economic Change and the New Masculinity* (Routledge, 2016).

Morten Kyed is postdoctoral in Sociology in the Department for Sociology and Social Work, Aalborg University, Denmark. His chapter is in parts based on his PhD thesis entitled 'John Wayne and Tarzan no longer work here: An ethnographic tale of masculinity, safety and "EMT-ship"' (2014). His main research interests are within the intersections of masculinity, work and cultural practice. Examples of his previous publications within this area are 'Distinction meets "dirty work": On the tracks of symbolic domination and autonomy among refuse collectors in a Danish city' in *Praktiske Grunde* (2011) and 'Masculinity, emotions and "communities of relief" among male emergency medical technicians', in *Gender, Emergency Work and the Rescue Services: Contested Terrains and Challenges*, Mathias Ericson and Ulf Mellström (eds), Ashgate (upcoming).

Jeppe Fuglsang Larsen is an external lecturer at the Department of Sociology and Social Work, and Research Assistant at the Department of Culture and

Global Studies, Aalborg University, Denmark. His research interests include ethnicity and intersectionality, masculinity, identity construction, right-wing populism, racism and qualitative research.

Xiaodong Lin is Lecturer in Sociology at the University of York, writing in the field of men and masculinities in China. He is the author of *Gender, Modernity and Male Migrant Workers in China: Becoming a 'Modern' Man* (Routledge). The book was shortlisted for the British Sociological Association *Philip Abrams Memorial Prize* 2014. He has published articles in *Gender, Work and Organization* and *Gender, Place and Culture*. He is a member of the editorial board of *Work, Employment and Society*.

Máirtín Mac an Ghaill works at Newman University, UK. He has published several texts with Chris Haywood, including *Men and Masculinities* and *Education and Masculinities: Social, Cultural and Global Transformations*. He has recently co-edited two collections: *East Asian Men: Masculinity, Sexuality and Desire* (with Xiaodong Lin and Chris Haywood) and *Muslim Students, Education and Neoliberalism: Schooling a 'Suspect' Community* (with Chris Haywood).

Jens Christian Nielsen, PhD, is Associate Professor and researcher in Youth Studies at Aarhus University, Denmark. His research interests and publications include youth studies on individualization, becoming, in- and exclusion, social interaction, learning and talent development.

Ylva Odenbring, PhD, is Associate Professor of Education, Department of Education, Communication and Learning at the University of Gothenburg, Sweden. Her main research interests are in the field of Gender Studies and Social Justice in education. Odenbring has participated in both national and international research projects on social justice and youth victimization in education.

Niels Ulrik Sørensen, PhD, is Associate Professor and Executive Manager at the Danish Centre for Youth Research at Aalborg University in Copenhagen, Denmark. His research and publications focus on youth cultures, new body cultures, young people's well-being, gender and masculinities.

Introduction

Chris Haywood and Thomas Johansson

Introduction

Across Europe we are witnessing a series of events that are drawing upon representations of men and masculinity that are rupturing the social fabric of everyday life. For example, media reports of social unrest, migration, misogynous hate crime, religious extremism, drug trafficking and political Far Right mobilization have often been at the centre of the discussion the figure of the apathetic, disenchanted, socially excluded young man. At present, discussions of men, social and political dysfunction remain highly dependent on media-led narratives that report on the problem *of* men in society. These media narratives are dovetailing with contemporary discussions about improving gender equality at global levels. More specifically, existing work on men and women suggests that there are reasons to be doubtful regarding a linear process towards gender equality. Many of the developments are contradictory and context-dependent (Haavind and Magnusson, 2005; Holter, 2007). For example, in recent Nordic research and political investigations there are indications that certain groups of men are particularly unlikely to identify with the political agenda on gender equality, and that certain groups of men even feel hatred towards feminists and politicians fighting for a gender-equal society. Today, these types of sentiment may be increasing, suggesting that gender equality may not be seen as advantageous 'from all points of view' but also that the pursuit of gender equality may not be possible. One of the interesting themes from broader discussions on gender and equality is an implicit assumption that men have power. At present, existing work on gender equality and masculinity often 'blames' men for their lack of awareness and reflexivity. In effect, gender equality is often viewed as a problem of men. However, more information is needed to explore men's specific needs and responsibilities to understand how gender equality is a problem *for* men.

In this introduction to the book we will frame issues of gender equality, power and exclusion by unpacking the concept of marginalized masculinities. Initially, we will discuss the concept of marginalization and focus on the dynamic and complex interaction between marginal and dominant. After that there is a section on class, gender and marginalization, pointing towards the importance of including intersectional perspectives in analysis of marginalization.

The following two sections focus on international and methodological perspectives on marginalization. The contributors in this book have used this introduction dialogically in order to frame the themes and issues being explored throughout the chapters. Therefore, each of the chapters has been written with the brief to engage with one or more of the following sections on marginalization in the context of how we theorize it, how we research it and what relevance the concept has at a global level. In doing so, we connect with four main guiding questions:

First, what do we mean by marginalized masculinities; how do we define these terms? What is involved in the process of investigating the relationship between gender equality, marginalization and hegemonic masculinities? Is it simply about men? Do boys have masculinities? What about female masculinities?

Second, what are the experiences of those who are marginalized and those who are doing the marginalizing? For example, are tendencies towards marginalization producing identification with political goals on gender equality, and is, for example, anti-feminism connected to certain groups and the social configurations of men (class, age, living conditions etc.)?

Third, how do patterns of marginalization and masculinity vary between different countries, regions and local contexts? Related to the previous point, it is important to explore who has the power to define what is marginal and how categories of marginality differ temporally and spatially.

Fourth, what does it mean to research marginalized masculinities? Underpinning each of the chapters is a critical reflexivity about how we research marginality. Intricately connected to research practices are the different ways in which marginalization is conceptualized, thus the theoretical lens of the research will shape the nature of the data being collected.

The dialogical basis for this collection was embedded in a project that sought to bring those working in the field of men and masculinity together to look at different areas of marginalization, including: Theorizing Gender; Unemployment and Whiteness; Fatherhood: The Art of Not Taking Paternal Leave; Internet, Hate-groups and Anti-Feminists; and, Lost Boys? Schooling and Marginalization. This group has an underlying commitment to equality in areas such as gender, 'race'/ethnicity, age, sexuality and disability, and as part of the dialogue we continued to explore how marginalization operated across and within different social categories. Although the contributors in this book are largely from Northern Europe, we aim to connect to a global agenda where the concept of marginalized masculinities might be critically explored and scrutinized in the pursuit of establishing its empirical viability and conceptual purchase in global, national and local contexts. The contributors are highly aware of how theories and concepts embedded in the West are often unproblematically applied to other, non-Western contexts. As a result, contributors have been asked to write their chapters to connect to the main themes underpinning this collection.

Theorizing Men, Masculinity and Marginalization

The questions raised, and the topics we have chosen to discuss in this volume, have their 'home' in the field of critical studies on men and masculinity (Hearn, 2004). This field of research has roots in the 1980s discussion on masculinity and gender in different countries, especially Denmark, Norway, Sweden, the United Kingdom, Australia and the United States. During the 1990s, this field of research expanded considerably and revolved mainly around theoretical issues and definitions of the field, but today we can see how a rich and extensive empirical field of research is gradually developing. Certain areas, such as fatherhood, violence, gender equality and sexuality have received a lot of attention, whereas others – alternative masculinities, subordinated men, marginalized men – have attracted little. Through the introduction of a number of important concepts, such as hegemonic masculinity and marginalized masculinities, Raewyn Connell (1987; 1995) initiated both a theoretical discussion on how to frame and understand developments in masculinity and actualized a number of important empirically oriented questions on gender, sexuality and identity. Another important influence came from Susan Faludi and her book *Stiffed: The Betrayal of the Modern Man* (1999) in which she focused on men in different precarious occupations and positions, including those who were unemployed and marginalized. Such work has been accompanied by a range of developments in the literature on men and masculinities. This field of research has become an established subfield within gender studies.

More recently, attention has also been given to issues on both transformations of hegemonic masculinity and, to a lesser extent, men who are not able to occupy or demonstrate qualities associated with this dominant position. In this book, we have directed out attention towards different forms of marginal and/or marginalized masculinities, but we maintain an overall dimension to knit these disparate fields together. This 'joined up' approach focuses on three different 'fields' in society: Crisis, Risk and Socialization; Transformations, Work and Unemployment; and Marginalization, Bodies and Identity. Our fourth 'field' or area of inquiry, Rethinking Marginalization, explores how we can begin to develop ways of thinking about marginalization. Through zooming in on atypical or marginal masculinities, we will get a closer picture of how men in precarious positions in different countries, social contexts and situations experience and relate to the political ambition to create gender-equal societies. In doing this, we will lean heavily on international research already completed in these areas, specifically in family research, gender and masculinity studies (Gavanas, 2001; Hearn and Pringle, 2006; Holter, 2007; Johansson and Ottemo, 2013). We will also frame these discussions in the context of developments in the welfare state, European discussions on gender equality and gender politics (Esping-Andersen, 1990; EIGE, 2012) and broader social and economic changes within a global context. In the book, we will furthermore focus on and discuss the theoretical and conceptual developments in the field of critical studies on men and masculinities. In particular, we will look closely at how central concepts such as hegemonic masculinity, homosociality, heteronormativity and marginalization can be developed, as well as adapted, to different countries and contexts. Recently there have been extensive discussions and elaboration on the concept of hegemonic masculinity (Connell, 1995; Hearn et al., 2012; Haywood and Mac an Ghaill, 2012; Johansson and Ottemo, 2013). The ambition is to follow up on these discussions and theoretical developments and also to make a considerable contribution to this field of research.

Although the focus in this collection is primarily on boys, young and older men, the contributors to the collection strongly emphasize masculinity as being a relational concept. It is relational in a number of ways. One of the themes of the book is to consider how marginalization is manifest at a generational level. It is important to see how masculinity as a concept can 'contain' male and female bodies of all ages. This means that when we think about masculinity it is often used indiscriminately and applied to males of all ages, assuming the same logic of identity and practices of a three-year-old child with those of a middle-aged man. We recognize how the concept of masculinity is used across a range of populations. The concept shifts from being analytical to being descriptive; we need to think about how gender explains marginalization in generational terms. This means that to understand masculinity we need to recognize the interdependency between masculinity and femininity. We need to hold in focus Raewyn Connell's (2000, p. 40) claim that 'masculinities do not first exist and then come into contact with femininities. Masculinities and femininities are produced together in the process that constitutes a gender order', which is echoed by Connell (2005, p. 27): 'We must remember that gender is relational, that women are as much involved in the formation of masculinities as men are'. But, where relationships between men and women are discussed there is a reductionism that suggests that it must take place either through codes of compulsory heterosexuality, in a sense of replacing homophobia, and/or the practice of antipathy or violence against women. Therefore, in this collection, masculinity and femininity act on each other in a relational manner, shaping and informing how they are lived out and experienced.

Approaches to Masculinity and Marginalization

Despite the rising attention paid to men and masculinity, relatively little work has been carried out on those men who occupy marginal spaces in society. This collection in particular makes a critical intervention into this discussion by responding to Jackson and Moshin's (2014, p. 2) question: 'How can men, who are often in positions of privilege be understood as marginal?' Central to this discussion is that it is not self-evident what is understood by 'marginalization' as this term covers a wide range of identities, communities and contexts (Danaher et al., 2013). A key definition of marginalization is provided by Cheng (1999, p. 295): 'When we speak of "marginalization," we are broadly referring to intergroup and/or intragroup relations, "activities between and among groups" (Alderfer, 1987, p. 190). Specifically, marginalization means peripheral or disadvantaged unequal membership, disparate treatment.' Schiffer and Schatz (2008,

p. 6) provide a more context-specific approach which argues that 'Marginalization describes the position of individuals, groups or populations outside of "mainstream society", living at the margins of those in the centre of power, of cultural dominance and economical and social welfare'. In many ways, marginalization can refer to a zero-sum notion of power where levels of marginalization can be understood along a continuum of those who have and those who have not. For example, marginalization may refer to men experiencing physical or mental disability (Gartrell, 2010). Totten (2003) talks about male youth as being marginal due to their lack of economic support, being subject to physical abuse by their families and living away from home often in poor housing conditions with low educational attainment. In relation to older men, economic change in many Western countries has led to a drop in the number of occupations within industry and other professional fields that have traditionally been occupied by men. Industries such as coal mining, ship building, engineering, car production, fishing and agriculture are undergoing transformations that have often resulted in their contraction, fragmentation or collapse (World Trade Organization, 2000). In other industries, it is suggested that there has been a feminization of various sectors including hotel, banking and other service-related industries (Breugel, 2000). As a result, there is a casualization of men's work that is often connected with high levels of labour turnover and organizational restructuring.

This focus of the discussion on marginalization connects a lack of access to social, economic and cultural opportunities and resources to a marginal status. Interestingly, in this approach there is little need to draw upon masculinity as an explanatory tool as men become subject to social, economic and cultural circumstances resulting in a range of positions that may include high levels of poverty, low educational opportunity and poor access to health and social welfare and housing provision. Thus, men may be marginalized because of their social, economic and cultural location rather than the version of manhood in which they invest and perform. Therefore, in this sense, marginalization is caused by the structural organization of social and economic relationships that affect men. From this explanation, there is little information on the problem of *being* a man who may be experiencing a high level of social exclusion. Therefore, rather than simply focusing on measuring rates and levels of exclusion/inclusion, we can also begin to understand marginalization as a *social process*. This focus on marginalized masculinities as part of a socially constituted process has been identified in a range of research settings that include race/ethnicity and the media (Jackson II and Moshin, 2013), sports (Hirose and Kei-ho Pih, 2010), schooling (Tischler and McCaughtry, 2011), health (Evans *et al.*, 2011) and crime (Abrams *et al.*, 2008). From this perspective, we need to locate often highly volatile responses to gender equality within the changing social and economic contexts such as the fragmentation of the material, cultural and symbolic structures through which men have traditionally asserted authority, legitimacy, control and dominance (Mac an Ghaill and Haywood, 2007).

One of the key theoretical contributions to understanding marginalized masculinities as produced through a social context has been Connell's (1995) approach to marginalization within a framework of hegemonic masculinity and the privileging of patriarchy. In this approach, marginalized masculinities are often referred to as 'outcasts' (Phillips, 2005) or, as Cheng (1999, p. 295) suggests, those men who have 'disadvantaged unequal membership'.

This unequal membership is produced in the process of making masculinities. Alongside this, Connell's concept of the 'protest masculinities' might be salient. This is a masculinity that is enacted by men who are in a dialectical relationship with the State. Although they mirror elements of the State, such as being tough, athletic and violent (qualities that often designate hegemonic masculinities) they exist in opposition to it (Curran and Abrams, 2000). What differs is their social, cultural and economic location, and as Connell and Messerschmidt (2005, p. 848) suggest, protest masculinity is:

> a pattern of masculinity constructed in local working-class settings, sometimes among ethnically marginalized men, which embodies the claim to power typical of regional hegemonic masculinities in Western countries, but which lacks the economic resources and institutional authority that underpins the regional and global patterns.

In this way, marginal masculinities are those masculinities that operate in ways that restore their lack of power. This can often be achieved through deviant behaviours such as criminality. The key point to recognize is that marginal masculinity is defined in relation to those men who have power. As Cheng (1999) suggests:

> The hegemonic definition of manhood is a man in power, a man with power, and a man of power. We equate manhood with being successful, capable, reliable, in control. The very definitions of manhood we have developed in our culture maintain the power that some men have over other men and that men have over women.
>
> (p. 300)

Thus, in many ways, marginalized masculinities are often located and defined in relation to men that hold cultural privilege. From this perspective, masculinity becomes the resource through which marginalization takes place.

More specifically, men's positionality as marginal is dependent on what is deemed as central. This approach suggests that we can know and understand marginal masculinities through their relationships with those masculinities that are socially, culturally and economically elevated. Importantly, it is those masculinities that are dominant that are able to define and sanction those which are deemed subordinate. As Champagne (1995, p. xxv) suggests: '… the Other functions as an oppositional term for the formation of a normalized subjectivity'. According to Champagne, the Other – that which is marginal – cannot be too radical in its composition as this would reduce it to a position beyond normalization.

Thus, the marginal has to be constituted in relation to the centre and the centre to the marginal. Therefore, the Other '… is not posited in a relation of absolute alterity to the center but rather is usefully maintained in a certain place of opposition on which the dominant depends' (ibid.; p. xxvi). In a similar vein, Jackson II and Moshin (2014) suggest that margins determine what the dominant is, not as the margins define identities in a negative manner. Or as Phillips (2005, p. 220) suggests: 'Marginalized masculinities or "outcasts" from the norm are constructed in the productive wake of the ideal, and as the conditions necessary for the ideal's production and "natural" appearance'. The implication of this is that the dominant and the marginal belong together in a relationship that mutually informs their status.

The issue here is that marginal masculinities remain framed through the dominant cultural logic of difference and how such processes of difference are experienced. In other words, we need to think about those who operate outside of that relationship. As Blagojević (2012) suggests:

> It seems to me that in a certain way we reduce *the other* to their (our?) otherness, we fix and 'freeze' their (our?) identities, and by doing so, we strengthen the binary model which reduces the other to the difference that reflects the normative identity, the forms and patterns imposed on us by culture itself.
>
> (p. 68)

Even then, Blagojević argues, cultures will produce their own spaces of alterity. This has particular implications for how we research, identify and explain the nature of marginal masculinities as the Centre will frame not simply what we know, but also what we are able to know. As such, a potential space emerges around issues regarding the potential for men to be elevated and marginalized at the same time. Thus, it is possible to be culturally elevated, such as black masculine hip-hop culture, and yet at the same time occupy a socially and economically marginal position. A similar situation is evident around masculinity and bodybuilding, where men with high levels of muscularity may be socially desirable, but the chemical enhancements may infract social and legal norms. An interesting theme emerges around the possibility of the marginal being outside of the official registers, for example, those of the State or institutions, which sanction the possibility of being marginal. Dahl-Michelson (2014) develops the notion of marginalized masculinities as not only those that could not meet hegemonic standards, but also did not operate or make sense of their identities through hegemonic gender norms. This means that men might recognize the Centre/Marginal dichotomy and occupy a position on the outside of the binary. Marginality, in this case, should not be interpreted as an array of inequalities embedded in categories such as gender, 'race'/ethnicity, sexuality or age. Rather, the emphasis is on the *systems* of signification that create the possibility of marginality, dominance and Otherness. The implication of this is that we should not simply consider the empirical characteristics or attributes of marginalized men, rather we need to begin to focus on the complex, often unstable, systems of signification and representation that sanction or warrant those attributes.

One of the difficulties of thinking through men, masculinity and marginalization is that there is a tendency for those approaches that focus on theoretical and conceptual dynamics as a cultural formation, to underplay how the materiality of the experience of marginalization is lived out across a range of different social contexts. It is this limitation to which we now turn.

Towards a Transnational Marginal Masculinity

At present, rather than an overarching global concept of marginalized masculinity, the concept has been used in a range of contexts beyond Europe, North America and Australia. For some, the concept of marginalized masculinity provides a useful approach to understanding within a range of contexts, such as Filipino seafarers (McKay, 2007), Pakistani eunuchs (Ahmad, 2010), men in Cuba attending a mental health centre (Hernandez *et al.*, 2014), men in poverty in India (Roy, 2011) and insurgency in Latin America (Ortega, 2012). Ratele's (2014) discussion on masculinity studies and South Africa suggests that the concept of hegemonic masculinity is becoming less appropriate as global capitalism marginalizes societies. Thus, we need to think about 'marginal hegemonies' or 'hegemonies within marginality' (ibid., p. 39). In many ways, we are brought back to Cheng's (1999) suggestion that men can be both dominant and marginal at the same time. Thus, although white middle-class men may have social and economic privilege on the one hand, they may at the same time lack the cultural valorization of the hyper-sexual black body on the other. It is interesting that the concept that has been able to explain masculine domination at global levels is Connell's Transnational Business Masculinity. This masculinity has been employed to describe those business and political executives who are involved in economic and political management at a global level. It is suggested that these men are egocentric, have less sense of loyalty and responsibility for others and have no permanent commitments. They are, however, involved in the subjectification of men and women in order to sustain their global hegemonic position. However, it appears that there is little discussion in the field about globalized marginal masculinities. This is revealing, because as processes of globalization intensify in areas such as finance, digital space and consumption, a question is raised about the relevance of the theorizing of marginalization within shifting relationships across the global North to the global South.

Furman *et al.* (2012) suggest that transnational flows from wealthy countries to those countries that are economically disadvantaged result in the distribution of Westernized versions of masculinity. They argue that, in the developing world, hegemonic masculinity operates through themes of corporate capitalism and that men are aspiring to meet such masculine ideals. The impact of this is that men experience gender role conflict where their aspirational masculinity cannot be realized. While they identify men in developing countries as having potential privilege over other men and women in a local context, at a global level they are located within transnational flows such as unequal labour markets. In these fluid scenarios, it is not self-evident what marginal masculinity means in relation to (dis)continuous access to masculine resources. For example, Donaldson and Howson (2009) consider what happens to men who migrate or are resettled, and how men reclaim their masculine subjectivities in light of the social and economic change. They suggest that migrant men, on entering their host country, redouble their efforts to be 'real' men and may adopt the same strategies and resources to make their 'new' masculinities. At present, in North Africa and the Levant, there are unprecedented levels of displacement of populations due to poverty and conflict. The impact of these issues has resulted in communities experiencing levels of marginalization not only within their local contexts but also in the process of migration. Such events provide a timely reminder about the adequacy and relevance of the theoretical frames and the concepts that we use and their applicability across space and time. However, despite concerns about migration across a wide range of global contexts, there has been little explanation of how to understand masculinity, marginality and migration. Ingvarsdottir's (2016) recent study of young male refugees in Athens, Greece, is one of the few contemporary studies to address the subject. Of particular interest is how the media projects these men as dangerous and/or lazy migrants, erasing their histories as working men with families in the process. In response, these refugees are resisting media motifs by making connections with global/local grassroots movements that promote the rights of women and marginal groups mobilizing around areas such as queer activism and disability. However, these young men are also trapped within local gender hierarchies of inequality, as well as those from their homeland, and those fashioned through travelling. Thus, whilst in this collection there are a number of local contexts, it is important to consider the relevance and transferability of the dynamics of marginalized masculinity at national and transnational contexts.

Finally, a discussion of the global context not only scrutinizes the relevance and applicability of the concept of marginalized masculinity, but asks questions about the adequacy of masculinity as a concept. The difficulties of simplistically applying masculinity to male bodies is identified by Janssen (2009, p. 85) who, in relation to childhood, suggests:

> At a fundamental level, one can ask whether the notions of boy and girl can be adequately conceptualised in terms of often adult-centric politicized rubrics such as masculinity/femininity, and whether they ethnographically tolerate notions of child and adolescent as generic, equivalent or 'neutral' terms.

Although much work has been focused on unpacking the meanings of maleness through multiple, differentiated and plural masculinities, there is scope to question the ubiquity of the concept of masculinity. One way in which this can be achieved is by considering how specific social and cultural context shapes and generates the specific resources for how to be a man, and how particular social and cultural interrelationships reshape the meanings of manhood. This feeds into a broader cultural sensitivity to the notion of gender and possibility that the theoretical concept of gender may also be part of a colonial practice. As Mirsky (1996, p. 30) explains:

> The importance of looking beyond a didactic notion of gender creates the possibility that: there may be areas or moments in men's lives in which masculinity is irrelevant; men might exist without or beyond masculinity; such possibilities are not comprehended in a men's studies approach which, against its stated intentions, theorizes masculinity as a necessary attribute of human males.

The important point here is that by focusing on masculinity as the conduit for understanding gender we may proscribe the possibility of understanding gender in alternative ways, especially in ways that may exist outside of Western theoretical frames of gender.

Methodology: Researching Marginality

The final area in this discussion of marginalized masculinity is one that remains relatively underexplored, namely how do researchers explore about marginalized masculinities? At a methodological level, researchers engaging with men and masculinity need to reflect on epistemology and ask 'Whose version counts?' There are major issues concerning who we talk to and how we talk to participants in the research, especially as conversations often involve emotionally difficult and sensitive issues. Such a discussion has been informed by the 'paradigm wars' (Bryman, 2008) where one epistemological position competes against others to prove that they are more adequate. It is often the case that the methodological approaches to marginalization will be connected, although not causatively, to how marginality is conceptualized. Those approaches that are able to measure marginalization through social and economic positioning are able to use quantitative data collection methods. Thus, it is not simply meanings or experiences that matter, but the preponderance of social and economic location and respective practices that become indicators of marginalization. Furthermore, such approaches do not always necessarily focus on individual experience, where information can be obtained at the level of social and economic collectives. For example, men's participation in particular labour processes can be measured and compared spatially and temporally and can then be used as evidence to measure how far someone is marginalized. In contrast, from an epistemology perspective, it is argued that knowledge about marginality emerges from men's experiences. Central to this approach is the claim that the experiential operates hermeneutically, with that knowledge, understandings and feelings being the source of knowledge. Thus, approaches to marginalization take place at a more local level. At the same time, we need to think about what it means to undertake research with those whose position is not cohered through the dominant/marginal dichotomies. In short, how do we represent those who remain unpresentable?

One of the major themes of undertaking research on marginality is the possibility of opening up a social world and exposing the researcher to alternative experiences and understandings to those of dominant institutional perspectives. In representing marginality, there is no simple 'reading off' from experience to a specific subject position. Rather, we suggest that, as with all accounts, such representations involve complex interpretations of social reality. In recent work, Haywood and McDermott (2018) carried out research on men with learning disabilities in day-care contexts; one of the difficulties in this research was gaining access to the research sites. Although deemed consenting adults with capacity, the service providers for the adults with learning disabilities were extremely suspicious of the research and protective of 'their' clients. Despite their adult status and capacity (many lived independently, had employment and had romantic relationships), they were positioned by the service providers as vulnerable. This group of men, who are often silenced at a societal level, were also being silenced by those providing the care. So, in this case, the process of researching this group not only involved reassuring the men themselves, but also those responsible for delivering the care provision. The practical challenges of researching marginalized groups therefore involves ethics as much as access. Consequently, in relation to conducting the research, it was important to employ a number of ethical and safeguarding protocols to ensure participants' understanding of the project and the concept of informed consent (clear and simple textual explanations, repeated reassurance, visual prompts and cues). In this scenario, consent was always an iterative process that was continually being confirmed. Alongside access and ethics, other concerns around the gendered nature of the research practice requires further consideration.

The gendered nature of the research relationship refers to the ways in which research practice may operate in itself as a marginalizing process, where those in the research may be seen as more powerful than others. This means that in order to understand the research process it is important to view masculinity not as something that is separate from the research process, but something that is operating as part of the research practice. We suggest that in order to understand the situation we need to understand research practice as the negotiation of masculine subjectivities that are (dis)located across traditional and contemporary gendered identity formations. Even in relation to a simple agreement of research it has been found that a male researcher had difficulty recruiting men because his desire to talk to men was read as a desire *for* men (Haywood and Mac an Ghaill, 1997). As Oliffe and Mro'z (2005, p. 257) acknowledge: 'Men don't volunteer – they are recruited'. Walby (2010, p. 654) suggests that when researching masculinity, a sexualization takes place where 'The researcher has an agenda-setting power (Hoffman, 2007), yet the respondent can swerve the encounter towards propositions and sexualization, which results from and contributes to meaning in the making'. In relation to females interviewing males, Schwalbe and Wolkomir (2001, p. 94) argue that 'Inappropriate sexualizing is a way that some heterosexual men try to reassert control when being interviewed by women. This can take the forms of flirting, sexual innuendo, touching, and remarks on appearance'. Other researchers have identified how participant disclosure depended on the attractiveness of the women interviewers. For example, Gailey and Prohaska (2011, p. 373) citing earlier work, quoted the hostile response of one of their male interviewees who stated: 'You should know that you're lucky that you're both in good shape or men wouldn't be talking with you about these things' (Gailey and Prohaska, 2006). Issues concerning researching masculinity require a reflexivity to recognize how masculinity is being enacted in the research process.

Structure of the Book

Over the past two years, contributors to this book have been working together to engage with men and masculinity and have provided new insights, developed new knowledge and have identified potential interventions to facilitate our understanding of men and masculinity. This collection focuses on and aims to examine men and masculinity and issues of marginalization. The intention is to bring together theoretical developments, empirical research and methodological innovation. With that in mind, the book has been divided into four key areas and these connect to the empirical focus of the different chapters.

The first section of the book concentrates on themes of Crisis, Risk and Socialization and focuses specifically on the category of 'boys'. Boyhood is a category that is held in critical tension with masculinity as the generational difference becomes a means of understanding how gender is lived out. This collection starts with Chapter 1 with research undertaken by Anette Hellman and Ylva Odenbring. This chapter explores how gender norms related to marginalized masculinity are constructed in the daily practice of early childhood education. It draws on ethnographic fieldwork from Swedish preschool and preschool class settings. In order to analyse and understand marginalized 'boyishness', the study is situated in critical masculinity research. In so doing, it identifies a critical tension between understandings of masculinity and 'boyness'. The chapter explores which positions are normalized for boys and, more specifically, sheds some light on so-called 'problematic boys'. A main point of the results in this chapter is that children occupy several positions related to gender. Some positions are made visible and are categorized by the teachers, whereas other positions are made invisible. The teacher's gaze on the children is connected to specific actions, norms and the children themselves. Most visible to the teachers are the rowdy boys and this behaviour is categorized as 'typical for boys'. This group of boys' noisy and aggressive actions clash with general expectations of order and discipline in preschool and, as a result, these boys are given low status by teachers and other peers. Consequently, these boys are marginalized and excluded from different play activities in peer–peer interaction.

In early childhood education, play is the most important space for children's social relations and identity constructions. Hence, to be categorized as problematic and excluded from play also means that these children are marginalized from social relations with other peers. Instead of discussing the place where the problems actually occur, in the educational setting, other explanations of the problem and how to solve it are discussed. This theme of location and who defines the problem is taken up by Marcus Herz in Chapter 2. He discusses how the profession of social work tries to manage marginalization amongst boys and men. Instead of an approach taking different discourses of masculinity into consideration, boys and men are simply seen as *being* a risk instead of being seen as exposed to risk. Marginalization could, as a result of this approach, take on two different expressions. First, it could lock people into positions of marginalization because gender is treated as synonymous with being in need of intervention by Social Services. This means being subjected to regulations and positions enclosed by the social services system, subjecting oneself to less freedom in exchange for support. On the other hand, the same approach to masculinity could be argued to conceal marginalization amongst men. This is the case when men do not comply with being a risk, but instead being at risk. Men being at risk from others does not coincide with the social worker's view on masculinity. Their situation is thus not taken seriously, which can hide marginalization amongst men. The chapter will also discuss how notions of masculinity need to be put into motion to be able to capture several positions of marginalization as well as more hegemonic positions.

The book then moves towards understanding marginalization and masculinity in the context of Transformations of Work and Unemployment. Moving from marginalization and boys, this section begins with notions of youth transitions and issues of marginalization involved in the process of becoming men.

Chapter 3, based on ethnographic research in an urban community in Greenland, looks into young men's changing identities from a cultural perspective with focus on the shift in rural–urban and tradition–modernity oppositions in the North. Firouz Gaini argues that many young men from Greenland are in turmoil because of incompatible demands and expectations from family and society: on the one hand, they should live up to the ideals of 'real' masculinities (referring to physical competence, toughness, etc.), while on the other they should be educated and urban in style. This chapter intends to analyze young Inuit men's identity negotiation, as well as their response to societal challenges and ideologies, by examining the distinct contexts within which they are located. The City is characterized by different groups of men in symbolic struggle for power and recognition, and marginalization of young men in Greenland is part of the modernization and urbanization of society. Man's traditional life and work as a hunter is not an option anymore. The City symbolizes a crack in the ice, a split without complete separation of conventional and contemporary identities and constructions of 'Greenlandness'.

The impact of socio-economic changes on men's lives is pursued further in the work of Peter Håkansson in Chapter 4 and explores the emergence of the new service- and knowledge-orientated society. For the working class and the low-skilled, transformation of the labour market has led to a transition of employment from low-skill manual work to low-skill service work. Thus, the research question becomes: How do men in Sweden adapt to this transition of the labour market? Have men become redundant (either by choosing self-exclusion or by normative exclusion categorizing them as 'unemployable')? Or are men adapting to the new low skill jobs in the service sector? The results show that men are underrepresented in the so-called 'high-touch' sector, but something else is happening. The low-skill service sector is increasing, just as stipulated, but it is men's participation that is increasing the most. Men's participation in relation to women's is increasing in retail, hotel/restaurants and in care. This change may challenge traditional occupational gender norms. Thus, are masculinities marginalized? As Connell and Messerschmidt (2005) point out, at times there can be a struggle between different forms of masculinities, and at present, due to labour market transition, the old masculinities, including masculinities with an industrial habitus, become excluded and therefore marginalized. In short, it is argued that in service jobs there is no room for these old masculinities, where other kinds of 'feminine' skills are needed.

The shift in the nature of men's work is further explored by Morten Kyed in Chapter 5, based on male Emergency Medical Technicians (EMTs) and their strong emphasis on socio-emotional competence. It explores how mundane processes of discursive marginalization are constructed in relation to socio-emotional skills amongst male EMTs in Denmark. EMTs in the Danish ambulance service is an interesting empirical setting for a study of socio-emotional skills because it is a male-dominated occupation with a strong working-class tradition. However, it is also a job that requires 'high-touch' care and bodywork, and which has been vastly upskilled with high-tech knowledge in recent years (McDowell, 2009; Håkansson's Chapter 4, this book). The aim of this chapter is to explore the meaning of socio-emotional skills in ambulance work and how these skills are used to construct hegemonic and marginalized subject positions amongst male EMTs in Denmark.

The final piece in this section, Chapter 6, explores the lives of a group of socially marginalized men – migrant workers. In the context of China, Xiaodong Lin explores marginalization through globally inflected internal migration. Through engagement with the concepts of 'suzhi' (quality) and 'benshi' (capability) within the context of fast-paced modernization in China, the chapter examines rural young men's narratives of their migrating experience in urban China with particular reference to their gendered experiences and practices in relation to their familial lives. In so doing, it sets out to respond critically to public representations of migrant workers as 'marginalized' others in the discourse of modernization, that is often marked by progress and development. In turn, the chapter contributes to an understanding of marginalization in the context of rural migrating men as both social exclusion and symbolic otherness, within the context of the reconfiguration of the relations between tradition and modernity at a time of rapid, globally-inflected changes.

Moving away from more structurally-led notions of marginalization, the third section of this book, Marginalization, Bodies and Identities focuses on the subjective experiences of marginalization. Niels Ulrik Sørensen in Chapter 7 undertook qualitative interviews with young boys who have had experiences with loneliness, eating disorders, self-harming behaviour and other manifestations of a lack of well-being. This chapter examines the ways the young boys understand and experience the self and how they link it to their lack of well-being. Fear of marginalization seems to be an important part of this link. The chapter shows how the young boys are struggling to live up to the expectations they experience in an increasingly individualized and competitive society and their fear of being lost and pushed out seems to have a destabilizing influence on their well-being. The young boys in the chapter are not socially excluded in terms of being outside 'mainstream society', rather their marginalization is that of insiders who feel that their insider position is fragile and on the verge of collapsing, which is why they are struggling all they can to avoid being pushed out or marginalized.

Masculinity and the experience of marginalization shifts to the online context in Chapter 8, where Jesper Andreasson and Thomas Johansson explore the internet forum Flashback. This chapter explores how fitness doping is negotiated and understood in terms of masculinity and marginalization. The chapter shows that the Internet community studied can be read as an example of a transformational process in which ordinary rules are questioned and partly put out of play. In the world of the bodybuilder, the marginal masculinity is, in certain senses, dominant. On the one hand, achieving a muscular and well-trained body is regarded as a core aspect of manhood within the community. Marginal masculinity is thus momentarily transformed into dominant and hegemonic masculinity. On the other hand, however, the findings also indicate that a drug-using, muscular masculinity is constructed in negotiation with other central masculine ideals, such as the employable man and the responsible father. Found within the community is a complex and dynamic interplay between subculture and common culture, and intersecting discourses of manhood.

The final section, Rethinking Marginalization, involves thinking through a number of issues surrounding marginalization. The main issue is the disconnection of masculinity and marginalization from other social and cultural categories. Although in previous chapters there has been an engagement with context, these final chapters focus on how we begin to understand how social and cultural categories inflect and intersect. In Chapter 9, the focus is on the emergence of 'dangerous Muslim young men'. Notions of marginalization are often co-opted with issues of public safety and danger and, in this chapter, Mairtin Mac an Ghaill and Chris Haywood examine how young Muslim men are subject to a state-led project of normalizing their masculinity that is underpinned by an implicit tension. It is argued that this tension is based on ascriptions of young Muslim men as a threat to the state through notions of radicalization and as a threat to themselves as being unable to resist terrorist recruitment. The chapter draws upon research data gathered during a three-year critical ethnography (2008–2011) and explores the experiences of third-generation young British Muslim men of Pakistani and Bangladeshi heritage. The chapter suggests that Muslim's social and economic marginalization is somewhat in contrast with an unreported assertive English nationalism, involving a forging of a renewed British identity. More specifically, the chapter explores this marginalization through the reification of particular social and cultural categories, namely that of religion. In response, the chapter suggests that these young men are experiencing alternative forms of gendering where masculinity and marginalization are being reconfigured outside of normative 'British' codifications of manhood.

In Chapter 10, 'Marginalized adult ethnic minority men in Denmark: The case of Aalborg East', Ann-Dorte Christensen, Jeppe Fuglsang Larsen and Sune Qvotrup Jensen focus on adult ethnic minority men in Denmark. The aim of the chapter is to address a blind spot concerning specific issues of marginalization amongst these men. The chapter analyses processes of marginalization amongst ethnic minority men in a specific multi-ethnic and underprivileged neighbourhood, Aalborg East. The chapter consists of three main sections. The first section presents the theoretical framework and four key concepts: hegemonic masculinity, intersectionality, class journey and othering. The second section presents the methods and data which are primarily based on interviews. The third section analyses specific processes of marginalization: local and contextual mechanisms; implications of downward class journey; and processes of othering. One of the main findings is that the marginalized position of these adult ethnic minority men is not related to one single category. Instead, it reflects the interplay between multiple and intersecting categories: gender/masculinity, class and race. For instance, the intersectional analysis indicates that the downward class journey and the processes of othering are intertwined and inseparable. The collection concludes with Thomas Johansson and Chris Haywood drawing together the main themes and offering ways forward for future research in the field.

References

Abrams, L. S., Anderson-Nathe, B. and Aguilar, J. (2008) Constructing Masculinities in Juvenile Corrections, *Men and Masculinities* 11(1): 22–41.

Ahmad, J. (2010) Sexuality and Gender in Conflict: Residential Patterns of Eunuchs (Hijra) in Pakistan, *Humanities and Social Sciences*, Researchgate.net

Alderfer, C. P. (1987) An Intergroup Perspective on Group Dynamics. In: J. W. Lorsch (ed.) *Handbook of Organizational Behavior*. Englewood Cliffs, NJ: Prentice-Hall, pp. 190–222.

Blagojević, J. (2012) The Ethics of Marginality: A New Approach to Gay Studies, *Belgrade Journal of Media and Communications* 1(1) 65–75.

Breugel, I. (2000) No More Jobs for the Boys? Gender and Class in the Restructuring of the British Economy, *Capital and Class* 71: 79–101.

Bryman, A. (2008) The End of the Paradigm Wars. In: P. Alasuutari, L. Bickman, and J. Brannen (eds) *The SAGE Handbook of Social Research Methods*. London: Sage, pp. 13–25.

Champagne, J. (1995) *The Ethics of Marginality: A New Approach to Gay Studies*. Minnesota: University of Minnesota.

Cheng, C. (1999) Marginalized Masculinities and Hegemonic Masculinity: An Introduction, *Journal of Men's Studies* 7: 295–315.

Connell, R. W. (1987) *Gender and Power*. Sydney: Allen & Unwin.
Connell, R. W. (1995) *Masculinities*. Cambridge: Polity Press.
Connell, R. W. (2000) *The Men and the Boys*. Cambridge: Polity Press.
Curran, L. and Abrams, L. S. (2000) Making Men into Dads: Fatherhood, the State, and Welfare Reform, *Gender and Society* October 2000 14: 662–678.
Dahl-Michelson, T. (2014) Sportiness and Masculinities among Female and Male Physiotherapy Students, *Physiotherapy Theory and Practice: An International Journal of Physical Therapy*, 30(5): 329–337
Donaldson, M. and Howson, R. (2009) Men, Migration and Hegemonic Masculinity. In: M. Donaldson, R. Hibbins, R. Howson and B. Pease (eds) *Migrant Men: Critical Studies of Masculinities and the Migration Experience*. London: Routledge, pp. 210–217.
Esping-Andersen, Gösta (1990) *The Three Worlds of Welfare Capitalism*. Princeton: Princeton University Press.
European Institute for Gender Equality (EIGE) (2012) *The Involvement of Men in Gender Equality Initiatives in the European Union*. Luxembourg: Publication office of the European Union.
Evans, J., Blye, F., Oliffe, J. L. and Gregory, D. (2011) Health, Illness, Men and Masculinities (HIMM): A Theoretical Framework for Understanding Men and Their Health, *Journal of Men's Health* 8(1): 7–15.
Faludi, S. (2000) *Stiffed. The Betrayal of the American Man*. New York: Perennial.
Furman, R., Kaufmann, E. and Ackerman, A. R. (2012) Men at Risk in a Global World – Challenges for a Transnational Social Work, *Transnational Social Review: A Social Work Journal* 2(1): 83–94.
Gailey, J. A. and Prohaska, A. (2006) 'Knocking Off a Fat Girl': An Exploration of Hogging, Male Sexuality and Neutralizations, *Deviant Behavior* 27: 31–49.
Gailey, J. A. and Prohaska, A. (2011) Power and Gender Negotiations during Interviews with Men about Sex and Sexually Degrading Practices, *Qualitative Research* 11: 365–380.
Gartrell, A. (2010) 'A Frog in a Well': The Exclusion of Disabled People from Work in Cambodia, *Disability and Society*, 25(3): 289–301.
Gavanas, A. (2001) *Masculinizing Fatherhood: Sexuality, Marriage and Race in the U.S. Fatherhood Responsibility Movement*. Stockholm: Department of Social Anthropology.
Haavind, H. and Magnusson, E. (2005) The Nordic Countries – Welfare Paradises for Women and Children? *Feminism and Psychology*, 15(2): 227–235.
Haywood, C. and Mac an Ghaill, M. (2012) 'What Next for Masculinity?': Reflexive Directions for Theory and Research on Masculinity and Education, *Gender and Education* 24(6): 577–92.
Haywood, C. and Mac an Ghaill, M. (2013) *Education and Masculinities. Social, Cultural and Global Transformations*. London: Routledge.
Haywood, C. and McDermott, V. (2018) Disability and Masculinity: Exploring Men, Bodies and Sexuality. Papworth Trust.
Hearn, J. (2004) From Hegemonic Masculinity to the Hegemony of Men, *Feminist Theory* 5 (1): 49–72.
Hearn, J., Nordberg, M., Andersson, K., Balkmar, D., Gottzén, L., Klinth, R., Pringle, K. and Sandberg, L. (2012) Hegemonic Masculinity and Beyond: 40 Years of Research in Sweden, *Men and Masculinities* 15(1): 31–55.
Hearn, J. (1998) *The Violences of Men: How Men Talk about and How Agencies Respond to Men's Violence to Women*. London: Sage.
Hearn, J. and Pringle, K. (2006) *European Perspectives on Men and Masculinities. National and Transnational Approaches*. London: Palgrave Macmillan.

Hernandez, S. F., Pita, I. H. and de Juan, T. F. (2014) Masculinities in Cuba: Description and Analysis of a Case Study from a Gender Perspective, *Masculinities and Social Change* 3(3): 220–247.

Hirose, A. and Pih, K. K. (2010) Men Who Strike and Men Who Submit: Hegemonic and Marginalized Masculinities in Mixed Martial Arts, *Men and Masculinities* 13(2): 190–209.

Holter, Ø. G. (2007) Men's Work and Family Reconciliation in Europe, *Men and Masculinities* 9(4): 425–456.

Jackson II, R. L. and Moshin, J. E. (2012) *Communicating Marginalized Masculinities: Identity Politics in TV, Film, and New Media*. London: Routledge.

Janssen, D. F. (2009) Where 'Boys' 'Are': Co-constructions of Maturities-Genders-Bodies-Spaces, *Children's Geographies* 7(1): 83–98.

Johansson, T. and Ottemo, A. (2013) Ruptures in Hegemonic Masculinity, *Journal of Gender Studies*. Online 27 June 2013.

Kimmel, M. S. (1996/2006) *Manhood in America*. New York: Oxford University Press.

Kimmel, M. S. (2005) *The History of Men. Essays on the History of American and British Masculinities*. New York: State University of New York Press.

Mac an Ghaill, M. and Haywood, C. (2007) *Gender, Culture and Society*. London: Macmillan.

McKay, S. C. (2007) Filipino Sea Men: Constructing Masculinities in an Ethnic Labour Niche, *Journal of Ethnic and Migration Studies* 33 (4): 617–632.

Mirsky, S. (1996) Three Arguments for the Elimination of Masculinity. In: B. Krondorfer (ed.) *Men's Bodies, Men's Gods: Male Identities in a (Post-)Christian Culture*, New York: New York University Press.

Oliffe, J. and Mro'z, L. (2005) Men Interviewing Men about Health and Illness: Ten Lessons Learned, *The Journal of Men's Health and Gender* 2(2): 257–260

Ortega, L. M. D. (2012) Looking Beyond Violent Militarized Masculinities: Guerrilla Gender Regimes in Latin America, *International Feminist Journal of Politics* 14(4): 489–507.

Phillips, D. (2005) Reproducing Normative and Marginalized Masculinities: Adolescent Male Popularity and the Outcast, *Nursing Inquiry* 12(3): 219–230.

Ratele, K. (2014) Currents against Gender Transformation of South African Men: Relocating Marginality to the Centre of Research and Theory of Masculinities, *Norma* 9(1): 30–44.

Roy, A. (2011) Re-Forming the Megacity: Calcutta and the Rural–Urban Interface. In: A Sorenson and J. Okata (eds) *Megacities: Urban Form, Governance, and Sustainability*. London: Springer.

Schiffer, K. and Schatz, E. (2008) *Marginalization, Social Inclusion and Health*. Amsterdam: Correlation Network.

Schwalbe, M. and Wolkomir, M. (2001) The Masculine Self as Problem and Resource in Interview Studies of Men, *Men and Masculinities* 4(1): 90–103.

Tischler, A. and McCaughtry, N. (2011) PE Is Not for Me: When Boys' Masculinities Are Threatened, *Research Quarterly for Exercise and Sport* 82(1): 37–48.

Totten, M. (2003) Girlfriend Abuse as a Form of Masculinity Construction among Violent, Marginal Male Youth, *Men and Masculinities* 6: 70–92.

Walby, K. (2010) Interviews as Encounters: Issues of Sexuality and Reflexivity when Men Interview Men about Commercial Same Sex Relations, *Qualitative Research* 10: 639–657.

Part I
Crisis, Risk and Socialization

1 Becoming a "Real Boy"
Constructions of Boyness in Early Childhood Education

Anette Hellman and Ylva Odenbring

> PRESCHOOL TEACHER ONE: The boys we have in our group this year are not so "typical," but rather very nice boys. They are calmer: they don't need the teachers' attention; they don't get into fights and conflicts but know how to get along with other children in play.
> PRESCHOOL TEACHER TWO: Yeah, we'd rather see the boys in our group this year as children, not as boys.
> (Field notes, Marigold preschool)

In this introductory quote, two preschool teachers are discussing what kind of boys and boyness they wish to have at their preschool. In early childhood education, strong discourses are manifested about gender-stereotyped norms concerning what are considered "real boys" as opposed to "real girls." Actions that certain children perform are categorized as "problematic boyness" and are understood as all boys' actions (Nordberg *et al.*, 2010; Thorne, 1993). According to Thorne (1993), this kind of hegemonic description, which she defined as *The Big Man Bias*, not only regulates boys by describing what practices can be considered normal and deviant, but also directs teachers' attention to certain boys and practices. Furthermore, it also produces and constructs the categories "boy," "masculinity" and "boys' practices" by excluding, marginalizing, and neglecting certain groups of boys and many of the situations in which boys act differently.

Boys who are categorized as, and perform the position of, "problematic boys" are often understood as lacking certain emotions or skills. This group of boys becomes what Ratele (2014) defines as "marginalized hegemonies" or "hegemonies within marginality." The research literature on early childhood education and children's skills has recognized that the so-called competent child is one of the most idealized positions for children. The child who is categorized as "the competent child" not only behaves in "the right way," but also knows what is considered "good" and acceptable behavior. This is not a neutral position, but rather a gendered one (Hellman *et al.*, 2014). One way this position is conformed to is through children acting and being constructed as "ideal pupils," which is one form of preparation arena for school. This child, often a girl, is either asked by the practitioners to act, or acts on her own initiative, as the teacher's little helper or assistant in daily practice (Odenbring, 2014; Odenbring and Lappalainen, 2013).

Care is another dimension that relates to certain skill expectations, but also to gendered positions. Violent and dominant actions are often unreflectively understood as "typical" for boys, whereas caring and competent actions performed by boys are categorized as "non-typical" for boys – even if most boys perform them every day (Nordberg *et al.*, 2010). Several Nordic researchers have argued that hegemonic masculinity has to be understood in relation to hegemonic discourses in society (Christensen *et al.*, this volume; Hearn *et al.*, 2012). From a Swedish educational perspective, this means that traditional discourses on masculinity intersect with gender equality as well as discourses on the competent child.

In this connection, the aim of the present chapter is to explore constructions of *boyness* in Swedish preschool and preschool class settings. The chapter draws on data from three different ethnographic studies conducted in two preschools, named Marigold and Ladybug respectively, and one preschool class, named Octopus, all located in Sweden. Methodologically, we take our point of departure in feminist ethnographic ideas concerning reflexivity and gender awareness (Skeggs, 2001). Initially, the data from the individual projects were collected and analyzed separately. For the present chapter, we have considered collective and meta-ethnography to be a fruitful point of departure (Beach *et al.*, 2013). The analysis is based on a collective process through which we have jointly read through our field notes and analyzed the data (Gordon *et al.*, 2006; Odenbring and Lappalainen, 2013).

Gender Equality and Early Childhood Education in Sweden

Historically, gender equality has quite a long tradition in Sweden (Hearn *et al.*, 2012). Policies aimed at men have often been a central part of Swedish gender-equality policy. Full-time work for women has been one side of the gender-equality coin, where the other side is the government encouraging men to play a greater role in housework and childcare (Nordberg, 2004). Swedish early childhood education has also been described as playing an important role in forming children's gendered identities. In Sweden, preschool education is provided for children aged one to five years, whereas preschool class education is provided for children aged six years.

Another important part of Swedish gender equality is providing early childhood education for all children. During the past four decades, the majority of children have attended preschool and preschool class, which means that these educational institutions have been, and still are, an important part of childhood. From an international perspective, Sweden has become a leading country when it comes to providing childcare across the country, regardless of the child's social background (SFS, 2010: 800; Tallberg Broman, 2010). The national curriculum specifically mentions practitioners' obligation to counteract gender stereotypes (Skolverket, 2010, 2011).

The Panoptic Gaze and Boyness

We have found the theoretical concept of *the gaze* (Foucault, 1977; Whitehead, 2002) to be a useful analytical tool for investigating how marginalized masculinities are manifested in the everyday practices of early childhood education. Whitehead (2002) identified a special and normalizing way of looking and searching for what are understood as truths about the observed individual: *the panoptic gaze.*

> In gendered terms we can see the gaze applied to both women's and men's bodies, whereby the discursive subject comes to discipline and manage her/his body as self-surveillance. So the gaze is not simply directed at us; we regulate our own bodies in the knowledge and presence of the authoritative gaze. However, the gaze itself is not neutral but invested with powers, in so much as it comes with a set of moral, social codes or assumptions; an "economy of looks" that places values on the body, and different values on different bodies.
>
> (Whitehead, 2002, p. 195)

According to this theoretical understanding, the normalizing gaze is not neutral, neither in terms of gender nor what is understood as suitable for boys' and girls' bodies' respective ways of talking and acting. Gaze also produces male or boy subjects. Some norms are given hegemonic status and construct a hegemonic order for how to interpret, desire, look, behave, and organize (Butler, 1993). These norms make certain ways of acting in early childhood education possible, recognizable, and labeled as normal. On the other hand, other ways of performing boyness are constructed as abnormal.

At the same time, there are always contradictions that lead to resistance and the reconstruction of norms. Several gendered norms are at work at the same time, and these might also be complex and contradictory, thus creating continuous negotiations about what constitutes acceptable or unacceptable behavior. Men's, boys', women's, and girls' valuations of how "a real boy" should behave may all be active in this process. Hence, individuals other than those categorized as "typical boys" also perform norms related to what is considered right, suitable, or natural. According to Connell (2000), hegemonic masculinity is seldom the most common masculinity, but rather an ideal seldom achieved by living individuals. However, this image of "the real man" and "the real boy" is a norm that individuals have to relate to. Other forms of masculinity are measured in relation to, as well as subordinated to, this normalizing masculinity.

In the present chapter, we use the concept of *boyness* (Haywood and Mac an Ghaill, 2013). Boyness relates to norms concerning masculinity and how boys are expected to act in certain ways if they are to become "real men" in the future. Yet norms related to masculinity and adult men are not necessarily the same thing as gendered expectations for boys. In this connection, becoming a "real boy," and later on in life a "real man," also intersect with hegemonic norms concerning age, such as competence and certain skills (Hellman *et al.*, 2014).

The Panoptic Gaze on Boys' Bodies

In our data, we have identified different gendered expectations for boys with regard to their biological body and processes of *the panoptic gaze* (cf. Foucault, 1977; Whitehead, 2002). This is something that the investigated children experienced during different daily activities, for example during play activities. In the excerpt below, the children in the Octopus preschool class are playing on a playground in a park. One of the boys, Erik, wants to try the most advanced climbing frame:

> Erik wants to reach the Roman rings in the climbing frame. Preschool teacher Helena says that it is too hard to reach and too difficult, but Erik claims that he won't get hurt if he falls down. Eventually Erik manages to reach the Roman rings. Helena comments on this by calling him a pack of muscles.
>
> (Field notes, Octopus preschool class)

Comments and categorizations such as those in the extract above relate to predominant masculine ideals and understandings and the expectation that boys should be strong and tough (cf. Connell, 2003). Through these bodily expressions and actions on the playground, the child male body conforms to occupying space (Whitehead, 2002). According to Connell (2000), dominant norms concerning masculinity are accentuated when boys' bodies are positioned at the center of attention, such as in sport activities. This often emerges when boys are supposed to behave like "real" boys. At preschool, these norms were also expressed during meals:

PRESCHOOL TEACHER: (placed mustard on his plate with his soup) This is really hot stuff; you have to eat it together with your soup.
TED: What is it?
PRESCHOOL TEACHER: It's mustard. Try some! It's really something for big, strong, and cool guys like me. *(Tommy flexes his biceps and points at each one of the older boys around the table).*
TED: Yeah, right *(He shows his biceps as well).* Yeah, this is stuff for strong boys like me and Tommy!
PRESCHOOL TEACHER: Ludwig and ... Emil.
EMIL AND LUDWIG: Yeah, we're also strong!
Emil and Ludwig show their muscles and put some mustard in their soup. Kalle, a younger boy, is sitting close to the older boys. He is looking at the mustard without tasting it.
KALLE: Maybe I'd like some of that too, then. Yeah, I'll have some!
PRESCHOOL TEACHER: That's my boy! Now that you've been so brave, I bet your muscles have grown already. Let me see! Wow! Just like your older friends!

(Field notes, Marigold preschool)

When strength, size and achievement norms were emphasized, the boys in Marigold preschool were often at the center of attention. The preschool teacher therefore creates a group of boys who are brave enough to try the mustard: "we strong boys." The preschool teacher also addresses *certain boys* around the table – namely the oldest and "big" boys, those with the highest status among the preschool children. Here, it is important to recognize the significance of age as a power structure working together with hegemonic masculinity in order to create "real boys." However, the position as a "real boy" was – like any position – a subject of constant negotiation. Connell (2000) describes how idealized norms concerning how to behave like a boy always need to be re-established and guarded, even if one is ascribed a high-status position like the boys in the excerpt above. This was expressed, for instance, when boys crossed gendered boundaries and moved toward what was labeled as feminine, such as when they whined, tried on dresses, or kissed other boys. Other actions were normalized in the public sphere. One situation was observed when the preschool class children were playing on a playground near the preschool class:

> The children are playing on the playground. While playing, Sven has to go to the bathroom. There are no toilets available so preschool teacher Monika tells him to walk over to a tree to pee. She also says that it might be complicated with all his clothes, but that he is better equipped because he is a boy.
> (Field notes, Octopus preschool class)

Here, *the panoptic gaze* is aimed at the male genitals, which are indirectly also compared to something that is their opposite, i.e., the female (and invisible) genitals. Regardless of whether this boy is comfortable with these actions, he is encouraged to conform to a specific form of (sexualized) masculinity in public, where the male child body and his genitals are exposed in a public space (cf. Whitehead, 2002). Not surprisingly, we have not found any notes about preschool teachers encouraging girls to conform to femininity and claiming space in a similar way.

In this section, we have highlighted how the gaze is directed at young boys' bodies. Already in preschool and preschool class, they are expected to conform to a sporty and masculine ideal. Moreover, to become a "real boy" or "real man" in the future, they also have to eat proper meals so they will develop big muscles and get strong.

Rowdiness and Male Role Models

According to the national curriculum, all practitioners working in Swedish preschools and preschool classes are obliged to counteract stereotyped understandings of gender (Skolverket, 2011). Hence, this strong discourse on gender equality is also manifested in the investigated preschools and preschool class. At the same time, stereotyped notions of "typical" boys and girls also emerge in all our preschools, and discourses on boys' natural (biologically or culturally inherited) actions – such as violence, dominance, and rowdiness – intersect with gender equality.

At Marigold preschool, violence and dominance were performed by all of the children. In conversations with practitioners, however, this was understood as something "natural" for all boys – even though just a few boys (and girls) behaved in this manner in certain situations. The preschool teachers often discussed the problems associated with the so-called rowdy boys and how to solve them. One suggestion was that an extra preschool teacher should be employed to help out with the rowdy boys, pointing out that this person should have certain qualifications:

> Some of the practitioners argued that boys, especially the "rowdy boys" who commonly oppose the rules set up by preschool teachers and other children, needed more discipline than the practitioners managed to uphold. According to some of the practitioners, female practitioners could not handle rowdy and problematic boys. One of the preschool teachers, Katarina, expressed that men often have more muscles, physical strength and more powerful voices, aspects she thinks are important in teaching children certain limits.
>
> (Field notes, Marigold preschool)

A recurrent discourse in the debate on the feminization of the educational system is that it has resulted in a lack of "male role models" for this group of boys (Baagöe-Nielsen, 2005; Haywood and Mac an Ghaill, 2013). It is also argued that female teachers only support girl-friendly practices, and as a result boys do not receive the support in their boyness that is necessary for them to become "real boys" (Haywood and Mac an Ghaill, 2013).

The practitioners at Marigold preschool argued that the boys need a certain kind of male role model – a man who can discipline them and be someone they can respect. These results correspond with findings from previous research on the moral panic debate concerning boys in school (Haywood and Mac an Ghaill, 2013). One recurrent argument in the moral panic debate is that female teachers lack the ability to discipline and that boys require a certain degree of discipline if they are to become proper future citizens. Another common argument in this debate, in relation to early childhood education, is that boys need a particular kind of male role model. These men must have certain skills and demonstrate a tough and aggressive form of masculinity (Nordberg et al., 2010). Yet, not everyone at Marigold preschool agreed with the argument that the presence of particularly strict men would solve the problem:

> Why do we need a man to do that job? That's just ridiculous. It's also problematic for the men we engage; who wants to be the bad guy all day long and what message does that send to our children about men?
>
> (Preschool teacher, Marigold preschool).

The preschool teacher quoted above not only expresses her concern about how these boys are supposed to be disciplined, but she also questions the notion of female practitioners' inability to maintain order and discipline among the children. What we can see is ambivalence with regard to how certain groups of boys are understood and how to give these boys adequate guidance and support. According to some of the preschool teachers, these boys need a strict and firm masculine hand and guidance, not a caring masculinity. Again, we can see a clash between caring and hegemonic understandings of becoming a "real boy."

Marginalized Boys

The normalized position of a "typical boy" is not necessarily connected to high status. Our results indicate that this is also a position with low status in the peer group. This notion is related to discourses on competence and incompetence, where incompetence is labeled as lack of self-control and not following the rules during play. Children who do not follow the established rules during play activities are understood as troublesome, and sometimes these children are excluded from other children's play activities and, thus, marginalized (Sutton-Smith, 1997). In child–child interactions during play or games, exclusion of children who interrupt the play or ignore the rules may have severe consequences. During a floor hockey game at Octopus preschool class, one of the boys, Oliver, repeatedly interrupted the game, which resulted in verbal harassment.

> It is an intense game and the boys hit hard balls at each other. The boys are both laughing and complaining about the hard balls. Oliver is playing, but is interrupting the play. Martin and Erik tell him to stop what he is doing. Erik tells Oliver to stop and says: "Stop it Olivia!" Martin repeats what Erik just said. Erik repeats the name Olivia twice when he addresses Oliver, but Oliver seems to ignore the other boys' verbal harassment.
> (Field notes, Octopus preschool class)

Claiming space is also incongruous for young boys. Although these boys occupy space with their bodies during the game (cf. Whitehead, 2002), it is also important to follow the rules and not interrupt the game. Name calling is a very powerful weapon used by the other boys to marginalize Oliver. By calling Oliver "Olivia," a girl's name, the other boys are not only marginalizing him, but also positioning and categorizing him as a "girl." Research (Connell, 1995; Epstein, 1998) has suggested that verbal harassment of this kind is often used among men in superior positions to legitimize their power over subordinated men (Connell, 1995). Using feminine categorizations, such as being called a girl or homophobic nicknames, is often part of this form of harassment.

In Oliver's case, his subordinated position in the peer group is likely of importance here. Previous research has shown that popularity plays an important role in children's daily gendered worlds. The popular child, despite gender, has greater possibilities to challenge traditional gendered expectations and can quite easily maneuver between gender borders without being questioned or teased by other children (Davies, 2003; Thorne, 1993). Part of becoming a competent preschool child is following routines and rules during play. Research (Johansson, 2008) also indicates that children, despite gender, emphasize rules during play. At Marigold preschool, the girls and boys who liked to play together created spaces of friendship. One example of this is of a girl, Bella, and a boy, Carl, both five years old, who really liked playing together.

CARL: Bella is my friend; it's so much fun to play with her. If we want different things when we play, then we do a little bit like she wants and a little bit like I want. We don't care if Tony teases us; we just keep on playing and ignore him.
INTERVIEWER: Does Tony tease you for playing with Bella?
CARL: No, not always, but if he can't play with us then he will start teasing me for playing with Bella or for playing with dolls. But Bella says: "Ignore him!" And then I just ignore him. Bella say nice things to me and I usually say nice things to her – that's what friends do. Real friends don't tease each other; they help and are nice to each other like me and Bella do.

(Interview, Marigold preschool)

Bella and Carl's friendship often worked as a kind of safety platform for the other children involved; a platform from which they could negotiate and play with norms. For the children at Marigold preschool, most important to achieving status and being included in friendship relations was having knowledge about how to play with peers. Having knowledge about play rules, the ability to negotiate with and care for others, self-control, humor, and creativity gave certain individuals high status and provided them with access to wider networks of relations, where girls and boys could negotiate predominant norms concerning age, gender, and behavior. Children who had gained this knowledge were categorized as "competent children," which was the most admired position for children in the investigated preschools and preschool class. However, preschool teachers and other children talked about the problematic boys as individuals who lacked competence and control. Uncontrolled actions and violence were thus at risk of being perceived as natural for boys, even if most boys, as well as most girls, performed the position of a competent child. The part of "rowdy and problematic boy," characterized by dominance, uncontrolled aggression, or uncontrolled actions, was strongly gendered. Boys were made visible, reprimanded, and recognized through this position. Even if most boys behaved in other ways, practitioners tended to overlook these other actions and to connect "rowdy-boy" actions to all boys, something which will be discussed further in the next section.

Normalization of Families

Research has shown how the highest status position for children in Swedish preschools and preschool classes is that of the so-called competent child (Hellman *et al.*, 2014). This position is not neutral, but linked to certain family backgrounds, as one of the Marigold preschool teachers expressed: "Nice boys are very calm and competent, but of course these children have a good home environment with good parents, not single mothers or parents who don't have time for their children."

According to our informants, the nuclear family is the ideal family for children to grow up in. By expressing this, informants not only maintain certain norms concerning what "the good" family is, but they also conform to classed aspects of the ideal family. When it comes to how family background and family constellations are described by our informants, intersectional aspects of the gaze emerge. The gaze is multiplied and embodied through gender, class, age, sexuality, and ethnicity as well as culture (Whitehead, 2002). The middle-class nuclear family represents the ideal family and good parenthood, where children get the right guidance and upbringing. Children growing up with single mothers are described and also classed in a different way. These children are considered problematic, and informants report that these children will not have the same life chances – in terms of economic conditions and present parents – as children growing up in a nuclear family.

At Ladybug preschool, the collective "us" was based on the idea that everyone should learn the Swedish language and traditions so as to become part of Swedish society. The practitioners discussed the importance of involving the children's parents in Swedish traditions and helping them "blend into" Swedish society (see also Haywood and Mac an Ghaill, this volume). Celebrating holidays such as Lucia (December 13th) and Christmas and explaining to the parents why Swedes celebrate these holidays were considered important parts of this process.

One way of working with the Swedish language and inclusion at Ladybug preschool was by encouraging the children to speak only Swedish at preschool. The main reason for this was, according to the preschool teachers, to get an overview of, and have control over, what the children were talking about. One of the Ladybug preschool teachers expressed her ideas in the following way: 'There are a lot of things going on here. Especially when you have children from Muslim countries, then you definitely have to control what is said so there isn't a lot of inappropriate talk in the preschool.'

The practitioner above talks about the need to control the children, especially children from Muslim countries, because so much is "going on." Understanding and learning "Swedishness" through language is not only a matter of inclusion for the children. It also seems as though the preschool teacher feels the need to be included in different language spaces at the preschool, in order to get an overview of what is going on. The same preschool teacher also stressed the importance of controlling these children and checking what they are doing:

> Boys from Muslim countries are more often troublesome [compared to "Swedish" children], but it's not only that they fight more. It's also the language, that they say inappropriate sexually discriminating things. That's why Swedish is the only language used, so we know what's going on and can organize the whole thing.
>
> (Preschool teacher, Ladybug preschool)

According to this preschool teacher, it is the sexually discriminating language that needs to be controlled. Given that this particular preschool teacher did not speak these children's mother tongue, she had no understanding of what the children were actually saying. The preschool teacher also pointed out this group of children as being more troublesome and violent compared to other children in the preschool. Thus, the incompetent child is someone who performs violent and unequal actions, and this position is ascribed to boys with a Muslim background.

In addition to this, the practitioners also discuss the importance of involving children's parents in Swedish traditions so that they can "blend into" Swedish society. Furthermore, gender equality also seems to be an essential part of becoming a "real" Swede. The Principal at Ladybug preschool gave one example of this:

> Once we had parents from a remote mountain village with a very narrow understanding of gender equality and a very strict understanding of Islam and religion. We had quite difficult meetings before they understood what it is like in Sweden in terms of gender equality. It's not easy to know how to handle this in preschool. It's important to show that women must be treated with respect, but at the same time you don't want to humiliate the parents. But it's not easy if you're an Iranian who believes in an eye for an eye and a tooth for a tooth.
>
> (Principal, Ladybug preschool)

The authoritative gaze and the construction of *the Other* are also directed at Muslim boys and Muslim families (cf. Whitehead, 2002). There seems to be a general understanding among the informants that they are capable of giving these boys and families the tools needed to become gender equal. Their understandings of gender equality are based on the notion that gender equality is typically Swedish and that all Swedes live up to gender-equality norms.

Conclusion

Children in early childhood education play several parts related to gender. However, the practitioners' *gaze* on the children is connected to specific actions, norms, and certain children, and most visible to the preschool teachers are the "problematic boys." We have shown that the "typical boy" is normalized through stereotyped notions about "real boys" (in the process of becoming "real men"). Here, the preschool teachers' gaze is directed at boys' bodies. We have discussed how ideals about strength and muscular bodies regulate boys' bodies when the young children are eating in preschool and engaging in sports and play activities in the preschool class. We have also shown that space is important in the construction of the "typical" boy. Typical boyness is linked to achievement in public space; there are expectations that boys will perform well in sport activities, and there are no restrictions on boys showing their genitals in public.

Typical and normal boyness also seems to include rowdy, violent, and dominant actions, even if such behavior was seen as problematic in the investigated preschools and preschool class. With regard to controlling boys, there was a discussion about the need to employ "real" men, that is, men who were expected to control and restrict boys in a firm and strict way. This was a form of control that, according to some of the preschool teachers, was made possible by strong bodies and strong voices – by bodily behavior linked to men rather than to women. But there were also voices that raised concerns about this gender-stereotyped picture.

We have also shown that status and certain knowledge are linked to inclusion and exclusion. Boys who use the "problematic boy" position are given low status. Consequently, they are marginalized and excluded from different play activities in peer–peer interaction. Our results indicate that *knowledge about how to play* is important if a child is to gain high status, be popular, and be included in play. Hence, certain competencies, such as negotiating and solving conflicts without violence or using playfulness, humor, and creativity, will generate high status and facilitate children's access to social relations with peers – where these competencies often are learned (Sommer, 2015). Children who use violence, interrupt, or break the play rules are not accepted by other children. It is therefore of great importance that teachers fulfill their responsibility (Skolverket, 2010), participate in children's play, and teach children who are marginalized from play the knowledge required to facilitate their inclusion.

Furthermore, central to inclusion and exclusion in early childhood education settings are discourses on competence and non-competence. Although rowdy actions and violence are normalized for boys, they are also understood as incompetence and as being in opposition to actions categorized as competent. The explanation for boys' rowdy actions is not discussed in relation to the preschool or the preschool class practice, but instead the responsibility is put on the families. Here we can see that the gaze on the non-competent child and *the Other* is related to class as well as ethnic background (Whitehead, 2002). Children growing up with single parents are particularly problematic, according to the practitioners. Non-competence is also tied to boys with an immigrant background – Muslim boys in particular. Muslim boys are not only categorized as problematic, but they and their parents also have to learn how gender equality works in Sweden.

The present study has generated new knowledge about the problematic boys in early childhood education. In order to be accepted and to play the "competent child," certain skills are required. Yet the messages sent to the boys are quite contradictory. On the one hand, they are encouraged to perform certain hegemonic expectations linked to masculinity: be active, be physically strong, and eat proper meals so they can become strong boys and future men. On the other hand, this position does not seem to be consistent with the discourses on competence and gender equality. We argue that, at least on the local level, different forms of idealized masculinity may exist at the same time. In the Swedish context, at least in some educational contexts, this means that "typical" boyness is normalized at the same time as a self-regulated and caring child – the competent child – is idealized and given high status.

References

Baagöe-Nielsen, S. (2005) Mend og daginstitutionsarbejdets modernisering – teoretiske, historiske og etnografiske perspektiver på sammenhenge mellem genus, pedagogisk arbejde og organisering av daginstitutioner [Men and the modernization of day care – theoretical, historical and ethnographic perspectives of gender, pedagogy and organization in day care]. Doktorsavhandling. Roskilde: Roskilde Universitetscenter.

Beach, D., Dovemark, M., Schwartz, A. and Öhrn, E. (2013) Complexities and contradictions of educational inclusion. A meta-ethnographic analysis, Nordic Studies in Education 4: 254–268.

Butler, J. (1993) Bodies that matter: on the discursive limits of "sex." New York: Routledge.

Connell, R. (1995) Masculinities. Berkeley, CA: University of California Press.

Connell, R. (2000) The men and the boys. Cambridge: Polity.

Connell, R. (2003) Gender (2nd ed.). Cambridge, MA: Polity Press.

Davies, B. (2003) Frogs and snails and feminist tales – preschool, children and gender. Cresskill, NJ: Hampton Press.

Epstein, D. (1998) Real boys don't work: 'underachievement,' masculinity and the harassment of 'sissies.' In D. Epstein, J. Elwood, V. Hey and J. Maw (eds) Failing boys? Issues in gender and achievement. Buckingham: Open University Press, pp. 96–108.

Foucault, M. (1977) Power/Knowledge: The birth of the prison. London: Allen Lane.

Gordon, T., Hynninen, P., Lahelma, E., Metso, T., Palmu, T. and Tolonen, T. (2006). Collective ethnography, joint experiences and individual pathways, Nordisk Pedagogik, 26 (1): 3–15.

Haywood, C. and Mac an Ghaill. M. (2013) Education and masculinities. Social, cultural and global transformations. London: Routledge.

Hearn, J., Nordberg, M., Andersson, K., Balkmar, D., Gottzén, L., Klinth, R., Pringle, K. and Sandberg, L. (2012) Hegemonic masculinity and beyond: 40 years of research in Sweden, Men and Masculinities 15(1): 31–55.

Hellman, A., Sundhall, J. and Heikkilä, M. (2014) Don't be such a baby! Competence and age as intersectional co-markers on children's gender, International Journal of Early Childhood Education 46(3): 327–344.

Johansson, E. (2008) "Gustav får visst sitta i tjejsoffan!" Etik och genus i förrskolebarns världar ["Gustav may also sit on the girls' sofa!" Ethics and gender in preschool children's daily practice]. Stockholm: Liber.

Nordberg, M. (2004) Flickor och pojkar [Girls and boys], Utbild 2: 10–18.

Nordberg, M., Saar, T. and Hellman. A. (2010) Deconstructing the normal boy: Heterosexuality and gender constructions in school and preschool. In L. Martinsson and E. Reimers (eds) Norm struggles: Sexualities in contentions, Newcastle: Cambridge Scholars Publishing, pp. 29–53.

Odenbring, Y. (2014) Gender, order and discipline in early childhood education, International Journal of Early Childhood 42(2): 345–356.

Odenbring, Y. and Lappalainen, S. (2013) In "the educational twilight zone": Gendered pedagogy and constructions of the ideal pupil in the transition from pre-primary education to compulsory schooling in Finland and Sweden, Nordic Studies in Education 33(4): 329–343.

Ratele, K. (2014) Currents against gender transformation of South African men: Relocating marginality to the centre of research and theory of masculinities, Norma 9(1): 30–44.

SFS 2010:800. Skollagen [Education Act]. Stockholm: Utbildningsdepartementet.
Skeggs, B. (2001) Feminist ethnography. In P. Atkinson, A. Coffey, S. Delamont, J. Lofland and L. Lofland (eds) Handbook of ethnography, London: Sage, pp. 426–442.
Skolverket. (2010) Läroplan för förskolan [Curriculum for preschool]. Stockholm: Skolverket.
Skolverket. (2011) Läroplan för grundskolan, förskoleklassen och fritidshemmet [Curriculum for the compulsory school, preschool class and the recreation center]. Stockholm: Skolverket.
Sommer, D. (2015) Barndomspsykologiska fasetter [Perspectives on childhood]. Stockholm: Liber.
Sutton-Smith, B. (1997) The ambiguity of play. Cambridge, MA; London: Harvard University Press.
Tallberg Broman, I. (2010) Svensk förskola – ett kvalitetsgrepp. In B. Riddersporre and S. Persson (eds) Utbildningsvetenskap för förskolan [Educational sciences for preschool] Stockholm: Natur and Kultur. 21–38.
Thorne, B. (1993) Gender play. Girls and boys in school. New Brunswick: Rutgers University Press.
Whitehead, S. M. (2002) Men and masculinities: Key themes and new directions. Malden, MA: Polity.

2 Being at Risk or Being a Risk?
Marginalized Masculinity in Contemporary Social Work

Marcus Herz

> SOCIAL WORKER 1: He's a boy, for starters.
> HEAD OF STAFF: Hmm.
> SOCIAL WORKER 1: Everyone knows about the case, right? We don't have to say too much about their background. So, where should we start?
> SOCIAL WORKER 2: Alright, risk factors … on an individual level. OK, he is a boy. Actually, we don't know that much more about him.
> SOCIAL WORKER 1: He's been a problem at school.
> SOCIAL WORKER 2: Mmm. He has difficulties at school.
>
> (Herz, 2012)

In the preceding dialogue, a couple of social workers are discussing a case concerning a young boy, together with their head of staff. The discussion took place during a staff meeting at a social services office with staff working with children in distress. To get an overview of the case, the social workers discuss different so-called risk and protective factors in the child's everyday life. This example is from the beginning of that discussion. The fact that, biologically, the client is a boy is highlighted and treated as synonymous with being at risk. When the social worker stresses that the client is a boy, this is noted on a whiteboard by the head of staff under the heading "risk." One reason the social workers put so much emphasis on the child being a boy is because the evidence-based assessment system they use states that boys are more likely to be exposed to and to get involved with "antisocial" behavior (Andershed and Andershed, 2005, 2010).

Two things seem to happen, and both are associated with an alleged connection between the systems, methods, and knowledge being implemented and evidence-based practice as "the best available knowledge" (Herz and Johansson, 2011a, 2012; Herz, 2012, 2013). First, gender is used as a static variable – that is, being a biological man supports certain assessments or decisions. Second, the use of methods, tools, and systems as part of an evidence-based practice (EBP) discourse is, by definition, "best available knowledge" – that is, that the tools, systems, and methods take on gender issues is automatically considered or treated as being based upon best available knowledge regardless of whether this is the case or not. This is what is happening in the dialogue above: being a boy is interpreted through the use of a method, marketed as being evidence based. By this logic, masculinity is only represented through the child's biological sex, and, as a static variable, it also predicts certain behaviors and social conditions.

Even if the assessment in some terms might be considered statistically valid, when translated down to individuals lives, the assessments and decisions based on this statistical assumption might lead to the same constructions of masculinity being constantly reproduced. For example, boys often receive treatment and other interventions to a greater extent than girls (Brunnberg, 2002). Furthermore, boys and girls tend to get different interventions based solely on gender assumptions, as is the case with so-called male role models sometimes used as an intervention method for young boys (Hicks, 2008; Johansson, 2005; see also Hellman and Odenbring's chapter, this book).

When discussed in relation to marginalized positions connected to social problems, social exclusion, or social vulnerability, masculinity often tends to be approached as a static and unquestionable position. However, what this approach often veils is, in fact, rather unclear and messy. For instance, this is the case as certain notions of masculinity are often approached both as the underlying cause of a problem and as something desirable. One might claim that certain notions of masculinity are both contributing to the "problem" and becoming part of the solution. This is, in turn, substantiated by masculinity being approached as static.

This chapter will discuss what happens when the social work profession tries to manage marginalization among boys and men. Instead of an approach that takes different discourses of masculinity into consideration, boys and men are interpreted through hegemonic discourses of masculinity and simply seen as *being* the risk, instead of being seen as exposed to risk. On the one hand, I will claim that such an approach could be argued to lock men into a certain position of marginalization, whereby gender is synonymous with being in need of help by social services. On the other hand, such a static approach could be argued to conceal marginalization among men since their situation, feelings, and experiences might be subordinated to their gender position. Furthermore, the chapter will discuss how notions of masculinity need to be put into motion to be able to capture several positions of marginalization as well as more hegemonic positions.

The chapter is based on an ethnographic study that took place at a social services office in Sweden over the course of one year (Herz, 2012). This material is discussed using official statistics and policies as well as current methods and systems used in social work. The reason for this approach is that the social workers taking part in the ethnographic study often referred to different methods, systems, and policies based on statistics and aggregated data in their work. To be able to understand the discussions, the assessments, and the decisions made by the social workers, their different narratives need to be read through the lens of the methods, systems, and documents referred to.

In the next section, I discuss masculinity as being a risk: Is there any truth behind the assumption that being a boy, or being a man, equals being at risk? Thereafter, gender and masculinity in general in social work will be discussed through previous research and empirical examples. I then discuss evidence-based social work and its possible effect on gender issues in order to understand the ongoing development of social work. In the following section, "It could be a risk, being a boy," we return to the social services office to see how this development tends to be interpreted and understood, as well as its effect on the practice of social work. Last of all, I discuss an alternative approach to masculinity and marginalization before concluding the chapter.

Boys and Men Being at Risk

To say the least, social work is a disparate field; for instance, social workers are to be found in schools, health care, and community work or in the fields of social services working with social vulnerability or social problems all over the world. In terms of social problems, men are almost always overrepresented as being the offender or being the cause of social vulnerability. Men are more likely to be convicted of indictable offences than women; they are more likely to both put themselves or others in danger; and a great majority of all sex offenders are male (Herz, 2014; "Offending and Masculinity: Working with Males," 1990).

Concepts such as risk, aggressiveness, power, contestation, or violence are all notions closely associated with masculinity or how men behave. Men and violent crimes are almost synonymous because men, as mentioned, are overrepresented as perpetrators. In Sweden, 83 percent of all prosecution decisions concern men, and in terms of who is sentenced to prison, this number is even higher, about 90 percent. The more serious and violent the crime, the greater the chance of it having a male perpetrator. Similar numbers are possible to see across large parts of the world (Herz, 2014). In Australia and in the United States, for instance, the proportion of men in the prison system is about 93 percent in both countries (Australian Institute of Criminology, 2015; Federal Bureau of Prisons, 2015).

However, being this strongly associated with being an offender or a risk-taker could put men in a position that makes them almost impossible to include in different notions of marginalization, regardless of their situation. In this section I will, as an example, mainly dwell on one statistical fact, namely, that of over-mortality among men in general and among young men or boys in particular. Mortality among men is higher than among women over the whole life cycle, but tends to peak between 20 and 24 years of age. The reason for this is often connected to lifestyle issues, manifest through, for instance, accidents, taking risks, and committing suicide. Although using an example from Sweden, similar patterns are seen in many other countries as well (c.f. Miniño, 2010).

When presented as aggregated data, over-mortality among young men or boys, in particular, could support the view that being a boy equals being at risk. In this case, the risk of dying prematurely is nearly 3 percent higher for men between 20 and 24 years of age (see Figure 2.1). There is a tension between interpreting this as an effect of men "being men" and of some men more than others being affected by dominant conceptions of masculinity. This data provides no tools on how to interpret this risk or how to transform this knowledge

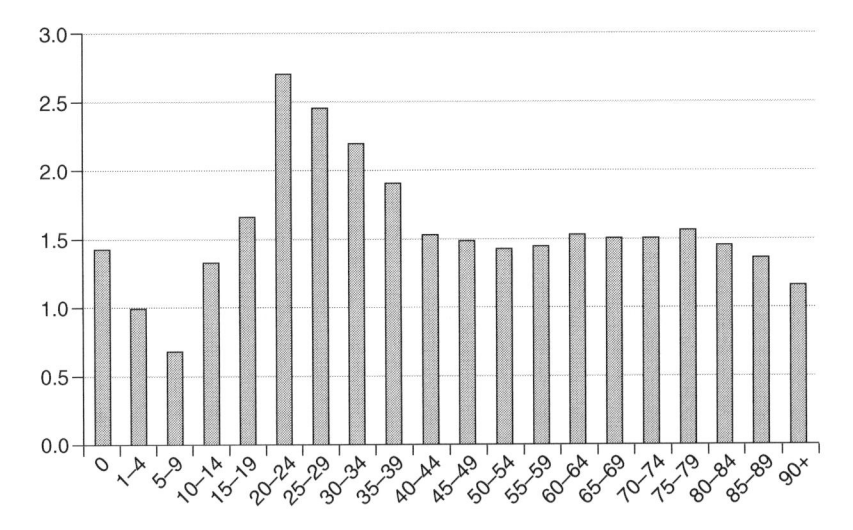

Figure 2.1 Over-mortality (in percent) among men (age) in Sweden, 2014 per year at time of death.

Source: Statistics Sweden.

into everyday professional practice with men or boys seeking help or support. To be able to interpret this phenomenon, we need to focus our attention elsewhere. One possible approach to understanding this peak in over-mortality is through masculinity studies. Thus, the lifestyle issues mentioned above, such as taking unnecessary risks, need to be understood in terms of different notions of masculinity, otherwise marginalization and exposure among men risks simply being interpreted or reformulated as an expression of a "lack of masculinity" based on static notions of masculinity and gender. In the everyday practice of social work, however, masculinity is seldom analyzed, instead it is often used and understood as a static position.

Gender and Masculinity in the Field of Social Work

Feminists and postcolonial theorists have, over the years, formulated a major critique of social work, accusing it both of being gender-blind and of neglecting critical perspectives on power (Herz and Johansson, 2011a, 2011b). An increasing number of academic studies on these issues show that social work practices often are influenced by stereotypical views on gender and ethnicity (Burck and Gwyn, 1995; Dominelli, 2008; Hicks, 2008; Sue, 2006). Often, gender is treated as a complementary fact in terms of two different categories of people complementing each other with their different traits and conditions (Mattsson, 2005). Gender is also often seen as being static, meaning that it is seen as unchangeable over time (Orme, 2003; Zufferey, 2009).

Scourfield (2003) has, for instance, studied how fatherhood is being constructed in social services in Great Britain. His results indicate that there are six different discourses on men and fatherhood used in the social services. The first one, "men as a threat," has to do with men being considered a threat toward the children or the mothers, which in turn tends to be transmitted to the social workers when talking about the men. Other discourses, which are not as common, include the following: "men as no use," "men as irrelevant," "men as absent," and, finally, the two more positively connoted, "men as no different [parent] from women," and "men as better [parent] than women." These two discourses are more positive toward the father but at the same time they claim the mothers to be inadequate. According to Scourfield, this is the only way fathers are being constructed as good, or as good enough parents. Masculinity becomes almost synonymous with being a bad father, which in turn prevents the fathers from being positioned as being in need of help and support. To be able to inhabit such a position, the mothers need to be interpreted as being bad parents. Another example of how gender is interpreted in social work is related to sexuality and masculinity. The expectations on men to always want sex and to feel confident about their sexuality tend to affect how these issues are approached in social work and in schools. In this case, there are two different approaches: one connected to the notion of male sexuality as being dangerous, and the other to how male sexuality also is seen as being desirable. Male sexuality as dangerous is connected to male violence, rape, and sexual dominance, whilst the second approach has to do with the aim to get girls to enjoy sex as much as men do (Bäckman, 2003; Mattsson, 2005). Mattsson (2005) conducted a study on addiction treatment centers in Sweden and found how male sexuality was interpreted as a possible danger regardless of whether it was a male resident meeting a female staff member or a male staff member meeting a female resident.

In the everyday practice of social work, these approaches to gender affect how treatments, decisions, and assessments differ according to gender where men tend to get different treatments compared to women (Bates and Thompson, 2002; Kullberg, 2002). In contrast, another visible example is related to how gender often is not at all present in analyses of the client's or patient's situation, which in turn risks reproducing an unreflective view of gender as static and complementary and of people as in need of gender-specific treatments (Dominelli, 2002; Herz, 2012). The workplace itself is also often organized in a way that further reproduces these patterns. Work assignments could, for instance, be organized based on gender or assigned to social workers of a certain gender (Mattsson, 2005; Nylander, 2011).

Together, these patterns create a situation where masculinity in social work is almost becoming synonymous with someone being active, in power, and, as we shall return to soon, a risk. The implications of this are that men, through this logic, almost cannot be in a more marginalized position. When someone is expected to be in control, in power, or dominant, they cannot at the same time be considered a victim. Sundaram, Helweg-Larsen, Laursen, and Bjerregaard (2004) call being a victim an antithesis of masculinity.

When talking about gender issues and social work, it is important to remember that social work is, by definition, a normalizing practice to a great extent, something that often seems to get forgotten both by social workers as well as researchers (Payne, Adams, and Dominelli, 2002; Payne, 2005). Social workers tend not to be on a mission to change society and resist power structures; nevertheless, they do have to confront and reflect upon these structures. Their profession is therefore stuck between upholding societal norms and practices and needing to confront and change some of these structures. Feminist and postcolonial critique of social work has focused on the strong tendencies of essentialism and naturalism inherent in this clinical field of practice. An essentialist view on masculinity is that of men and masculinity being associated with, for instance, being in power, and agency challenges the ability for men to be in a marginalized position or even to be in need. Because of this, social work practice needs to remain critical and reflexive toward gender stereotyping, especially since the profession's close connection to the welfare state and how social work is normalizing to such a degree that it tends to influence and affect society at large (Tilly, 2000).

Aggregation as Evidence

Recent developments in social work practice all over the world have been geared toward implementing EBP. Although there is no agreement on how to define EBP, or even evidence, the most common definition is probably one where evidence is seen as "scientific support" on the effects of treatments, assessments, or the use of specific methods. EBP is, to this same logic, seen as the accurate, openly reported, and judicious use of the best available evidence (at the time) on decision making regarding treatments to individuals or families. In professional social work, EBP is often translated into three parts: best available knowledge; the client's experiences and preferences; and the professional's experiences and abilities (Gambrill, 2010; Haynes, Bryan, Devereaux, Guyatt, and Gordon, 2002; Morago, 2006; Mullen and Streiner, 2004).

Although the definition often used is actually open to a variety of different kinds of science or knowledge, what is considered evidence based is, despite this, often connected to certain kinds of studies, which could be traced back to the concept's origin in medicine. Randomized studies (RCT studies) are often ranked and valued higher, and methods or tools based upon these studies or meta-studies consisting of several RCT studies are being promoted to a greater extent (Herz, 2013; Humphries, 2003; Soydan, 2011). This often means that different systems, methods, and knowledge are being integrated into social work practice based on this kind of data, which in turn has consequences regarding how issues such as gender or masculinity are approached. Although the tools differ between countries, the implementation of different, more or less systematic tools and EBP can be noted in countries such as Sweden, Denmark, Finland, the United States, Canada, the UK, Australia, and New Zealand. Furthermore, other countries such as China seem to be moving in the same direction (Gray,

Plath, and Webb, 2009; Herz, 2012; Krejsler, 2013; Kufeldt, Vachon, Simard, Baker, and Andrews, 2000; White, Hall, and Peckover, 2008).

As mentioned previously, two things seem to happen in relation to the alleged connection between the systems, methods, and knowledge being implemented and EBP being interpreted as "the best available knowledge" (Herz and Johansson, 2011a, 2012; Herz, 2012, 2013). First, is how "being" a biological man is interpreted to support certain assessments or decisions. Second, using evidence-based methods, tools, and systems is, by definition, "best available knowledge," which tends to include the methods, tools, and systems' perspective on gender. The first point is what happened in the introductory quote: being a boy was interpreted through the use of a method, marketed as being evidence based. By this logic, masculinity is only represented through the child's biological sex, and being a static variable, it also predicts certain behaviors and social conditions. The second point is more complex: When EBP is being implemented into the everyday practice of social work through the use of different methods, systems, or tools, these often say something also about gender and masculinities. Even if statements made on gender are not to be considered based on "best available knowledge" or if it is unclear what knowledge or research they are based upon, they are still able to be interpreted as stemming from best available knowledge and thus as evidence based. This is possible because of the symbiotic relationship between EBP as a concept and the idea of "best available knowledge."

One such example is the way gender is approached in the widely used system "Looking after Children" (LAC or LACS). Different versions of LAC are being used in the UK, Sweden, and Canada, among other countries. The LAC system states that children need positive same-sex role models to develop a positive identity (Basarab-Horwath, 2001; Socialstyrelsen, 2006). Because the system is being implemented as part of an EBP discourse, it could be interpreted by the social workers as being based upon the "best available knowledge," regardless of whether or not this is the case. Indeed, researchers actually question the use of same-sex role models because they tend to reproduce a "traditional", static and "hegemonic" masculinity (Hicks, 2008; Johansson, 2005).

The implementation of EBP in social work seems to affect the view on gender in both ways, from notions of gender being static based on aggregated data, to gender issues being considered evidence based regardless of whether or not this is the case. Previously, I claimed that men are often overrepresented in terms of being the offender or the cause behind social problems and that the most highly rated available data used by social workers is aggregated data, where masculinity is approached as static. With this in mind, it is easy to draw the conclusion that because of boys and men being statistically overrepresented, being born a male contains an inherent risk or that being a boy *is* a risk.

"It Could Be a Risk, Being a Boy"

Being male means an increased risk of antisocial behavior, and gender differences can be observed as early as after the age of two.... Many studies have shown that antisocial behavior is more common and more pronounced among boys than girls during childhood.

(Andershed and Andershed, 2005, p. 49, my translation)

This quote is from another evidence-based tool, called Ester, which is used for assessing children and youths at risk of either developing, or already showing signs of, antisocial behavior (see Andershed and Andershed, 2010; Andershed *et al.*, 2010). With the statistics in mind, this statement is reasonable. The question is, however, how this statistical fact and these kinds of statement are being transferred into the everyday practice of social work and whether it affects the agency and possible assessment outcomes for men and boys (and, by extension, for women and girls).

MARCUS: But do [you] approach gender at all?
BIRGITTA: We talk about it [when we do] risk and protective, when we do assessments based on risk and protective factors, or when we consider it.
MARCUS: In what way?
BIRGITTA: But it could be a risk being a boy that is something we can talk about sometimes.
MARCUS: This makes me a bit confused; this is from "Ester" [an evidence-based assessment tool] isn't it? And you don't work with "Ester," do you? But you've got the data from there, haven't you?
BIRGITTA: Mm. They've established how being a boy is a risk factor.

(Herz, 2012, p. 121 my translation)

This interview with Birgitta, who works with children in need at a social services office, is interesting since it highlights how knowledge from different systems, tools, and methods could spread across the workplace; knowledge that could be used by social workers even if they themselves lack specific knowledge on the tools in question. Birgitta has not been trained in using this specific tool, but she uses the knowledge "they've established" in her work with clients.

For the boys themselves, this means that they are seen as a risk or as inheriting a biological risk factor based solely on their gender – a "fact" that could be used to argue for specific assessments, decisions, and treatments. That is, men are receiving care and support customized to their needs (i.e., gender). Gender-specific treatments are, as mentioned, common in social work. This means that although masculinity is seen as an underlying cause and even though it influences the kind of support that is made available, it is, at the same time, impossible to change as long as it is considered as being something intrinsic and static connected with being a boy. An approach whereby masculinity, by definition, results in being a risk makes it hard for boys or men to free themselves from such a position. One might even say that they risk being *locked into a marginalized position*. Being a man equals being a client or a patient.

However, this is not the only approach to masculinity as a risk that becomes problematic. Although using the same explanatory models, the result becomes somewhat different. In the following conversation with two social workers working with family violence at a social services office, the close connection between masculinity and being in power or being a risk becomes observable. The result, however, is that men who are not in power and who are exposed to risks afflicted by others could find it hard to inhabit a marginalized position at all.

SOPHIA: I mean, I had, but it was one of the "gangsters" so to say, but he came to me once and told me, very frankly, how his woman had beat him, and she had probably done it quite substantially here over the ear, and he was probably in some pain. He wasn't scared or anything like that, but it was very…. And I started laughing, and that wouldn't have happened [if it were a woman].
INGRID: And then you say, "But what had you done [to deserve that]?" *(said in a sententiousness voice).*
SOPHIA: Yes, exactly, and then it's, well…. You would, of course, not have acted like that if it was a woman telling you the same thing.

(Herz, 2012)

Sophia describes how, when a man told her about being beaten by his partner, she breaks out in laughter in response, even though traces of violence were clearly visible on his face. The man in this example might be at risk, from his partner, but the situation is interpreted through a hegemonic and static view on masculinity where men are not at risk, but rather pose a risk. There are a couple of effects from this way of dealing with gender. First, there is a "lack of language" for men to talk about being a victim or in need of help without, at the same time, disrupting certain norms of masculinity (Herlof Andersen, 2008; Knutagård, 2009). This is what's happening when the man tells Sophia he had been hit by his partner. Second, it is possible to see how social vulnerability that is not associated with masculinity is reformulated or reinterpreted to fit existing models of explanation (Herz, 2014). This is what's happening when Ingrid talks about how the blame for what happens in these kinds of situation are often placed back on the man. When already existing models of explanation for – in this case, family violence being equal to men abusing women – can't be used, the situation needs to be reinterpreted. This is what happens when Ingrid says that if a women abuses a man, he must have done something to her first that caused her to hit him. Although not being able to inhabit a marginalized position, it is likely that this approach could lead to men's *experiences being marginalized.*

These approaches to masculinity tend to strengthen already rather static images of gender (Hicks, 2008). But an approach where the men themselves are problematized rather than notions of masculinity is also sometimes supported, to some extent, by researchers of men and masculinity. For instance, this is the case when claiming that it is important to attribute the violence of men toward men. Jeff Hearn (1998) is one of the researchers who used to emphasize the importance of using the term "men's violence," although this was later further nuanced (see Hearn and Whitehead, 2006). The reason for using "men's violence" was, according to Hearn, its preciseness. It is men being violent, and it does not propose anything being biologically male, nor does it propose a "specific" male violence. Instead, he continues, it acknowledges the plurality of men's violence (Hearn, 1998).

On the one hand, Hearn makes a valid point when he argues for the use of "men's violence," since masculinity is often used by men themselves as a defense or as an explanation to their actions (Catlett, Toews, and Walilko, 2010; Hearn, 1998). However, on the other hand, a focus solely on men's violence does not in itself disrupt the confusion between men, males, and masculinity and their relationships to violence or to marginalization, social vulnerability, and social problems in general.

Notions of Masculinity as Risk – an Alternative Approach

> During assessment with men, social workers are encouraged to actively address not just the concept of gender, but the patient's perception of what it means to be a man – and what aspects of masculinity most inform their behaviors, serve as sources of strength, present them with challenges, and most accurately characterize who they are, regardless of whether or not other people would necessarily understand those same traits as "masculine."
> (Winnett, Furman, and Enterline, 2012, p. 320)

In this final section, I claim that, rather than focus solely on boys and men or being biologically considered a male, it is important to take people's own notions of masculinity, gender, and identity into consideration. Too great a focus on "being" a man without at the same time deconstructing masculinity does not open up for change, but, rather, the opposite. I claim that it is important to openly address gender and discourses of masculinity with the client or patient as well as what Winnett *et al.* (2012) propose: to examine and deconstruct the client's or "patient's perception of what it means to be a man." This is not the same thing as downplaying men's violence or their own liability as perpetrators; this could still be important, but for social workers it is just as important to create spaces for change. If a man behaves "like a man," according to what social workers consider to be masculine behavior, and thus receives treatment for being a man or behaving like a man, then what kind of change is possible? Rather than focusing on specific discourses of masculinity and taking their impact for granted, social work needs to shift toward putting discourses in motion together with the client or patient being subjected to social work.

> Actually you know what – with this girl, I mean she like brought out like the anger, I don't know. It's just I turned into a whole different person when I was with her. It like, you know, she woman, and she the man, you know what I'm saying? She wear the pants and I wear the skirt. I can't have that,

you know what I'm saying? I wasn't raised up like that, you know? So I had to tell her and put her in her place.

(Catlett *et al.*, 2010, p. 114)

Let's return to men's violence. As mentioned, it is common that men in treatment use masculinity as a way to exonerate themselves from responsibility (Catlett *et al.*, 2010; Hearn, 1998). The man in the quote above does exactly this by emphasizing how she became the man and he the woman ("wearing the skirt"), ending up in him feeling he had to react. Although it could be argued that discourses of masculinity could be used to alienate men from their actions, there is a difference between *being* a discourse and to understand and change the way discourses act through subjects (Hearn and Whitehead, 2006). This is an important difference; social workers need to embrace different discourses on masculinity and how people actively relate to them in their everyday life to be able to affect their behavior and, in the long term, maybe change discourses on what it means to be a man altogether. Instead of handling the over-mortality among boys as boys being a risk, because of their gender, it means that social workers actively approach how boys relate to their identity and possible notions of masculinity. This opens up for men being both in positions of power and agency as well as being in more marginalized positions.

Research on suicide and depression among men has shown a similar approach being valuable. Suicide and depression among men sometimes seems to be related to their masculine identity, or more accurately, to their loss of certain kinds of masculine ideals. This could manifest itself through a loss of a job or maybe not being able to care for the family, but mostly through the fact of being depressed in itself. Depression is still often interpreted as being weak or powerless, something far from more dominant views on masculinity. Emslie *et al.* (2006) show how some men approach these issues by trying to recreate a masculine identity where being strong and in power are included. Although this strategy actually could relieve depression, it also seems to lead to these men committing suicide to a greater extent than men using other strategies. Men that do not try to reconstruct their masculinity but instead try to reformulate it toward an inclusion of feelings such as weakness, powerlessness, or maybe even marginalization commit suicide less often. Strategies whereby an adjustment to dominating masculine ideals take place seem to be more harmful than ones where other ideals are being included into masculinity (Emslie, Ridge, Ziebland, and Hunt, 2006). By the same logic, it is possible to understand why suicide among men is higher in organizations based on certain masculine ideals, such as in the U.S. military (Braswell and Kushner, 2012).

What this shows is that if social work is going to be able to help men and boys, and help others victimized by men and boys, it cannot be through a practice whereby certain masculine ideals are reproduced. A social work where being a man, without considering masculinity, in itself is a risk and thus a reason for treatment – which, moreover, is a gendered treatment customized to fit men – is a social work that unreflectively risks reproducing specific masculine ideals. It is a social work where men and boys are being attributed a specific masculine ideology, rather than taking specific individual positions, negotiations, ambivalence, resistance, and movement between discourses of masculinity and gender (Emslie et al., 2006; Mac An Ghaill and Haywood, 2012). Here lies the challenge for social work: to increase knowledge about the relationship between masculinity and different kinds of social problems without, at the same time, presuming that all men and boys relate to masculine ideals the same way.

Hans-Herbert Kögler (2007) suggests that social workers need to change their approach to discourses from assuming their relevance to instead discussing the client's approaches and relationships to them. Let us use fatherhood as an example: Instead of assuming the father is the breadwinner and an absent father, because this might be considered common or an ideal among many fathers, different discourses on fatherhood need to be approached together with the client. What is important is not whether or not the client could be positioned within a certain discourse, but, rather, how he relates to these discourses. What is important, what strategies are used, how is resistance done, and what other notions of fatherhood exist? This approach, where people are active toward discourses rather than being determined by them, does not lock someone in a presupposed version of masculinity – it creates a space for change.

Conclusion

To summarize, being a boy or a man is not in itself a risk. Being influenced by or feeling trapped by certain dominating notions of masculinity is. There is a difference. Being a risk does not permit any change since the *being* in itself is made the problem, and we cannot *un-be* and still remain alive. Being affected by certain ideals permits us to change the ideals and our relation to them and, finally, to creating new ones that do not risk harm to yourself or others, instead of adapting or feeling pressured to adapt.

In terms of masculinity and marginalization, an approach to masculinity or to "being" a man as something static and unchangeable produces challenges for men to feel – or be considered – vulnerable or marginalized since this is not consistent with what a man "is." A hegemonic view on masculinity often conforms to men being in power, having success, or being in control. This view, as suggested by Cheng (1999), tends to contribute to some men having power not only over women but also over other (more marginalized) men as well. The approach in which social workers, on the one hand, tend to interpret masculinity as a static risk factor and, on the other hand, seem to consider the same masculine ideals as being part of the solution, does not open up for any changes. As a result, it could be argued that instead of decreasing marginalization, the interventions might even be involved in reinforcing marginalization.

First, it is possible to claim that men and boys could become trapped in a marginalized position because of their gender. This is possible if all that is needed for becoming a client or a patient is being gendered as male. Thus, masculinity could be argued to actually put men into a marginalized position of being subjected to the different regulations and positions enclosed by the social services system. Second, however, this static approach to gender and social issues could be used, somewhat paradoxically, to conceal marginalization. When gender becomes more or less synonymous with certain needs or social situations, the men's or boy's own experiences, needs, and social rights risk being marginalized.

Therefore, social work needs to apply a more nuanced, attentive, and fluid view to masculinity and gender to be able to pay attention both to different ways of doing, interpreting, and relating to masculinity and to the different outcomes and effects these approaches to masculinity might have. It must be possible both to be or feel marginalized and at the same time be empowered, or even in power, in other contexts, without the one position overriding the other (e.g., Cheng 1999).

References

Andershed, H., and Andershed, A.-K. (2005) *Normbrytande beteende i barndomen: vad säger forskningen?* Stockholm: Gothia.

Andershed, H. and Andershed, A.-K. (2010) Risk-need assessment for youth with or at risk for conduct problems: Introducing the assessment system ESTER, *Procedia – Social and Behavioral Sciences 5:*377–383. doi:10.1016/j.sbspro.2010.07.108

Andershed, H., Fredriksson, J., Engelholm, K., Ahlberg, R., Berggren, S., Andershed, A.-K., Lauka, K., and Seppo. J. (2010) Initial test of a new risk-need assessment instrument for youths with or at risk for conduct problems: ESTER-assessment, *Procedia – Social and Behavioral Sciences*, *5*: 488–492. doi:10.1016/j.sbspro.2010.07.129

Australian Institute of Criminology (2015) *Age and gender of prisoners*. Retrieved May 4, 2015, from www.aic.gov.au/statistics/criminaljustice/age_gender.html

Basarab-Horwath, J. (ed.) (2001) *The Child's World: Assessing Children in Need*. London: Jessica Kingsley Publishers.

Bates, J. and Thompson, N. (2002) Men, Masculinities and Social Work. In C. Gruber and H. Stefanov (eds) *Gender in Social Work: Promoting Equality*, Dorset: Russell House Publishing.

Braswell, H. and Kushner, H.I. (2012) Suicide, social integration, and masculinity in the US military, *Social Science and Medicine* 74: 530–536.

Brunnberg, E. (2002) *Are boys and girls treated in the same way by the social services?* Retrieved from www.diva-portal.org/smash/record.jsf?pid=diva2:221681

Burck, C. and Gwyn, D. (1995) *Gender and Family Therapy*. London: Karnac Books.

Bäckman, M. (2003) *Kön och känsla : Samlevnadsundervisning och ungdomars tankar om sexualitet*. Göteborg: Makadam.

Catlett, B. S., Toews, M. L., and Walilko. V. (2010) Men's gendered constructions of intimate partner violence as predictors of court-mandated batterer treatment drop out, *American Journal of Community Psychology* 45: 107–123.

Cheng, C. (1999) On the functionality of marginalized masculinities and femininities: An ethnography on organizational power and gender performances, *The Journal of Men's Studies* 7: 415–30.

Dominelli, L. (2002) *Feminist Social Work Theory and Practice*. Basingstoke: Palgrave Macmillan.

Dominelli, L. (2008) *Anti-Racist Social Work, Third Edition (Practical Social Work)* (3rd ed.). United Kingdom: Palgrave Macmillan.

Emslie, C., Ridge, D., Ziebland, S., and Hunt, K. (2006) Men's accounts of depression: reconstructing or resisting hegemonic masculinity? *Social Science and Medicine* 62:2246–57. doi:10.1016/j.socscimed.2005.10.017

Federal Bureau of Prisons. (2015) *BOP Statistics: Inmate Gender*. Retrieved May 4, 2015, from www.bop.gov/about/statistics/statistics_inmate_gender.jsp

Gambrill, E. (2010) Evidence-informed practice: antidote to propaganda in the helping professions? *Research on Social Work Practice*, 20: 302–320. doi:10.1177/1049731509347879

Gray, M., Plath, D., and Webb, S.A. (2009) *Evidence-based Social Work: A Critical Stance*. New York: Routledge.

Haynes, B. R., Devereaux, P. J., and Guyatt, G. H. (2002) Physicians' and patients' choices in evidence-based practice: Evidence does not make decisions, people do, *British Medical Journal* 324: 1350–1351.

Hearn, J. R. (1998) *The Violences of Men: How Men Talk About and How Agencies Respond to Men's Violence to Women*. United Kingdom: Sage Publications Ltd.

Hearn, J. R. and Whitehead, M. (2006) Collateral damage: Men's "domestic" violence to women seen through men's relations with men, *Probation Journal* 53: 38–56. doi:10.1177/0264550506060864

Herlof Andersen, T. (2008) Speaking about the unspeakable: Sexually abused men striving toward language, *American Journal of Men's Health* 2: 25–36. doi:10.1177/1557988307308107

Herz, M. (2012) *Från ideal till ideologi. Konstruktioner av kön och etnicitet inom socialtjänsten*. Örebro: Örebro University.

Herz, M. (2013) Live social work: How to bring life back into social work, *Australian Social Work* 1–15. doi:10.1080/0312407X.2014.910676

Herz, M. (2014) Män och social utsatthet: en översikt. In Statens offentliga utredningar (ed.) *Män och jämställdhet: betänkande av utredningen om män och jämställdhet*. Stockholm: Fritzes.

Herz, M. and Johansson, T. (2011a) Critical social work: considerations and suggestions, *Critical Social Work* 12: 28–45.

Herz, M. and Johansson, T. (2011b) *Maskuliniteter: Kritik, tendenser, trender*. Malmö: Liber.

Herz, M. and Johansson, T. (2012) "Doing" Social Work: Critical Considerations on Theory and Practice in Social Work, *Advances in Social Work* 13: 527–540.

Hicks, S. (2008) Gender role models ... who needs 'em?! *Qualitative Social Work* 7: 42–59.

Humphries, B. (2003) What else counts as evidence in evidence-based social work? *Social Work Education* 22: 81–91.

Johansson, H. (2005) *Pojkar behöver manliga förebilder? En studie av socialsekreterares tankemönster och arbete med söner till ensamstående mödrar*. Göteborg: Göteborgs Universitet.

Knutagård, H. (2009) *"Men du har ju blivit våldtagen" – om våldtagna mäns ord-löshet*. Malmö: SRHR:s rapport 2009: 4.

Krejsler, J. B. (2013) What works in education and social welfare? A mapping of the evidence discourse and reflections upon consequences for professionals, *Scandinavian Journal of Educational Research* 57: 16–32. doi:10.1080/00313831.2011.621141

Kufeldt, V. K. J., Simard, M., Baker, J., and Andrews, T. (2000) *Looking after children in Canada: Final report*. Retrieved from www.unb.ca/fredericton/arts/centres/mmfc/

Kullberg, C. (2002) Gender and social work: Research on gender differences in the treatment of clients in welfare institutions. In C. Gruber and H. Stefanov (eds) *Gender in Social Work: Promoting Equality*. Dorset: Russell House Publishing.

Kögler, H.-H. (2007) Die Macht der Interpretation: Konturen einer kritischen Sozialwissenschaft in Anschluss an Foucault. In *Foucaults Machtanalytik und Soziale Arbeit. Eine kritische Einfürung und Bestandsaufnahme*, edited by Roland Anhorn, Frank Bettinger and Johannes Stehr. Wiesbaden: VS Verlag für Sozialwissenschaften.

Mac An Ghaill, M. and Haywood, C. (2012) Understanding boys': Thinking through boys, masculinity and suicide, *Social Science and Medicine* 74: 482–489. doi:10.1016/j.socscimed.2010.07.036

Mattsson, T. (2005) *I viljan att göra det normala. En kritisk studie av genusperspektivet i missbrukarvården*. Malmö: Égalité.

Miniño, A. M. (2010) Mortality among teenagers aged 12–19 years: United States, 1999–2006. *NCHS Data Brief* 37:1–8. doi:10.1016/j.yane.2011.01.023.

Morago, P. (2006) Evidence-based practice: from medicine to social work, *European Journal of Social Work* 9: 461–477.

Mullen, E. J., and Streiner, D. L. (2004) The evidence for and against evidence-based practice. *Brief Treatment and Crisis Intervention* 4: 111–121. doi:10.1093/brief-treatment/mhh009

Nylander, P. Å. (2011) *Managing the Dilemma: Occupational Culture and Identity Among Prison Officers*. Örebro universitet.

Offending and Masculinity: Working with Males (1990) *Probation Journal* 37: 106–111. doi:10.1177/026455059003700302

Orme, J. (2003) 'It's feminist because I say so!': Feminism, social work and critical practice in the UK, *Qualitative Social Work* 2: 131–153. doi:10.1177/1473325003002002002

Payne, M. (2005) *Modern Social Work Theory* (3rd edition). New York: Palgrave.

Payne, M., Adams, R., and Dominelli, L. (2002) On being critical in social work. In R. Adams, L. Dominelli, and M. Payne (eds) *Critical Practice in Social Work*. New York: Palgrave.

Scourfield, J. (2003) *Gender and Child Protection*. New York: Palgrave Macmillan.

Socialstyrelsen (2006) *Grundbok barns behov i centrum (BBIC)*. Stockholm: Socialstyrelsen.

Soydan, H. (2011) Editorial: A glimpse into contemporary American social work research. *Journal of Social Work* 11: 4–7. doi:10.1177/1468017310384662

Sue, D.W. (2006) *Multicultural Social Work Practice*. New Jersey: John Wiley & Sons.

Sundaram, V., Helweg-Larsen, K., Laursen, K. B., and Bjerregaard, P. (2004) Physical violence, self rated health, and morbidity: Is gender significant for victimisation? *Journal of Epidemiology and Community Health* 58: 65–70. doi:10.1136/jech.58.1.65

Tilly, C. (2000) *Beständig ojämlikhet*. Lund: Arkiv.

White, S., Hall, C., and Peckover, S. (2008) The descriptive tyranny of the common assessment framework: Technologies of categorization and professional practice in child welfare, *British Journal of Social Work* 39: 1197–1217. doi:10.1093/bjsw/bcn053

Winnett, R., Furman, R., and Enterline, M. (2012) Men at risk: Considering masculinity during hospital-based social work intervention, *Social Work in Health Care* 51: 312–326. doi:10.1080/00981389.2011.650843

Zufferey, C. (2009) Making gender visible: Social work responses to homelessness, *Affilia* 24: 382–393. doi:10.1177/0886109909343559

Part II
Transformations of Work and Unemployment

3 'Crack in the Ice'

Marginalization of Young Men in Contemporary Urban Greenland

Firouz Gaini

Prologue

Today the polar bear is under threat, not from the arrows and bullets of Inuit hunters, but from irreversible climate and environmental change in the Arctic. The bear's untamed life, ending with a violent death, is today replaced by a condition of persistent starvation and subsequent dishonourable death. The great hunting grounds are out of reach. The bear is, nevertheless, still an icon of Greenlandic culture – treated as an extremely powerful and terrifying creature that Inuit feel deeply attached to and dependent on. The prosperity of the Inuit is, symbolically speaking, relying on the bear's freedom. When Karen Blixen (1937) says that the neighbouring lion makes African villagers feel 'alive', it is a parallel to the sense of unity and continuity that the polar bear galvanizes in Inuit hamlets. The dazed bear that we have seen on television lately, weak and alone on a small drifting ice flow, without any sense of place, is especially shocking because of its contrast to expected images of the bear and the nature of the farthest north. The unusual heat, breaking and melting the immemorial ice, makes the furry giant seem out of place, helpless and useless in a nature in transformation, and even, as was the case in the town of Sisimiut during my fieldwork in Greenland, heading to town in search of food or attention (a kind of suicide). In Sisimiut, an elderly man with the reputation of being a 'great hunter' got the honour of killing the desperate bear that, of course, posed a real danger to townspeople. It is ironic that even wild animals from the endless Greenlandic scenery end up in the tiny urban communities accommodating most of the population of the world's largest island. It is, for sure, tragicomic to see the normal hero turn into an unsteady loser in the animal kingdom. Then, what about the huntsmen confronting the bear on the ice; how have they adapted to life in the city? How are they affected by the crack in the ice?

The Hunter

What used to be the main characteristics of a 'real man', an independent hunter following the traditions of his ancestors, lie beyond the modern town's typical repertoire of styles and work, and man's fortune and prospects as citizen of an urbanized society depends very much on his social and cultural capital. In this chapter, I will discuss young Greenlandic men at risk with a focus on their changing masculinities and quite ambivalent relations to the old hunting culture in the context of the town/city. The hunter is, like the polar bear, feared and admired by people at the same time. The hunter in the city is additionally, anyhow, 'matter out of place' (Douglas, 1966). He is a persona non grata tainting this Arctic cityscape. This represents the reversed outlandish image of the hungry bear coming to town. He has entered a place not fitting his way of life or mindset. His presence is symbolically polluting the place, hence representing a danger to others. The others are the Insiders; he is the Outsider. He is the migrant leaving everything that he knew behind in the search for a new life. This could have been the story of any poor peasant moving to the large city in the global South. In Greenland, rural-to-urban migration (especially migration from remote villages to the capital, Nuuk) has been like moving to a foreign country – clearly, like moving to Denmark. The culture, the language, the food; everything is different. Nobody moved the opposite way, from the main towns to the small villages, so nothing was sent back to the periphery, which thence was bereft of any societal development (Nuttall, 1994). The intended centralization of Greenland, with forced relocation of people from small communities doomed to extinction, started in the 1950s as Danish authorities estimated it to be too expensive to uphold the geographically dispersed – and partly nomadic – Inuit hamlets in their ambitious modernization plan (Høiris and Marquardt, 2011). The contrast between urban and rural place is now sharp, and suspicion towards the counterpart flourishes. The 'real hunter' stereotype, for instance, is often used in constructions of binary oppositions between rural and urban men, but also between ethnic Inuit and ethnic Danish men. Defining the rural as the Other is also a way of consolidating inner inequalities in diverse urban settings. Very few men actually conform to the rigid depiction of the way of the traditional hunter, even if some groups of men – most obviously elderly villagers – feel closely linked to the work and life of previous generations. In the city, on the other hand, many people are being labelled as huntsmen without consent, and this is often regarded as a social stigma rather than as a compliment. The city is characterized by different groups of men in symbolic struggle for power and domination, a contest which has the definition of (ultimate) masculinity as a combat zone. This chapter intends to analyse young men's (gender) identity negotiation, as well as their responses to societal challenges and ideologies, by examining the distinct contexts within which they are located.

The Migrant

There are no hunters in the city, not of the kind that grandparents remember and old tales narrate, but many people, women as well as men, go hunting at weekends and on public holidays. An IT expert, for instance, says Greenland Today (no. 19, 2013), 'can easily spend his spare time hunting reindeer and fishing for Arctic char'. Hunting is very important as sport and tradition all over Greenland,

and nobody wants to change that. Fishing and hunting is *comme il faut* and something children at an early age become familiar with. A boy's first hunt – and first kill – is a day to remember with joy; it is nothing less than a 'cornerstone in the life of the family' (Sejersen, 2004, p. 77). It represents a rite of passage paving the way to respectable manhood, and men should actively help boys through the initiation.

> The bear jumped onto a small ice floe, and Angutidluarssuq was standing beside it with his spear without killing it. He was waiting for a small orphaned boy that never had got a bear because he didn't have dogs [...] Angutidluarssuq helped him to kill it.
>
> (Freuchen, 1953, p. 52)

The hunt associates with freedom, vitality and what we could call Inuit cosmology. In the city of Nuuk, the capital with its elite driving posh cars, people buy a lot of fresh food from the hunters at the market: fish, whale, seal, bear, reindeer and musk ox, etc. The trade at the open impromptu food market – at a corner just outside a supermarket – connects people otherwise living in totally different worlds; even their languages are different (Danish and different Greenlandic dialects), making the bargaining a ritual without much small talk. People in the capital like the hunted food – they value the hunt as a cultural product – but they usually keep the huntsman and his family at arm's length. They are afraid of them, because these people often live without a fixed job and salary, without a fixed home or daily rhythm. They are categorized as part of the diverse group of rural migrants not 'belonging' to the city. Most residents of Nuuk have, logically, roots in the villages, if not in Denmark. Danish citizens are considered urban per se, wherever their childhood home is located, and they are therefore treated, a priori, as models of the modern urban citizen. Nuuk and most other Greenlandic towns were established as Danish colonies (serving as trading centres and religious missions), thereby having an exclusive group of Danish envoys as their founders, and many people would still argue today that the towns are more Danish than they are Greenlandic. As mentioned earlier, the village/ town contradistinction is amazing, making it a tough task to conquer the city for any newcomer from rural areas. The stranger flying in from a foreign country, with a working contract in his suitcase, will on the other hand immediately be safely channelled into the field of the privileged classes: with housing, shopping, fitness, transportation, etc. at his disposal. The male Inuit rural-to-urban migrant will easily fail to get recognition as an Insider belonging to the city because of his language, his clothes, his walk, his education, his knowledge, etc. Even ethnic identity might be a barrier in some contexts. He might start feeling like a stranger in his own country, unable to break the codes that open doors and invite him into social networks. Usually, the cultural shock will be much more severe than he could have imagined. How could he know beforehand? He will also quickly find out that he is not alone; he is just one amongst a large and growing group of people coming from different parts of the country, all located on the same side of the divided city. What he thought would help him in the new place – his competences and skills – turn out to do just the opposite: they tell Insiders what they have experienced: that he does not fit. He is beyond their frame for proper urban masculinity. He doesn't know their cultural capital. Then the naïve young man with his wishful thinking, whether he likes it or not, will get labelled as (yet another) hunter in the city, or just as a social loser, and this situation will force him to rethink his strategies, or otherwise to risk sinking slowly but steadily to the bottom of society. Does he have the mental and cultural resources to initiate change and adapt to new requirements? Too many young men – much more than is the case for young women – vanish in the city.

New Life

Some important differences between boys and girls should be mentioned, before we continue the discussion about the hunter in the city. In Greenland, boys cannot cry or ask for help; they are supposed to find their own way out of any crisis. Their pride is resolute to a degree that can lead to dangerous and self-destructive behaviour. Of course, such a generalization overlooks interesting changes in society, especially in multicultural urban environments, but amongst men at risk it is a very persistent part of their personality and masculinity. It is, as a matter of fact, often a part of their social 'problem'. It keeps them out of attractive career prospects associated to modern lifestyles and family values. Another difference is that man's traditional life and work as hunter is not an option anymore. It has disappeared and nobody seriously expects it to return. So, everything that constructed man the 'heroic' hunter, that defined his masculinity and identity, basically, his *raison d'etre*, has lost meaning. He has to bet on an alternative career now, and it will most likely be of a very different nature. Who can help him prepare for this shift – the parents, peers or the school? Women had traditional duties – for instance chores in and around the house – more easily transferred to the context of contemporary society. They seem less bound to history, liberated from the burden of having to keep up a heritage from the hunting culture of the past. Everybody was dependent on men's hunting, he could not be substituted by anyone, but he was also worthless without a woman. If his clothes, made by the women, were loose at the seams, the hunter could face death while on the hunting grounds. He would freeze to death, hence not be able to bring vital meat home to the hamlet. Looking at gender differences in the hunting culture, I believe, is a bit like comparing oranges with apples. There was a relation of interdependence between man and woman, sharing equal status. Presumed male dominance, says Sonne (2000, p. 2), 'was kept relatively at bay by the complementarity of the male and female labour skills'. The predicament of the hunter in the city is not that contemporary women can earn their own money and be the breadwinner of the family (which is often the case in families of men fishing and hunting), but that he does not find a way out of his societal marginalization and isolation. In many cases, curiously, the woman with a well-paid full-time job will invest in her husband's fishing boat and equipment, even if his independent fishing business (sometimes combined with hunting) is not profitable. She will, as the only one in the household with a stable income, at the same time take care of the main living expenses. In this way, she helps him keep alive a 'dream' rejected by modern society. So, even if women do not represent a direct threat to men's dignity and power in society, many embittered men will blame or abuse women as a result of their own weakness and defeat. Many women and children pay a high price for their husbands and fathers' crisis. In everyday life and social interaction in the city, the Inuit man is under repeated investigation as fellow citizens query his personality, his masculinity and his distinction: what can this man achieve? Is he a hunter or an urban man? He can be both, or neither, but the point is that he will have to perform and negotiate his masculinity in the quest for respect and honour amongst men. He must prove his worth to a critical judge. Urban masculinity is, however, partly racialized, so the young Inuit man will be prevented from admission to some of the circles of men due to his physical appearance. Modern society, says Gutmann (1997, p. 403), considers it an obligation to 'domesticate' men.

The Capital of Greenland

Greenland, the world's largest island, was a closed Danish colonial territory from 1721 to 1953, and a Danish County until 1979 when it was granted Home Rule. The Self-Governing Act of 1989 gave Greenland a greater degree of independence, but short of full independence as sovereign state, within the Kingdom of Denmark. The population totals 56,000 of which almost 90 per cent is Greenlandic Inuit (including Danish/Greenlandic mixed persons). Most people, around 48,000 inhabitants, live in urban communities. To indigenous people of the circumpolar north, 'Greenland provides a model of regional self-government for which there is no precedent' (Nuttall, 1994, p. 16).

My fieldwork in Greenland (2014) disclosed traits of a complex society in shift, looking at its past the way a refugee looks at his birthplace and at its future the way a mountaineer looks at the captivating peak ahead. Times change fast; places in memory disappear but the imagined future is promising.

My data collection took place over five intensive weeks in Nuuk in the spring of 2014. I conducted eight individual semi-structured interviews with boys aged 12–15, outside of school hours. In addition, I conducted a small survey using open questions on two sixth grade classes from a public school and a class from an upper secondary school based in the capital. In addition to this, my fieldwork included interviews and discussions with fishermen, youth workers, social workers, youth researchers, teachers and senior advisers at the Home Rule administration. This fieldwork was done as part of an ethnographic research project on boys' identities and masculinities in Greenland.

Greenlanders, I learned rapidly, are much more interested in the present than in the past, still they cannot hide unhealed wounds from the colonial age of the second half of the twentieth century. Many young people say they are tired of media's incessant depressive narratives about violence, substance abuse and suicide in Greenland since the 1960s. They are fully aware of the tragic human cost of the demanding and antagonistic modernization project orchestrated by Danish authorities, yet most of them do not regret half a century's social developments in general. It seems to me that many young men have had a feeling of being caged and misrecognized in colonial discourses; now they want to deconstruct and reinterpret the lost Inuit. Let us take a closer look at the city of Nuuk now.

Strolling through Nuuk gives a strange feeling of being in a place that has no relation to its majestic surroundings. At first, the stranger will find the sensation surreal and a bit provoking, but thereafter he will slowly acclimatize to this rare Arctic urban environment. Is this city only a mirage? No, it is real, the home of a third of Greenland's population. For many Greenlanders, Nuuk was a symbol of decay in colonial times when large numbers of Inuit were forced to leave their remote settlements and start anew in the capital's infamous concrete apartment blocks, but lately it has changed to become what some local scholars have called in goodwill a vibrant self-confident micropolis (Rygaard, 2010). Nevertheless, the urban design and architectural make-up of Nuuk still seems as disconnected from the old Inuit habitat as Dubai's glittering skyline is from the modest tents of the Arab Bedouins of the surrounding desert. Greenlanders are, generally, proud of their expanding capital, but what should they compare it with? Nuuk is Nuuk. They seem to be amazed by its structure and magnitude, its up-to-date facilities and foreign (European) aura, not of its aesthetic character. In conversation with residents of the city, I noticed that many people define Nuuk as a difference from the small villages, rather than as a place with its own character. Nuuk is an ugly city, says Jørgen Chemnitz, 'that never managed to find its identity as a small city' (2013, p. 7). When the biggest and most emblematic – and probably also most ugly – apartment block in Nuuk was demolished a few years ago, it signified a very important event for thousands of people, especially for the men and women who once, for a shorter or longer period, had been Block P residents themselves. Block P, accommodating more than 500 souls, was like a reversed gated community in the city, feared by Outsiders as a dreary ghetto and appreciated by most Insiders as a pleasant and friendly place. It was a kind of refuge for displaced Inuit. It was an outlandish construction, like a colossal concrete iceberg full of small nests not matching the dwellers' practical spatial requirements – e.g. 'for drying fish on the balcony and slaughtering seal and reindeer in the bathroom' (Rasmussen and Tierney 2013, p. 46). This Arctic concrete jungle could, in principle, have been in a poor neighbourhood of any large segregated city, for instance in the Bronx (New York City) or in East Berlin, and many Greenlanders continue to consider it to be a prime breeding place for serious sociopsychological problems and illegal activities – especially amongst men from displaced underprivileged families – that have marked Greenland ever since the blocks were erected. An enraged journalist warned against irresponsible population 'concentration' policies in Nuuk in a 1992 newspaper article, saying:

An army of young social losers will flourish in front of the shops. They will stand silently with a beer in their hand, like guilty of the G-92 [national report, FG]. One of the workplaces which will be busiest in the hectic town will be the national hospital and especially the psychiatric ward.

(in Rygaard, 2010, p. 233)

Unfortunately, his prophecies were not completely false; even if this scenario, indeed, is more elegiac than reality is. If Block P was the symbol of the lost Inuit in the city, his confinement between the past and the future, then where do we find marginalized man today?

White Working Men

During the 1960s and 1970s, many Greenlanders felt, against their own will, ostracized from major construction projects transforming their towns in the name of modern progress. Inuit men got the dubious honour of being inactive bystanders watching foreign manpower, mostly Danish artisans and builders, engage in lucrative round-the-clock working enterprises launched by the authorities (Høiris and Marquardt, 2011). Inuit men's feeling of powerlessness against dominant groups of workers created an unexpected sense of unity amongst them. In the 1975 poem 'Suppressed', a young Greenlander describes his unpleasant sense of being worthless in his hometown:

With hand in the pocket. He looks at the building – no work for me. Too lazy – with black hair – bowlegged. Poverty draws my clothes. Incapability hangs over my head. Unemployed – underpaid in my country. Where strangers swim around in money – black vultures passing through. Darkened horizon – bland spit – tomorrow there is debt again.

(Jens Geisler, in Weyhe, 2011, p. 254)

At that time the move to town 'implied a move from a world of equals to a world of inequality with Danes as those holding superior positions and power' (Dahl, 2010, p. 129). Greenlanders were swiftly converted to 'detraditionalized' urban citizens yet did not, as pointed out earlier, feel that the ethnically segregated city belonged to them, because the city was 'where the white man's culture reigned' (ibid., p. 132). Even if times have changed, and many young citizens of Nuuk avoid talking about any Danish/Inuit cultural clash today, it is difficult to ignore the deeper meaning of ethnicity in discussions on the (colonial) history of gender and gender relations in Greenland. Some people would even argue that colonialism revolves around the topic of men and masculinities (Reeser, 2010). The Danish unskilled worker hired for projects in Greenland might have been performing his masculinity in a fashion quite different from what is considered to be 'mainstream' masculinity in Denmark. The foreign worker was assigned a symbolic role as nation builder in the colonial context. In the heyday of the modernization project, most foreign workers came to Greenland without their wives and children, thus often performing their masculinity in decadent style, something that would have been sanctioned as distasteful and improper behaviour in the workers' home countries. In Greenland, workers could – without anyone at home being aware of it – experiment with alternative masculinities that 'their former cultural context disavowed' (ibid., p. 194). Most of them were only planning to work in Greenland for a few years before returning home with their savings and some good (and even secret) memories. Many workers performed their masculinity as if there was no native masculinity of any sort in the colony. They did not recognize Inuit men as masculine men fitting their masculine modernization project in Greenland. In Greenland – most clearly from the 1960s and up to the 1980s – foreign (mostly Danish) workers held a powerful position that they as blue-collar workers could never have achieved at home. They shared a feeling of being totally free and invincible amongst Inuit. The demasculinization of Inuit men, together with the hypermasculinity of Danish men, displays a gendered expression of what could be called 'white supremacy' (Stoler, in Gutmann, 1997, p. 389). Hypermasculine men 'assert power and dominance over women by engaging in various behaviours […] that serve to uphold the macho personality' (Parrott and Zeichner, 2003, p. 70). Outlining colonialism from a gender perspective, Todd Reeser points out that:

> [t]he colonizer might also see the 'oriental' as childlike, as prepubescent, and thus as not having achieved masculinity and as not developed like the more mature European. This adult/child opposition resembles a male/female opposition since the child and the woman hold the same half of the binary opposition by analogy, as both are dominated by men …
>
> (2010, p. 186)

Inuit men were commonly presented as effeminate, but this was never done with reference to their culture and lifestyle. It was simply a way of uplifting the dominant masculinity of the colonizers. In the city, the foreign worker was like a fish in water; he had the job, the behaviour and the attitudes considered urban and modern. Danish workers, in short, fulfilled expectations of how 'real men' should be in this setting. Men in dominant position will normally try to block menacing change by 'monopolizing definitions of masculinity' (Coles, 2009, p. 6). It was, as mentioned, practically impossible for Inuit men, as individuals or as part of a group, to become included in the dominant (hegemonic) masculinity of the city. Their body capital (physical appearance) prevented them from recognition as 'real men' amongst the foreign migrant workers of the city. Whiteness was a central characteristic of dominant urban masculinity until the 1980s. Another hurdle was the language barrier as few Inuit men mastered the Danish language to its full extent – an unconditional requirement for cultural recognition by fellow men in dominant positions (Weyhe, 2011). It didn't make things easier that Danish language classes at most primary and secondary schools, especially in rural areas, were of very poor quality. Actually, it helped dominant groups resist social change for many years.

New Elite

For many Greenlanders old enough to remember the 1970s and 1980s, the most depressive era characterized by pandemic social and cultural disorder is now over. Society, they claim, bottomed out then and is now consolidating previous tensions. In simple words, I heard several times in discussions with adults mostly, that Greenlanders fought back imperialism and are now taking full responsibility of their own fate. This narrative is indeed part of a project rethinking Greenlandic identities. Many Greenlanders regret negative (mostly Danish) portrayals of their society as spoiled and dysfunctional and would rather see their country presented as a young and progressive partner amongst free nations. This branding and process, turning Greenland into an 'almost independent' nation in a globalizing world and eager to earn recognition rather than sympathy, has indeed changed (power) relations with Denmark. In Nuuk, it is easy to spot the societal elite composed of a Danish minority and a group of (mostly well-educated) Greenlandic political leaders promoting a social model responding to legislative lessons from Nordic neighbours (the Danish welfare state policy mainly), but also its contrast – the poor men from families associated with hunting and fishing lifestyles loitering around outside the main supermarket and other small shops and bars (Pedersen, 2008).

Before Home Rule was introduced, virtually all Greenlanders felt more or less stigmatized as second-rate citizens in their own country; today a different social division has appeared as many Greenlanders from the main towns have climbed up the social ladder to become part of the previously almost exclusively ethnic Danish ruling class. The sense of togetherness and unity as common victims (from the pre-Home Rule years), keeping the colonial 'intruder' responsible for all misery, has been replaced by a more fragmented arena with some groups of people enjoying the benefits of the new urbanized society, while others feel left in the limbo of lost dreams.

At the beginning of the twenty-first century, a time of great optimism in Greenland, the influential politician Jonathan Motzfeldt even exclaimed, 'There is no way back. The sled has departed. Greenland is a modern industrial society which competes on the world market. We must forget the old dream about the kayak' (in Kentorp, 2002: 3, my translation).

Jack the Fisherman

At the cafeteria of the Seamen's Home (Hotel), located at the busy commercial port of the city, I met Jack, a retired weather-beaten fisherman with a great interest in the education and future of young men from (dinghy) fishing families. Jack is a very knowledgeable man with a large social network, including practically all the dinghy fishermen of Nuuk. Dinghies are small boats with powerful outboard motors used for fishing in the sea close to Nuuk. When I entered the cafeteria, he was just going to conclude his daily coffee meeting (exchanging news about the work and life of fishermen) with a small group of senior dinghy fishermen. Jack went straight to the topic of formal schooling when the others had left the table and we started our discussion – and he was ruthless in his criticism of the education system. Referring to family and friends, especially the boys and young men, he recounted long dramas of neglect and despair. Many boys, he said bitterly, feel rejected on their first day at school. They feel that the school does not fit to them, he added, and they quickly lose all motivation. The boys are smart; they are clever; they just don't fit school, Jack stressed with a very serious facial expression. Confronting him with counterarguments about the need for children to adapt to modern school, Jack did not hesitate to admit that a part of the problem lies in the traditional fishing families' exaggerated admiration of the sons, the little 'hunter-heroes' enjoying extensive freedoms and few obligations, giving them the wrong impression of their place in contemporary society; boys are rarely given any chores or responsibilities in the house (Condon and Stern, 1993, p. 410).

Jack, a hard-boiled man happy to speak his mind, expressed disappointment at recent developments in Nuuk by recounting a series of tragic case stories sharing the same ending: the sons of dinghy fishermen 'die young – or end up in prison or psychiatric wards'. Time and again during my stay in Nuuk I heard people talk about the sons' very special position in Greenlandic families (most pronounced in 'traditional' families, but also in other Inuit families), offering them royal treatment as the saviour of the family (Condon and Stern, 1993). This kind of parenting, preparing boys for life on the great hunting grounds, probably fits well to the society of the past, but not for contemporary realities in urban communities. Even if just a few hundred Greenlanders are considered breadwinning hunters today, most Greenlanders still love to go hunting for reindeer, fox and seals, etc. as seasonal recreation.

As a habitué, Jack greeted most guests (most of them male workers wearing warm coveralls) entering the cafeteria while we had our talk sitting at his regular table. The cafeteria, with a nice view of the harbour and sea, acts as a kind of 'People's Parliament' where you're unlikely to find customers wearing business suits and ties. 'No one really cares about these boys', Jack said in calm, understated manner, 'they will not be able to live as dinghy fishermen'. He made me think of Paul Willis' lads from the West Midlands, but the English working-class boys could at least take over their fathers' blue-collar jobs (Willis, 1977). That does not seem to be the case for the fishermen's sons in Nuuk. Additionally, their resistance at school, at least according to Jack's narrative, is more self-destructive. The fishermen's sons are unable to mobilize collective action against the schools and authorities. I left the cosy cafeteria with a feeling that this group of people, a small hidden group of urban hunters, comprises young men that others stay away from. They are heroes at home, within their poor yet proud fishing families, but losers at school and elsewhere. If they will be fishing from dinghies in the future, it will most likely be supported by the income of their women, in the same way as in the Holman region in Arctic Canada: 'While hunting and trapping continue to be male-dominated activities, income generated by wives in generally secure wage-labor jobs often provides capital for husbands to purchase the equipment and supplies used in subsistence hunting and trapping' (Condon and Stern, 1993, p. 395).

Sons Without Future

Dinghy fishermen are very easy to spot in public in Nuuk, says the Greenlandic scholar Per Lynge (2012), because of their workwear, their gait, their expression, their jargon and even their skin colour. They don't look like other people in the street. They are few in numbers and mostly from older generations. Most fishermen, says Lynge, are 'tanned and more weathered than the rest of the native population in Nuuk' (ibid., p. 116). Hunting knowledge is more important than anything else in the fishermen's community:

> It is very simple: the families enjoying greatest respect are the families that have the greatest knowledge on our hunting culture. The dinghy fishermen, who enjoy great respect, must therefore also be able to present the necessary collective knowledge – [and] they can. Their real knowledge is, mildly speaking, tremendous. By listening and listening, over and over again, it appears increasingly clear that while most men in the group have the necessary knowledge, not everyone has the right to express that knowledge. You have to earn the honour and respect [that] it is to express [yourself] in the group.
> (Ibid., p. 134)

Dinghy fishermen's families are few in numbers today, however they are often treated as a memento of the general problem of marginalization amongst young unskilled men in urban communities in Greenland. On the one hand, they are, together with hunters' families from some of the remote villages in the north, enjoying respect as representatives of the community with the closest (unbroken) link to the styles and values of the hunting culture of the past. They are therefore the subject of admiration and exoticism in difference cultural discourses all over Greenland. On the other hand, they are also viewed as misfits with very poor prospects in society (Weyhe, 2011). According to Lynge (2012), the girls have, in most cases, been skilful and able to adapt to new societal requirements and demands, and some have even succeeded in ambitious ventures in higher education. On the other hand, he says it has gone horribly wrong for the boys. Most families are ashamed and blame themselves for the adversities of their sons. They feel disgraced and avoid seeking help, while at the same time realizing that the loss of a boy, literally, implies the downfall of the whole family (ibid.). The boys end up as social losers considered useless in the modern labour market as well as in their father's very specialized dinghy fisheries. They fit neither to school with its (Danish/Western) individualized view on pupils nor to the dinghy fishermen's fraternity with its strong collective values. The resilience and pride of the autonomous fishermen, ironically, becomes a major hindrance against social mobility. It represents a limitation in men's negotiation of masculinity in everyday life situations. Stressing cultural opposition between the (traditional)

Greenlandic and the (modern) Danish lifestyles of the city, Lynge (ibid., p. 139) declares gloomily that the fisherman 'is drowned in his own country'. While the problems of the boys from dinghy fishermen's families seem almost insurmountable, turning former heroes into present-day untouchables, the boys fit quite easily into a broader category of marginalized men in the modern city.

Young people's identities, Jens Dahl (2010, p. 137) claims, 'are no longer rooted in the notion of an imagined traditional Greenland culture'. The losers in society, he adds, are obviously 'those with little education and limited Danish (and English) language skills' (ibid., pp. 137–138). Interestingly, he blames the problems on the Greenlandic authorities that, he says, 'forgot the language requirements of any kind of education on the other side [sic] of the primary school' (ibid.). This assumption reflects a peculiar ignorance of the question of cultural continuity and societal rupture, seeming to believe that a future can be built without any connection to the past. More than any other institution, the school has reproduced social inequalities in Greenland through affirmation of dominant cultural models formulating what is defined as good and respectful for everyone. The school, founded on Danish culture (and language), has been associated to a progressive youth with taste and high ambition. Fluency in Danish is a relevant example of cultural capital, reconstructing inequality as a consequence of the differences in social agents' ability to master the codes of the culture. Prestigious schools have Danish teachers and bilingual pupils who are used to Danish language at home as well as at school. Most families would like to send their children to these schools (only available in main towns) as they are fully aware of these institutions' fame and status in society. Parents want the children to get recognition and success, but at the same time they know that the children might not fit into the dominant culture's styles and values. Social agents, says Bourdieu (1995), will often have a bodily sense (habitus) of what is fitting behaviour in a given context. If they don't, their lack of cultural capital will be uncovered and they will end up feeling stigmatized or marginalized. Clothing style and body language can also communicate young people's cultural capital, as smart modern outfits will normally be regarded as better style than practical traditional clothing associated with life in Greenlandic villages or the hunting culture of the past (Rygaard, 2010).

Fear and Loathing

Young men are unfortunately often presented as 'though they existed outside of and opposed to the rest of "society"' (Amit and Dyck, 2013, p. 5). Widespread demonization of young, uneducated Inuit men is also leading to action designed to persuade them to change from 'primitive' to rational and more 'civilized' conduct and values. Making young blue-collar men the scapegoat of modern Greenland's social problems is only bolstering existing stereotypes of the lost hunter in the city. Many young men feel culturally alienated and socially excluded in this societal context, which breeds youth marginalization and potential danger in the form of violence and other destructive activities.

Man's life and work was the strongest symbol of the hunting culture, and therefore it now also epitomizes failure in relation to the modern transformation of Greenlandic society. Now, how do we perceive the problem of marginalization? Malik Kleist from the Nuuk rock band, Chilly Friday, says in an interview:

> We don't write nationalistically [...]. Our texts are more personal and much stronger. Deeper, isn't that what you call it? They are about suicide, drunkenness and children being left on the streets, or children playing out in the middle of the night because they don't dare going home. So far a lot of people have hidden behind the excuse that the Danes destroyed our hunting culture. That became an excuse for drinking and wallowing in self-pity, but in modern Greenland we have to move on. Greenlandic youth wishes to live a proud and good life instead of being pathetic. We don't want to use our parents' bad excuses.
>
> (in Pedersen, 2008: 95)

Texts from local rap and rock songs inspire children and young people from all over the country. Many songs represent a bitter speech – after 'too long' a time with silence – to the many parents who failed to protect and guide their offspring. Some of the songs are, says Alex Andersen, like 'regular bombshell[s] on society' (ibid., p. 96). The children and young people of today represent the first generation without memory of the old rural settlements. Painful memories of suffering in childhood turns young people's anger against their own parents rather than towards authorities. In this way, young people learn that they are not alone in their misery, but also that they should not put the blame for all the problems on themselves. Nuuk is the perfect scene for graffiti and rap; there are countless dreary concrete walls to be painted and marked. And on the other side of the same cracked walls, you will find many of the boys and girls that 'cannot walk alone without fear'.

Maasi's Story

Under the headline 'It is my fault, and only mine', the bilingual lifestyle magazine *Anu Una* (2014) presented the story of the life of Maasi, a young man from Nuuk. His story reflects the life of many Greenlanders from the same generation – born in the decade after the introduction of Home Rule. It was a serious car accident in June 2012 that brought an end to Maasi's long-standing alcohol and marijuana abuse. He was 26 years old at that time and had been an addict for more than eight years. Maasi became famous in Greenland when his band, Prussic, released the innovative album 'Misiliineq Siulleq' (The First Test) in 2013. Three young friends rebelled against their parents, against abuse and neglect. People were amazed as nobody had written such accurate texts about painful 'realities' before. Maasi was rapping about his childhood and adolescence with an alcoholic father.

> Again I am alone, again father is drinking, what can Maasi otherwise put up with, he is too small to do anything but to watch while father is drunk. The youngest siblings are crying, the stepmother has escaped long time ago. Maasi is the only one to take care of the children.
>
> (from the piece 'Angajoqqaat')

His first four years were spent together with his father in Qaqortoq in Southern Greenland. Maasi doesn't know why his mother moved to Nuuk and left him with his abusive father. His father tried to commit suicide when Maasi was six years old. Then the boy stayed with his grandparents for a while, before returning to his father. When he was ten years old he moved to be with his mother in Nuuk. His traumatic childhood filled him with anger and he had problems in adolescence. He started smoking marijuana aged 17 but tried to limit the smoking to weekends as he had vowed not to end up like his father. That promise was broken after a short while. Maasi and his girlfriend had a son when he was 22 years old. Now he was drinking and smoking marijuana every day. His girlfriend had to take care of everything at home. He smoked so much that he didn't have any clear concept of time when he was 18–23 years old. He was also gambling. When, one night, he was very angry and started yelling and screaming at his terrified girlfriend, his four-year-old son came into the bedroom to protect his mother. Another day the son gave his father this advice: 'Ataata, move out of our house, so that you stop quarrelling'. When he survived the car accident in 2012, Maasi started thinking about his life. He stopped his abuse of alcohol and marijuana and recently resumed his journalism studies. 'I failed my son, and the fault is only mine', Maasi says. 'It was very hard to admit this.' This young Greenlander, with a life story similar to many of his peers, does not want to blame his parents or other relatives and friends for his troubles, but he is the child of a generation that went through huge societal and cultural transformation. He is a young man who enjoyed great success in popular music but grave misfortune in the transition from adolescence to 'respectable' adulthood. Maasi was admired as a streetwise and cool guy within the sub-field of urban hip-hop masculinity, but he was subordinated as a social loser in the field of 'modern' masculinity in the city. He could still focus on his music in order to get recognized as talented, but he has decided to invest in formal education as it seems to represent cultural capital more relevant for a young Greenlandic adult seeking a stable future as a family man. In this way, Maasi, trying to organize his chaotic life in order to save his closest family, is negotiating his masculinity and identity by asking: What can I do and what can I not do?

Summary

The city symbolizes a crack in the ice, a split without complete separation of conventional and contemporary identities and constructions of 'Greenlandness'. A minor crack may be followed by larger cleavage and separation, distancing different groups from each other. The risk of falling between ice floes will thereby grow. Nonetheless, ice floes have always been drifting and crashing in the Arctic.

Nuuk is a city of contrasts. It is a microcosm of the whole world, reflecting continuity and discontinuity in time and space. People are aware of what is happening on the global stage as well as at the outermost Arctic settlement. Ultima Thule is not inaccessible anymore. 'There are quite a few of us', says Pia Arke (in Meredith, 2013), a Danish/Greenlandic artist, 'who belong neither in the west, nor in the marginalized rest'. She portrays a society where many, maybe most, people fall between two elaborate categories: Danish and Greenlandic. Where to belong? 'We will', she says, 'have to create that place ourselves' (ibid.). Others, like the young artist Bolatta, believe it is necessary to uphold 'our culture' because 'everything is melting together around us' (Høegh and Havsteen-Mikkelsen, 2006, p. 48).

The case of Greenland is interesting because it shows how indigenous people at the edge of Europe in postcolonial times struggle to gain cultural recognition, and how closely this process is connected to the negotiation and performance of gender identities. Marginalization of young men in Greenland is part of the modernization and urbanization of society – and Inuit man's loss of work and identity in this process. Greenlandic marginalized masculinities reflect concussions in society, redefining the name of wanted and needed men. The social metamorphosis of Greenland has emancipated people from old ties and attached them to others. Man, the symbol of the 'natural order of things' in the premodern era, has had to completely rethink his role and status in Greenland, something that has turned out to be an extremely difficult adaptation with huge costs, not only for man himself, but also for his family and hence for the whole society. Has he now and for all eternity lost the dream about the kayak? I think it still pops up occasionally, but in a new shape and reminiscent of something he has experienced recently. Most men know very well that they cannot become hunters like their fathers or grandfathers once were. What many men have experienced, like Maasi for example, is a childhood where the 'order of things' was non-existent and the impression of moral and social disintegration paramount. For these men, the intersection of 'problems' influencing everyday life was mayhem, breeding outrage and antisocial behaviour. With this is mind, the boys were, to put it mildly, ill-prepared for the 'new normal' in the modernized city. While their sisters did not have an easier upbringing, their achievements later in life unveil young men's special challenges prompting this question: Why do so many Greenlandic men end up in marginalized positions in society? This chapter has discussed the question and suggested some answers.

References

Amit, V. and Dyck, N. (2013) Introduction. In: V. Amit, and N. Dyck (eds) *Young Men in Uncertain Times*. New York and Oxford: Berghahn, pp. 1–32.

Anu Una [Lifestyle Magazine] No. 19 (2014) It is my fault, and only mine. Nuuk.

Blixen, K. (1937) *Den Afrikanske Farm* [Out of Africa]. Copenhagen: Gyldendal.

Bourdieu, P. (1995) *Distinction. A Social Critique of the Judgement of Taste*. Cambridge, MA: Harvard University Press.

Chemnitz, J. (2013) Mikropolis. *Blok P – En boligblok i Nuuk*. Copenhagen: The North Atlantic House, pp. 4–20.

Coles, T. (2009) Negotiating the Field of Masculinity. The production and reproduction of multiple dominant masculinities, *Men and Masculinities* 12(1): 30–44.

Condon, R. G. and P. R. Stern (1993) Gender-role preference, gender identity, and gender socialization among contemporary Inuit youth, *Ethos* 21(4): 384–416.

Dahl, J. (2010) Identity, urbanization and political demography in Greenland, *Acta Borealia: A Nordic Journal of Circumpolar Societies* 27(2): 125–140.

Douglas, M. (1966) *Purity and Danger. An Analysis of Concepts of Pollution and Taboo*. London: Routledge and Kegan Paul.

Freuchen, P. (1953) *Min grønlandske ungdom*. Copenhagen: Fremad.

Greenland Today. (2013) Journal. Nuussuaq.

Gutmann, M. C. (1997) Trafficking in men. The anthropology of masculinity, *Annual Review of Anthropology* 26: 385–409.

Høegh, I. S. and Havsteen-Mikkelsen, A. (2006) Melting barricades [Arts Project] In F. Hansen and N. Tone Olaf (eds) *Rethinking Nordic Colonialism* [Rethinking-nordic-colonialism.org]

Høiris, O. and Marquardt, O. (eds) (2011) *Fra vild til verdensborger*. Aarhus: Aarhus University Press.

Kentorp, M. (2002) Mr. Grønland. *Berlingske Tidende* [Newspaper] 16 October. Copenhagen.

Lynge, P. K. (2012) *Myten om de elskede sønner* [Masters Dissertation]. Nuuk: University of Greenland.

Meredith, A. (2013). Northern Lights. Greenlandic Art in the 21st Century. *FirstAmericanArt Magazine*, Spring 2013 [firstAmericanartmagazine.com] pp. 64–68.

Nuttall, M. (1994) Greenland. Emergence of an Inuit Homeland. In Minority Rights Group (ed.). *Polar People. Self-determination and development*. London: Minority Rights Publications.

Parrott, D. J. and Zeichner, A. (2003) Effects of hypermasculinity on physical aggression against women, *Psychology of Men and Masculinity* 4(1): 70–78.

Pedersen, B. K. (2008) Young Greenlanders in the urban space of Nuuk. *Études/Inuit/Studies* 32(1): 91–105.

Rasmussen, K. (1962) *The Bear in the Ice Hole*. Copenhagen: The Royal Danish Ministry of Foreign Affairs.

Rasmussen, M. and Tierney, S. B. (2013) In: *Blok P – En boligblok i Nuuk*. Copenhagen: The North Atlantic House.

Reeser, T. (2010) *Masculinities in Theory*. Malden, MA; Oxford: Wiley-Blackwell.

Rygaard, J. (2010) 'Proxemic Nuuk'. Town and Urban Life with Nuuk as Example. In K. Langgård (ed.) *Cultural and Social Research in Greenland*. Nuuk: Ilisimatusarfik, pp. 229–248.

Sejersen, F. (2004) Horizons of sustainability in Greenland: Inuit landscapes of memory and vision, *Arctic Anthropology* 41(1): 71–89.

Sonne, B. (2000) *Gender perspectives in Greenlandic stories*. Seminar paper. Nuuk: Ilisimatusarfik.

Weyhe, T. (2011) Finanskrisen og arbejdsmarkedet i Grønland. In S. B. Nielsen (ed.) *Nordiske mænd til omsorgsarbejde!* [Report] Roskilde: Roskilde University, pp. 248–261.

Willis, P. E. (1977) *Learning to Labour. How Working-Class Kids Get Working-Class Jobs*. Farnborough, Hants: Saxon House.

4 Marginalized Masculinities and Exclusion in the New Low-Skill Service Sector in Sweden

Peter Håkansson

Introduction

After the structural crisis of the 1970s, the industrialized countries entered a new phase in which innovations of the third industrial revolution changed structures of production and the labour market (Lundh, 2010; Schön, 2007). The new labour market contains more services. This new phase of late modern society has been called 'the new service and knowledge-oriented society'. This process, however, has also led to a polarisation. Although employment in services in the EU increased from 56 per cent in 1991 to 70 per cent in 2012 (World Bank, 2014a), the increase – between 2011 and 2013 – was amongst the low-wage and high-wage service jobs, while the number of middle-wage jobs decreased (Eurofound, 2014). In addition to women having numerically dominated these low-wage service jobs, the occupations have also been gender coded as female work (Leidner, 1991; McDowell, 2009). However, what is considered masculine work or feminine work is not a given; rather, it depends on the *gender of the typical incumbents*.

This chapter analyses low-skill service jobs in Sweden from a gender perspective. The aim is to analyse marginalization of masculinity by studying how the transformation from an industrial economy to a service- and knowledge-based economy has changed the labour market. For the working class and the low skilled, this has led to a transition of employment from low-skill manual work to low-skill service work. Consequently, the research questions are the following: How do men in Sweden adapt to this transition in the labour market? Have men become redundant (either by choosing self-exclusion or by normative exclusion placing them as 'unemployable')? Or are men adapting to the new low-skill jobs in the service sector?

The questions bring about some interesting perspectives on marginalization. As some scholars seem to suggest (McDowell, 2003a, 2003b, 2009; Robertsson, 2003), men may choose not to participate in the low-skill feminine-coded service sector. This may lead to men with industrial habitus being marginalized/excluded either by self-exclusion (they do not feel they fit in) or by normative exclusion (they are seen as unemployable). However, there is also a third possibility which may be seen as a contradiction: if they do fit in and they do obtain employment in the low-skill service sector, this would also lead to a kind of marginalization because of the low status of the work, the low earnings, the insecure working conditions and the temporary employment contracts. This third possibility would be another kind of marginalization, not one based on exclusion but one based on a polarised and segmented labour market where some groups may become locked in on the secondary labour market. Further, this marginalization would not be based on gender; rather, it would be based on class, affecting both men and women in the low-skill service sector. This highlights that marginalization is not only a question of gender but also often a question of class, education and ethnicity, amongst other factors.

The question of how masculine work and feminine work are defined is central to this chapter. As pointed out earlier, the question of whether the work can be considered masculine or feminine depends on the gender of who can be considered the typical incumbent. However, the typical incumbent of a specific occupation can, of course, be observed in different ways. One way could be to analyse people's ideas and norms of who they believe to be the typical incumbent. Another way, which is the chosen method for this chapter, is to count the number of men and women in the occupation. This does not give any straight answers about marginalization, however. The concept of marginalization carries much more than just the number of men and women in specific occupations. However, change in the norms of what is considered masculine and feminine work can be essential because it may affect masculine exclusion, whether it is self-exclusion or normative exclusion. One way of observing a change of norms is to observe the numbers of men and women who work in this sector; specifically, when it is linked to who is the typical incumbent, as in this case. Further, if work in the service sector is the only work to be found and men are/have choosing/chosen to be excluded from this work, then these men may face marginalization. Exclusion from the labour market not only leads to an economically worse situation for the individual, it may also lead to a backlash when it comes to social status and power.

To summarize, the question of how to observe marginalization adds to questions on methodology, specifically regarding epistemology: How can we gain knowledge and understand marginalization by using quantitative methods? Can marginalization be measured quantitatively at all? It is important to point out that it is not the numbers per se that measure marginalization; the numbers have to be understood in their context and their theoretical framework. Without a theoretical framework, quantitative methods cannot contribute to any understanding of complex issues. As pointed out above, the numbers tell us whether men participate in the low-skill service sector or not, if there has been any change in this participation over the years, and if this participation is correlated with other factors (e.g. age, education, ethnicity); however, the numbers do not tell us why.

From Industry to Service: The Development of the Labour Market after the 1970s

When the economies of the industrialized countries entered a new phase, the labour market also changed. The new service- and knowledge-oriented society contains more services and less industrial work. In this process, masculine gender-coded occupations within industry have, to some respect, disappeared, resulting in rising unemployment and alienation. In the EU, employment within industry dropped from 34 per cent of total employment in 1991 to 25 per cent in 2012 (World Bank, 2014b). When specific professions within metal, machinery and related trades are analysed and combined with educational level, the picture is even clearer.[1] In Sweden, these occupations have lost 20,000 employees between 2001 and 2013. However, as Figure 4.1 shows, the number of employees with a primary education has been most affected – from 28,000 employees in 2001 to 15,000 in 2013 – while the number of employees with a tertiary education has increased by around 1,000 (Statistics Sweden, 2015). To some extent, this follows the general upgrading when it comes to formal education, but it also shows the transition of these occupations. The occupations have not disappeared; they have been upgraded.

On the other hand, the transition of the economy from being industrial-based to service- and knowledge-based has led to an increase in service jobs. However, a lot of these service jobs are of an unskilled nature. These jobs have sometimes been described as McJobs – de-skilled, low-quality service jobs – and they are

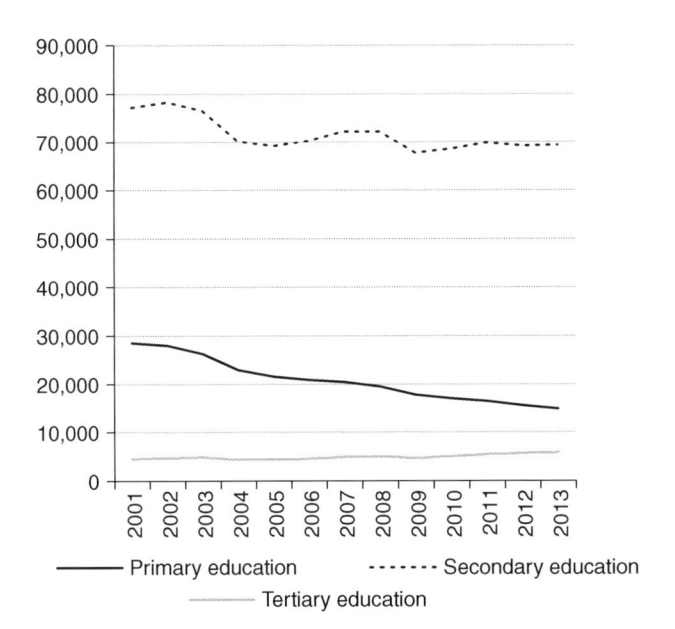

Figure 4.1 Number of men and women employed within metal, machinery and related trades work in Sweden. Year 2001–2013.

viewed as offering poor pay and conditions and few opportunities for development (*The Economist*, 1996; Lindsay, 2005). Goos and Manning (2003) differ between McJobs and MacJobs, where McJobs are considered 'bad jobs' and depend on warm bodies where the work, and specifically the pay, does not permit a decent living standard. The MacJobs, on the other hand, are considered 'good jobs', that is, high-tech and high-skill jobs that depend on high-skill performance.

Another taxonomy used by Linda McDowell (2003a, 2009) for the new polarized service sector is high-tech versus high-touch. High-tech jobs are those in high-quality service production, for example in finance and information and communications technology (ICT), whereas high-touch jobs can be defined as low skilled, generic and customer-oriented (D'Agostino *et al.*, 2006; Florida 2006; McDowell, 2003a, 2009; Sassen, 2001). Jobs in the high-touch sector include low-skill jobs in restaurants, hotels, retail and care. These low-skill jobs in the service sector can be an entry to the labour market for many young people. According to Statistics Sweden (2015), the young, specifically young women, are highly represented in low-skill jobs in the retail, hotel and restaurant industries. In retail, 20 per cent of all employees in low-skill jobs are women aged 16–24, whereas 12 per cent of the employees are men aged 16–24. Correspondingly, in hotels and restaurants, 13 per cent are women and 6 per cent are men; while in the care sector, 11 per cent are women and 2 per cent are men.[2]

Masculine work has been socially constructed as being dangerous, hard, dirty and sweaty, all of which has created a strong working identity. This construction lies far from the service-oriented social construction of high-touch work. However, the transition of the economy from industrial- to service-based affects both working-class men and women. Low-skill service jobs include lower wages and more insecure employment contracts than the manual, industrial work that was available previously; however, it is often the only employment available for both men and for women. Because (what can be considered as) masculine work is decreasing by numbers and feminine work is increasing, it has sometimes been asked if men, specifically working-class men, have become redundant, i.e. there is no room for working-class men in the new service and knowledge economy (McDowell, 2003b). In this discussion, different forms of exclusions are important to investigate.

Redundant Masculinities and Exclusion

Traditionally, personal services have been gender coded as female work, where attributes such as adherence, docility, timidity, politeness, subordination, caring and personal attractiveness have been necessary to adopt (Leidner, 1991; McDowell, 2009). McDowell shows that white working-class young men find it difficult to accept high-touch working conditions. They have grown up in places where work traditionally has been related to the mining industry and other basic industries where the male working-class identity has been forged (McDowell, 2003a, 2003b, 2009). This male work identity is far from the docile and service-oriented social construction of high-touch occupations. Young men cannot have access to service-based occupations unless they are able to embrace the personal skills that are needed in a service occupation. According to McDowell (2003b), who studied young men in the UK, young working-class men seem to have problems adopting those skills. Therefore, men that cannot adopt the personal skills and attributes needed in service-based occupations are excluded, which can be viewed as normative exclusion. According to McDowell (2003b), 'New forms of masculinity more in tune with the dominant attributes of a service-based economy ... have yet to find any expression among the young men here' (p. 226).

There are major differences between the UK and Sweden concerning, for example, the breadwinner norm (European Social Survey, 2010).[3] However, Robertsson (2003) finds similarities in Sweden, where unemployed men with experiences from industry prefer to stay unemployed rather than take a job in the healthcare sector: a sector which has severe difficulties recruiting staff. One could say that these men choose self-exclusion rather than taking a job in the healthcare sector. According to Robertsson, male nurses are given professional advantages but, on the other hand, they risk having their masculinity or sexuality questioned.

Accordingly, even though there are differences between the UK and Sweden, we cannot ignore that both work duties and work are also gender coded in Sweden. According to Leidner (1991), 'One of the most important determinants of the meaning of a type of work, as well as of how the work is conducted and rewarded, is its association with a particular gender' (p. 155). The reason for this is that gender is a strong denominator for identity, and the connection between the work you do and the identity you can accept is important for most people. However, what is considered as masculine work versus feminine work is not a given, as stated previously. Rather, it depends on the gender of who is considered to be the *typical incumbent*. Further, gender norms are changed and reinvented wherever they fit. According to Leidner (1991), '... employers and workers retain the flexibility to reinterpret them [gender norms of work] in ways that support jobholders' gender identities' (p. 171). Some working-class men might argue that masculine work is sweaty, dirty and dangerous but, in reality, occupational gender norms can be elastic. Furthermore, according to Connell and Messerschmidt (2005), it is important to acknowledge the role of change. There is a continuous struggle for hegemony '... and older forms of masculinity might be displaced by new ones' (Connell and Messerschmidt, 2005, p. 833). However, we cannot ignore historical heritage and path dependency when it comes to the gender coding of work. Work life has been gender segregated through legislation and traditions, and we can see its continuation in today's labour market where jobs are still constructed as either feminine or masculine (Leidner, 1991; Robertsson, 2003; West and Zimmerman, 1987).

Dual Labour Market Theory from a Gender Perspective

Dual labour market theory describes the labour market as dual and segmented. To analyse the gendered labour market from this theoretical perspective gives valuable contribution to understanding the polarized service sector. According to the theory, jobs fall into either the primary or the secondary labour market. Jobs in the primary sector are good jobs, characterized by high wages, job security, substantial responsibility and ladders where internal promotion is possible. Jobs in the secondary sector are unqualified and are characterized by low wages and insecure, temporary employment. Historically, groups that are underprivileged in the labour market – women, immigrants and youths – were to be found in the secondary sector (Doeringer and Piore, 1971; Reich *et al.*, 1973; Bulow and Summers, 1986; Boje and Grönlund, 2003). The taxonomy of high-tech and high-touch sectors can be understood as a dual and segmented labour market.

One important contribution of the dual labour market theory is the existence of this segmented labour market. Recruitment to the primary and secondary sector follows different logics. The primary sector is open only for persons with the correct education (but personal attributes and contacts can also be important). Therefore, it is not possible to use the secondary sector as a stepping stone and occupational transition. In short, if the outcome for feminine gender coding is equal to work in the secondary labour market (with unsecure working conditions, low wages and poor career development), there will be difficulties in recruiting men to these jobs. One reason, besides the obvious one, is that men have the breadwinner norm to live up to (Robertsson, 2003). Therefore, if female-coded jobs are devalued, low paid and have insecure employment contracts, it is then understandable that men do not want these jobs. The problem is that the kinds of job young working-class men traditionally have had are diminishing. The sector that is increasing is the service sector. According to data from Statistics Sweden (2015), the number of low-skill service occupations within retail (store cashiers, demo, market salespersons) has increased by 22 per cent from 2005–2013, and the number within hotels/restaurants (receptionists, catering personnel, waiters) has increased by 23 per cent during the same time period. As shown previously, the numbers of male working-class professions like welding, founding, tinsmithing, and so on, has decreased. This transition, which led to an exclusion of men from the labour market, can also be observed in the unemployment rates. Between 1976 and 1989, the rate of unemployment for young men (aged 20–24) was, on average, 5 per cent *less* than that of young women. In 1990 we can observe a break from this trend; from this year on, the rate of unemployment for young men has been, on average, 20 per cent *more* than that of young women. This can be interpreted as exclusion in the labour market having led to marginalization (i.e. unemployment). The question is, however, whether men are increasing their participation in high-touch jobs, i.e. if there is a change when it comes to exclusion?

Male Participation in High-touch Jobs

The data from Statistics Sweden (2015) show that male participation in high-touch jobs has actually increased in the country, both in absolute terms and in relation to the increase with its female counterpart. The number of men in these occupations increased by approximately 60 per cent during the time period. Figure 4.2 shows men's participation in low-skill occupations within retail, hotel/restaurants and care in relation to women's participation from 2005 to 2013. For example, men have increased their participation rate in relation to women from less than 0.4 in 2005 to approximately 0.55 in 2013.

When it comes to young people (16–24 years), it is the same trend in retail: the number of young men employed in retail increased by 60 per cent, while young women remained at the same levels. In the hotel and restaurant sector, the number of young men in employment increased by around 35 per cent, while the number of young women increased by 40 per cent. The number of people employed in low-skill occupations in care (nursing assistants, personal assistants) did not increase as rapidly compared to retail and hotel/restaurants: there was an increase of around 8 per cent during this time period. However, men primarily contributed to this increase as well. The number of men (in general) increased by 33 per cent, compared to the number of women who increased by 4 per cent. Young men

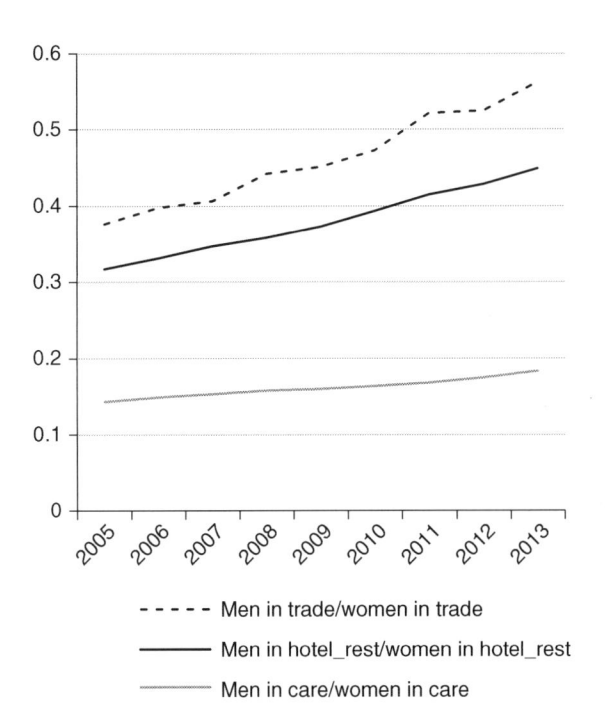

Figure 4.2 Men in low-skill occupations within retail, hotel/restaurants and care in relation to women. Year 2005–2013.

(16–24 years) increased by 31 per cent, while young women increased by 18 per cent. In short, the general picture is that the number of low-skill service jobs in Sweden is increasing, with the number of men compared to women in these occupations contributing significantly to the increase, which clearly indicates that male exclusion is diminishing in the low-skill service sector. However, we need to know more about *who* works in the high-touch sector and run variables for socio-economic status simultaneously with the development in the different occupations. To do this, data from the Swedish SOM Institute and regression analysis will be used.

Who Works in the Low-Skill Service Sector?

When it comes to the definition of low-skill jobs within the service sector, the standard occupational codes (ssyk) are used, as before. These codes are constructed in the survey from the respondents' open answers on occupation. The occupations studied here are the same as previously mentioned: low-skill service occupations within retail (store cashiers, demo, market salespeople), hotels/restaurants (receptionists, catering personnel, waiters) and care (nursing assistants, personal assistants). The sample used is fairly large – over 20,000 respondents over a period of seven years – and will give fairly good estimations of who works in the high-touch sector. The sample may look skewed when it comes to age distribution (there are few respondents aged 15–29 or 65–85), as pensioners and students are omitted, which affects age distribution. When it comes to education level, three levels are used: primary education (less than nine years or nine years of elementary school attendance); secondary education (studies at secondary school, graduation from secondary school or studies at post-secondary school without graduation); and tertiary education (university degree, research education). Moreover, the question of whether the respondent lives in an urban or rural location is examined, for which four different levels are used: rural (pure rural); minor urban; cities; and Stockholm/Gothenburg/Malmö. Except for the last category (where register data is used), it is the respondents' own perception of their neighbourhood that is expressed in the answers.

A variable is constructed to estimate the respondent's origin, or rather, the respondent's parents' origin. Responses to the question 'Where did your parents mainly grow up?' were divided between one group of respondents whose parents both grew up outside the Nordic countries and the other group with at least one of their parents growing up in a Nordic country. In the sample, only 8 per cent say that both their parents grew up in another country in Europe or in a country outside of Europe, which is a clear under-representation of this group. Even though the number of jobs in the high-touch sector as a proportion of the total labour market have increased, their numbers are still fairly small.[4] As Table 4.1 shows, only around 4 per cent of the total employment rate is made up by low-skill jobs in hotels and restaurants. Although 9 per cent comprises low-skill care jobs, only 1 per cent comprises low-skill jobs within retail. However, both the retail and hotel/restaurant sectors represent a fair amount of job opportunities for

Table 4.1 High-touch jobs (retail, hotel/restaurant, care) and other jobs in Sweden 2007–2013 in the sample Riks-SOM 2007–2013

Age	Retail	Hotel/rest	Care	Other	Total
15–29	81	175	268	2,104	2,628
	3%	7%	10%	80%	100%
30–49	50	300	788	8,332	9,470
	1%	3%	8%	88%	100%
50–64	21	261	847	6,768	7,897
	0%	3%	11%	86%	100%
65–85	0	9	15	363	387
	0%	2%	4%	94%	100%
Total	152	745	1,918	17,567	20,382
	1%	4%	9%	86%	100%

Sources: Riks-SOM 2007, Riks-SOM 2008, Riks-SOM 2009, Riks-SOM 2010, Riks-SOM 2011, Riks-SOM 2012, Riks-SOM 2013.

young people. When it comes to young people (15–29 years), around 10 per cent of all employed young people work in these kinds of job, in comparison to the 4 per cent of those aged 30–49. It is specifically young women who work in the retail and hotel/restaurant trades. Care, on the other hand, tells another story. The jobs are highly dominated by women. However, young people are not keen to work there, specifically young men. However, it is not enough to look at the numbers in one dimension. We also have to include other variables, like education and ethnic background, to get a picture of *who* works in these jobs. Therefore, a multinomial logit regression is used to estimate these jobs. The following variables are used: gender; age; rural/urban place of residence; parents' origin (growing up); and education level.[5]

Three different regressions were run: the first was run with all respondents; the second with women only; and the third with men only. The regressions show that men are working less than women in the low-skill jobs in retail, hotel/restaurant and care sectors. Moreover, and not very surprisingly, for retail and hotel/restaurants, the younger the respondent is, the higher probability for him or her to work in these sectors; but as we know from before, this is not valid when it comes to low-skill jobs within care. Some of the significant results for men and women respectively are shown in Figures 4.3–4.7. These figures show the probability of a man or a woman working in the hotel/restaurant sector, respectively the care sector, if he or she possesses some specific characteristics. Both Figure 4.3 and Figure 4.4 show that the probability of men and women in low-skill jobs within the hotel/restaurant and care sectors having tertiary education is lower compared to the probability of them having primary education.

However, when it comes to secondary education, the results are mixed. For men, the probability of having secondary education within the care sector is higher than the probability of them having primary education. For women in care and for men in hotel/restaurant trades, the results regarding secondary education do not significantly differ from the results regarding primary education.

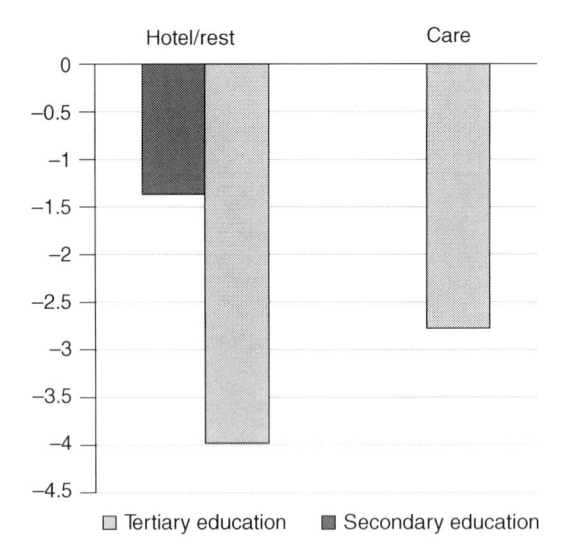

Figure 4.3 Significant differences in probability between women with secondary resp. tertiary education working in hotel/restaurants resp. care *compared to women with primary education.*

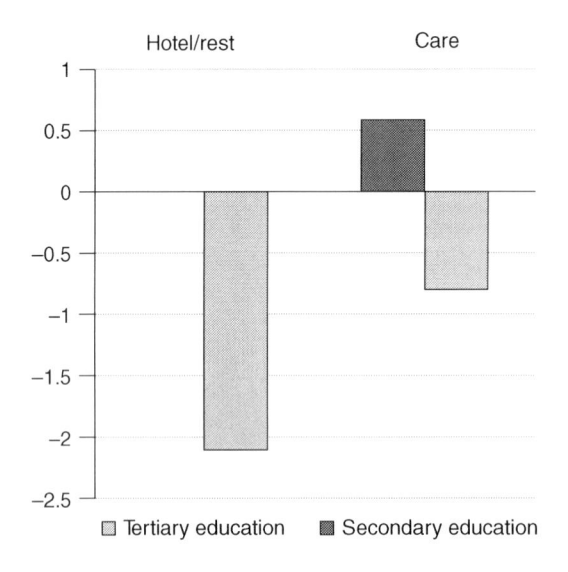

Figure 4.4 Significant differences in probability between men with secondary resp. tertiary education working in hotel/restaurants resp. care *compared to men with primary education.*

Note
* All shown results are significant on at least 5% level. No. of observations=9,803, adjusted $R^2=0.0762$, Prob>chi^2=0.0000

More interesting, though, is when we look at parents' origin and the respondents' place of residence. As Figure 4.5 shows, a respondent whose parents grew up outside of the Nordic countries has a higher probability of working in the hotel/restaurant or care sectors than a respondent with at least one parent brought up in a Nordic country.

When it comes to place of residence, there are some interesting results to comment on. When all the respondents are included in the analysis (i.e. men and women in the same data set), low-skill jobs in care seem to be less important in the urban areas – cities or major urban areas and in Stockholm/Gothenburg/Malmö – than in the minor towns and rural areas. However, as Figures 4.6 and 4.7 show, when the regression is run exclusively on women, the results show that the larger the city, the fewer the women that have low-skill jobs within hotel/restaurant and care. Consequently, these jobs seem to be more important for women in rural areas. The result for women (shown in Figure 4.6) is contradicted by the result for men in low-skill jobs in hotel/restaurant trades (Figure 4.7). Here, it is men from the major urban areas, specifically in Stockholm/Gothenburg/Malmö, who mostly work in these kinds of job. One could believe

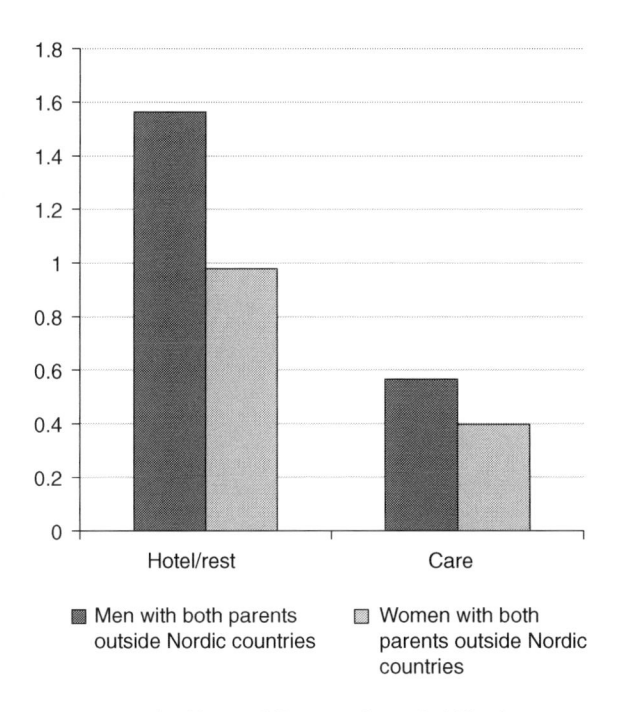

Figure 4.5 Significant differences in probability between men/women with *both* parents brought up outside of the Nordic countries working in hotel/restaurants resp. care *compared to men/women with at least one parent brought up in the Nordic countries.*

Note
* All shown results are significant on at least 5% level. No. of observations=9,803, adjusted $R^2=0.0762$, Prob>chi^2=0.0000

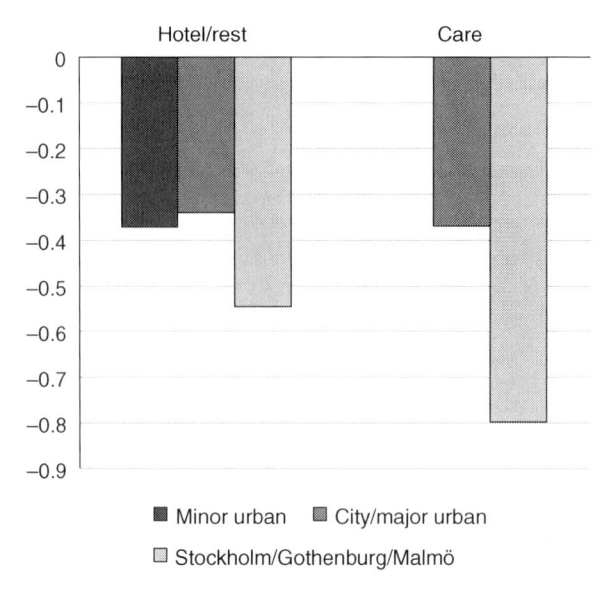

Figure 4.6 Significant differences in probability between women in urban locations working in hotel/restaurants resp. care *compared to women in rural locations.*

Note
* All shown results are significant on at least 5% level. No. of observations = 10,389, adjusted $R^2 = 0.1466$, Prob > chi^2 = 0.0000

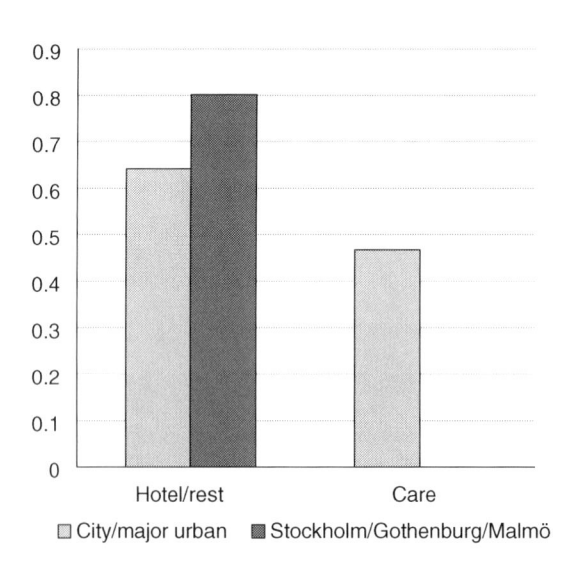

Figure 4.7 Significant differences in probability between men in urban locations working in hotel/restaurants resp. care *compared to men in rural locations.*

this would be so because these jobs exist to a higher extent in urban areas, but in that case it would be the same for women. Rather, the results show a *lower* probability for women from Stockholm/Gothenburg/Malmö compared to women from rural areas working in hotels/restaurants, while men from Stockholm/Gothenburg/Malmö *increase* their probability of working in this sector.

It is interesting to note that when it comes to men there is no significant difference between minor urban locations and rural locations, neither in hotels/restaurants nor in care. Furthermore, there is no significant difference in the probability of working in the low-skill care sector for men in rural areas and in Stockholm/Gothenburg/Malmö.

Conclusion and Discussion

The new service and knowledge society has led to an increase of jobs in the service sector. This increase in jobs covers both high-wage and high-skill jobs in ICT and finance, as well as low-skill service jobs within the retail, hotels/restaurants and care sectors. Meanwhile, the number of middle-wage jobs has decreased. The low-skill service jobs have been defined as high-touch; that is, they are low skilled, generic and customer-oriented jobs, and they often offer low pay and an insecure employment situation. Traditionally, these service jobs have been gender coded as female work where attributes such as adherence, docility, timidity, politeness, subordination, caring and personal attractiveness have been necessary to adopt.

In this chapter, high-touch jobs in Sweden have been analysed. These jobs are here defined as low-skill jobs within the retail, hotel and restaurant and care sectors. In the literature, there is a concern that there is no room for working-class men in the new service and knowledge economy. The old masculine-coded low-skill jobs in industry are disappearing, while the new low-skill service jobs are not attracting young working-class men, according to the literature (for example McDowell, 2003a, 2003b, 2009; Robertsson, 2003). However, Linda McDowell (2008) has pointed out that the feminized low-skill service jobs now are coming to represent the entire workforce as working-class men are forced to accept generic service employment '... that is not congruent with their sense of self as masculine but which is often the only employment available' (McDowell, 2008, p. 155). Therefore, it is important to analyse to what extent this is happening in Sweden. How do men in Sweden adapt to the transition of the labour market? Are men in Sweden excluded in the new service economy?

The results show that men, including those in Sweden, are under-represented in the high-touch sector, but something is happening. Both in absolute terms and as a share of the total labour market the high-touch sector is expanding, as stipulated, but it is men's participation that is increasing the most. Their participation in relation to women's is increasing in the retail and hotel/restaurant trades as well as in the care sector. This change may challenge traditional occupational gender norms or, as McDowell (2003b) puts it in *Redundant Masculinities*: '... economic restructuring and growing income inequalities are as likely to reinforce, as challenge, long-standing masculine attitudes and traditional gendered relationships in working class communities' (p. 226).

Therefore, are masculinities marginalized? As Connell and Messerschmidt (2005) pointed out, at times there can be a struggle between different forms of masculinities; and at present, and due to the labour market transition, the old masculinities, covering masculinities with an industrial habitus, become excluded and, therefore, marginalized. Basically, there is no room for these old masculinities in service jobs because other kinds of, what can be viewed as feminine, skills are needed. However, the question about marginalization when it comes to the labour market is complex. To be excluded (or to choose self-exclusion) obviously leads to marginalization. However, a more intriguing question might be: Is it not the high-touch sector per se that could lead to marginalization because of low incomes and insecure, temporary employment? In a dual or segmented labour market, these jobs belong in a secondary sector, a sector that traditionally employs groups that are underprivileged in the labour market: women, immigrants and youth.

Who then is working in the high-touch sector? More specifically, who are the men that, to a greater extent, are employed in low-skill service jobs? When it comes to low-skill jobs in the hotel and restaurant industry, it is more common that men from major urban areas work in these jobs. The participation is most common in Stockholm/Gothenburg/Malmö, followed by smaller cities. One might believe that the social stigma would be less in urban areas, or if you want, the transition of masculinity from the old kind to the new kind would have progressed further in the larger cities. When it comes to the care sector, men in the major urban areas and cities are participating more than men in rural areas. Moreover, when comparing major urban areas (except Stockholm/Gothenburg/Malmö) to rural areas, we might believe that less of a social stigma is important in explaining why men from major urban areas prefer to work in care than men from rural areas. Furthermore, there is no significant difference between men in low-skill care jobs in Stockholm/Gothenburg/Malmö and men living in rural areas. This can be explained by the care sector, in general, playing a less important role as an employer in urban areas than in rural areas. This is shown clearly in the women's regressions, where the more the urban area, the less important the care sector is.

Regarding those respondents whose parents grew up in a country outside the Nordic countries, the results show that these respondents more often work in the low-skill service sector, and this applies to both men and women. Furthermore, the results show that men in Sweden are increasing their participation in the low-skill service sector, and it is specifically urban men and men of foreign origin that work in this sector. Considering the late modern trends on urbanization and migration, the feminine gender coding of low-skill service jobs is facing change, as is masculinity. Likewise, if we agree that what is considered masculine work or feminine work depends on who is considered to be a typical incumbent, and that this typical incumbent is changing, then we must agree that the norms of a gendered labour market are changing. In the future, there may not be the strong gender coding we face today and the transition of the labour market will most likely change values and gender norms in general.

Notes

1 Three occupational codes (ssyk 3-digit level) were analysed: 721 sheet and structural metal workers, moulders and welders and related workers; 722 blacksmiths, toolmakers and related trades workers; 723 machinery mechanics and repairers. The Swedish classification SSYK 2012 is equivalent to the International Standard Classification of Occupation 2008 (ISCO -08).
2 The definition of low-skill occupations within these sectors will in this chapter derive from SSYK 2012 and contain the following: retail = store cashiers, demo, market salespersons; hotels/restaurants = receptionists, catering personnel and waiters; and care = nursing assistants and personal assistants.
3 On the statement 'Men should have more right to jobs than women when jobs are scarce' in European Social Survey 2010, over 17 per cent of the UK respondents 'agreed strongly' or 'agreed' with the statement. In the Scandinavian countries, 5–7 per cent 'agreed strongly' or 'agreed'.
4 ... based on SOM data.
5 In addition, the year in which the survey was conducted is used as a control variable.

References

Boje, T. P. and Grönlund, A. (2003) Flexibility and employment insecurity. In T. P. Boje and B. Furuåker (eds) *Post-industrial Labour Markets: Profiles of North America and Scandinavia*. Routledge: London, pp. 186–212.

Bulow, J. I. and Summers, L. H. (1986) A theory of dual labor markets with application to industrial policy, discrimination, and Keynesian unemployment, *Journal of Labor Economics*, 4(3): 376–414.

Connell, R. W. and Messerschmidt, J. W. (2005) Hegemonic masculinity: Rethinking the concept, *Gender and Society*, 19(6): 829–859. doi:10.1177/0891243205278639

D'Agostino, A., Serafini, R. and Ward-Warmedinger, M. (2006) Sectoral Explanations of Employment in Europe: The Role of Services, Working Paper Series No 625: May 2006, European Central Bank.

Doeringer, P. B. and Piore, M. J. (1971) *Internal Labor Markets and Manpower Analysis*. Lexington, Mass.: Heath.

Economist, The (1996) *Backlash against McJobs*. (October 19, 1996): S10.

Eurofound (2014) *Drivers of recent job polarization and upgrading in Europe: European Jobs Monitor 2014*, Publication Office of the European Union, Luxembourg.

Florida, R. L. (2006) *Den kreativa klassens framväxt*. Diadalos: Stockholm.

Goos, M. and Manning, A. (2003) McJobs and MacJobs: The growing polarization of jobs in the UK. In R. Dickens, P. Gregg and J. Wadsworth (eds) *The Labour Market under New Labour* (pp. 70–85). Basingstoke: Palgrave Macmillan.

Leidner, R. (1991) Serving hamburgers and selling insurance: Gender, work, and identity in interactive service jobs, *Gender and Society*, 5(2): 154–177.

Lindsay, C. (2005) 'McJobs', 'good jobs' and skills: Job-seekers' attitudes to low-skilled service work, *Human Resource Management Journal*, 15(2): 50–65.

Lundh, C. (2010) *Spelets regler: institutioner och lönebildning på den svenska arbetsmarknaden 1850–2010*. (2. uppl.) Stockholm: SNS förlag.

McDowell, L. (2003a) Masculine identities and low-paid work: young men in urban labour markets, *International Journal of Urban and Regional Research*, 27 (4): 828–848.
McDowell, L. (2003b) *Redundant Masculinities? Employment Change and White Working Class Youth*. Malden, Mass.: Blackwell Pub.
McDowell, L. (2008) The new economy, class condescension and caring labour: Changing formations of class and gender, *NORA – Nordic Journal of Feminist and Gender Research*, 16(3), pp. 150–165.
McDowell, L. (2009) *Working Bodies*. Chichester, UK: Wiley-Blackwell.
Reich, M., Gordon, D. M. and Edwards, R. C. (1973) Dual Labor Markets: A Theory of Labor Market Segmentation, *The American Economic Review*, 63 (2), Papers and Proceedings of the Eighty-Fifth Annual Meeting of the American Economic Association (May, 1973), pp. 359–365.
Robertsson, H. (2003) *Maskulinitetskonstruktion, yrkesidentitet, könssegregering och jämställdhet*. Diss. (sammanfattning) Stockholm: Univ. Stockholm.
Sassen, S. (2001) *The Global City: New York, London, Tokyo*. Princeton, NJ: Princeton University Press, cop.
Schön, L. (2007) *En modern svensk ekonomisk historia: tillväxt och omvandling under två sekel*. (2., [rev.] uppl.) Stockholm: SNS förlag.
West, C. and Zimmerman, D. H. (1987) Doing gender, *Gender and Society*, 1(2): 125–151.

Data

European Social Survey (2010). ESS5–2010, ed.3.2
Göteborgs universitet, SOM-institutet. RIKS-SOM 2007 [datafil]. Göteborgs universitet, SOM-institutet [producent], 2009. Göteborg, Sverige: Svensk Nationell Datatjänst (SND) [distributör], 2011. http://dx.doi.org/10.5878/002329
Göteborgs universitet, SOM-institutet. RIKS-SOM 2008 [datafil]. Göteborgs universitet, SOM-institutet [producent], 2010. Göteborg, Sverige: Svensk Nationell Datatjänst (SND) [distributör], 2011. http://dx.doi.org/10.5878/001129
Göteborgs universitet, SOM-institutet. RIKS-SOM 2009 [datafil]. Göteborgs universitet, SOM-institutet [producent], 2011. Göteborg, Sverige: Svensk Nationell Datatjänst (SND) [distributör], 2011. http://dx.doi.org/10.5878/002327
Göteborgs universitet, SOM-institutet. RIKS-SOM 2010 [datafil]. Göteborgs universitet, SOM-institutet, 2011. Göteborg, Sverige: Svensk Nationell Datatjänst (SND) [distributör]. http://dx.doi.org/10.5878/002316
Göteborgs universitet, SOM-institutet. RIKS-SOM 2011 [datafil]. Göteborgs universitet, SOM-institutet [producent], 2012. Göteborg, Sverige: Svensk Nationell Datatjänst (SND) [distributör], 2013. http://dx.doi.org/10.5878/002326
Göteborgs universitet, SOM-institutet. RIKS-SOM 2012 [datafil]. Göteborgs universitet, SOM-institutet [producent], 2014. Göteborg, Sverige: Svensk Nationell Datatjänst (SND) [distributör], 2014. http://dx.doi.org/10.5878/001872
Göteborgs universitet, SOM Institute. NATIONAL SOM 2013 [data file]. University of Gothenburg, SOM Institute [producer], 2014. Gothenburg, Sweden: Swedish National Data Service (SND) [distributor], 2015. http://dx.doi.org/10.5878/002630
Statistics Sweden (2015). *Yrkesregistret med yrkesstatistik*, Statistikdatabasen. www.scb.se.
World Bank (2014a) www.quandl.com/WORLDBANK/EUU_SL_SRV_EMPL_ZS-European-Union-Employment-in-services-of-total-employment.
World Bank (2014b) www.quandl.com/data/WORLDBANK/EUU_SL_IND_EMPL_ZS-European-Union-Employment-in-industry-of-total-employment.

5 Masculinity, Socio-emotional Skills and Marginalization Amongst Emergency Medical Technicians

Morten Kyed

Introduction

More than two decades ago, Maurizia Boscagli observed that 'a new generation of sensitive men has come of age' (1992/3, p. 64). Yet, too many accounts of men's emotional lives and capabilities remain crudely one-sided and tend to focus on either men's aggressive emotions or their 'emotional alienation' (Seidler, 1992, 2007). However, a few strands of masculinity research are now exploring men's emotional complexities; examples of such new research fields are studies of 'new' or 'involved' fatherhood (Brandth and Kvande, 1998; Johansson and Klinth, 2008) and studies on men's homosocial emotions (Anderson, 2009; Hammarén and Johansson, 2014). This has caused more nuanced scientific understanding of men's multifaceted emotional lives and practices to emerge, especially within the private sphere.

Cultural critics argue that the era in which we live is characterized by a 'therapeutic culture' and 'emotional capitalism' (Furedi, 2004; Illouz, 2008; Madsen, 2012). The foundation of emotional capitalism was laid at the onset of the industrial society, with industrial psychologists entering large organizations and causing managers and management techniques to become softer and more communicatively sophisticated (Rose, 1989; Illouz, 2008). In the post-industrial society, however, not only the managers but most of the workforce are governed by ideals of socio-emotional skills. Eva Illouz (1997; 2007; 2008) argues that emotions have become a form of capital, mobilizing the least reflexive and most embodied aspects of the habitus. The

> emotional habitus lies at the intersection of three domains of social experience: the interactional, the bodily, and the linguistic. It reflects and signals one's social class position at these three junctures. Emotional habitus shapes the ways in which one's emotions are bodily and verbally expressed and used in turn to negotiate social interactions.
>
> (Illouz, 2008, p. 214)

The emotional habitus is a stratified and stratifying asset, and the particular composition of the emotional habitus may be decisive in determining the chances of social actors in the post-industrial economy. As psychologist, journalist, management consultant and emotional intelligence guru, Daniel Goleman argues:

> The rules for work are changing. We're being judged by a new yardstick: not just how smart we are, or by our training or expertise, but also by how well we handle ourselves and each other. This yardstick is increasingly applied in choosing who will be hired and who will not, who will be let go and who retained, who passed over and who promoted.
>
> (Goleman, 1998, p. 3)

If we are to believe Goleman (1995, 1998), socio-emotional skills and emotional reflexivity are not only decisive for our chances of success, but also for the risks of marginalization and exclusion in the post-industrial service economy. However, classification of social-emotional skills is by no means a neutral act. According to Illouz, ideals and perceptions of social and emotional competence have become fundamentally androgynous: 'in the therapeutic era, men and women are called upon to reconcile "masculine" attributes of assertiveness with the "feminine" capacity to monitor relationships and emotions' (Illouz, 2008, p. 240). Moreover, these cultural frames of emotional competence are more consistent than previously with the 'soft and psychological' 'emotional make-up' of middle-class men, and thus at risk of marginalizing men with a conventional working-class emotional habitus and 'rugged' models of emotionality (Illouz, 2008, p. 235; see also Furedi, 2004, p. 33ff.).

This argument about socio-emotional skills as a key factor in social stratification – especially for men – seems to fit well with empirical studies suggesting that men with industrial working-class emotional habitus are more likely to become marginalized (Lindsay and McQuaid, 2004; Lupton, 2006; Nixon, 2006, 2009), displaced (Nayak, 2006) or redundant (McDowell, 2003): The reason is that their embodied dispositions do not encompass, or are insufficiently flexible to adapt to, the 'unequal exchanges' (Hochschild, 2003: 85f.) and *feminized* socio-emotional skills and 'aesthetic labour' required in much post-industrial front-line service work (Adkins, 2001; Witz *et al.*, 2003; Lloyd and Payne, 2009; Grossman, 2012; Nickson *et al.*, 2012). These studies indicate that gendered perceptions of service work pose a dual risk of male exclusion; some men are *deemed inappropriately embodied*, but many men also *exclude themselves* as they do not see themselves as appropriate for service work. However, no social tendencies are one-dimensional. Many men – especially those belonging to the middle classes – do not experience difficulties in the interactive service economy. Studies have emphasized how they preserve masculinities by carving out and negotiating masculine spaces in front-line service work (Leidner, 1993; Hall, 1993; Alvesson, 1998; Robinson and Hockey, 2011).

This chapter aims to inform the debate on men's socio-emotional skills and identities by way of an empirical study of male emergency medical technicians (EMTs) in Denmark. Male EMTs in Denmark constitute the basis for an interesting study of socio-emotional skills because the ambulance service is a male-dominated occupation with a strong working-class tradition. Moreover, it is an occupation that performs 'high-touch' care and bodywork, and which has been vastly upskilled with 'high-tech' knowledge in recent years (McDowell, 2009; Håkansson's Chapter 4, this book). The aim of this chapter is to explore: (1) the meaning of social-emotional skills in ambulance work; and (2) how these skills are used to construct hegemonic and marginalized subject positions amongst male EMTs in Denmark.

Marginalization and Discursive Positioning

In order to study mundane constructions of hegemonic and marginalized masculine subjectivities at a local workplace level, the analysis in this chapter follows Connell (2005) in seeing masculinity as a relational configuration of practice with multiple, interrelated positions. My primary focus will be on positions that are regarded as hegemonic and marginalized within the EMT 'community of practice' (Lave and Wenger, 1991). According to Connell, 'marginalization is always relative to the *authorization* of the hegemonic masculinity of the dominant group' (2005, p. 80f.). Another important point in Connell's framework is that masculine positions are not only related internally in any given point in time; they are also historically embedded. Hence, 'any one masculinity, as a configuration of practice, is simultaneously positioned in a number of different structures of relationships, which may be following different historical trajectories' (Connell, 2005, p. 73). In relation to the societal transformations towards emotional capitalism – as discussed in the introduction – different configurations of masculinity, or masculinity positions, may therefore be expected to follow different historical and structural paths within the occupational community of the EMTs.

While Connell's framework is powerful in terms of seeing masculinities as structural practices, assistance is needed to shed light on more dynamic and interactionist elements of gender practice. Therefore, the analysis also draws on positioning theory in analysing how the EMTs position themselves and their colleagues discursively (Davies and Harré, 1990, Edley, 2001). According to the original formulation of Davies and Harré (1990, p. 48), positioning should be seen as 'the discursive process whereby selves are located in conversations as observably and subjectively coherent participants in jointly produced storylines'. Davies and Harré distinguish between two modes of positioning; the *interactive* 'in which what one person says positions another' and the *reflexive* 'in which one positions oneself' (ibid.). Social actors carve out positions for themselves and others during conversations through their use of subject positions and culturally available storylines. Thus, when studying men's positioning strategies, it is important to focus on

> not only the ways in which men are positioned by a ready-made or historically given set of discourses or interpretive repertoires, but also at the ways in which these cultural resources are manipulated and exploited within particular rhetorical or micro-political contexts.
>
> (Edley and Wetherell, 1997, p. 206)

However, cultural repertoires and storylines are also morally and normatively loaded. It is therefore important to look for the legitimizing 'accounts' (Scott and Lyman, 1968) inherent in the situated preferred self-position. Moreover, 'when people speak, their talk reflects not only the local pragmatics of that particular conversational context, but also much broader or more global patterns in collective sense-making and understanding' (Wetherell and Edley, 1999, p. 338). Hence, when particular modes of discursive and normative positioning or, more specifically, the dominant vis-à-vis the subordinated reflexive or interactive position are investigated, marginalized masculine positions that entail 'disadvantaged unequal membership' at the local level come to fore.

The Empirical Setting

The data and original analysis in this chapter originate from an ethnographic study of male EMTs in two ambulance departments in Denmark (Kyed, 2014). The data material consists of 575 hours of participant observation studies and 20 qualitative in-depth interviews lasting between 90 and 150 minutes. The original focus of the study was the relationship between masculinity and safe practice. However, in order to explore the situated cultural meaning of safety and masculinity, the study focused intensively on the cultural identities of the EMTs in general during the data collection. Here, socio-emotional skills continued to emerge as an interesting finding and a key element for the male EMTs' identity formation.

As mentioned above, ambulance work is a particularity interesting area in which to study gender practice; this is an occupation with core characteristics that are both strongly associated with conventional masculinity (risk, heroism, physically and mentally demanding work environment, etc.), yet also associated with femininity (emotional labour, bodywork, etc.). As a result, ambulance work provides a rich variety of possible gendered positions. Moreover, ambulance work is situated in the intersection between three realms of work and class positions (Kyed, 2014): traditional craftsmanship; 'high-touch' interactive service work; and 'high-tech' quasi-professional knowledge work (McDowell, 2009). Until the middle of the 1990s, Danish ambulance workers received little formal education. However, as the ambulances became increasingly well equipped – and especially with the introduction of the defibrillator – a Basic EMT vocational education (Level 1) was introduced. Subsequently, an additional five-week EMT education (Level 2) was introduced and, in 2004, a formal 11-week paramedic (Level 3) education was introduced. Unlike the practice in many other countries, e.g. Sweden and Poland, Danish ambulances are not staffed by university-educated nurses. Danish legislation requires that ambulances must be staffed with at least two persons, one of which must be an EMT (Level 2), and the other must have passed an exam as a Basic EMT. The increasing educational upskilling has also affected the types of habitus that are recruited for the ambulance service. Not very long ago, the typical EMT had work experience as a craftsman and/or from the military before joining the ambulance service.

However, given the increased academic requirements within EMT training, as well as an organizational ambition that everyone entering the occupation today should possess the academic skills to pass the paramedic exam, most, but not all, apprentices now hold A-level exams as a basis for entering the ambulance service. In addition, many have some work experience from care professions. As a result of this change in recruitment practice, many apprentices now have stronger school backgrounds and less practical skills when entering the occupation. This creates ideological tensions and continuous negotiations in the everyday working life between forms of masculinities and masculine positions rooted in different structural and historical trajectories (Kyed, 2014).

Masculinity and Care Work

Because of the conventional gendering of emotions in society in general, men in care jobs are often faced with a series of challenges in preserving a desired gender identity. A common finding is that male nurses are typically homosexualized, marginalized and seen as 'matters out of place' (Widding Isaksen, 2002; Simpson, 2009, Harding, 2007; Harding *et al*., 2008). Moreover, as Ruth Simpson observes, men in feminized care work often find themselves in a 'double bind': 'If they perform masculinity through, for example, authoritarianism, emotional distance and control, their "caring skills" are questioned; if they perform femininity through nurturance and care, their masculinity and their sexuality are called to account' (Simpson, 2014, p. 118). For men in caring occupations, a common strategy to secure masculinity is to 'gravitate' towards more either merely prestigious, technically specialized or less care-oriented areas of nursing to secure masculine positions and identities (Williams, 1989, p. 95; Simpson, 2009). Another finding is that while female nurses are typically expected to be *naturally* caring, male nurses – even in a gender-egalitarian Scandinavian context – are not faced with expectations of a naturally embodied care disposition (Husso and Hirvonen, 2012). This provides male nurses with the agency to position themselves according to discourses of a 'new manhood' and to position their emotional labour as a gift to the patient and as a special professional skill that is not typical of most men (Simpson 2014, p. 127f.).

Ambulance Work as an Emotional Arena

In an attempt to place emotions on the organizational agenda, Stephen Fineman suggested that 'organizations can, indeed should, be regarded as emotional arenas' (Fineman, 1993, p. 10). Organizations providing prehospital ambulance services are specimens of multidimensional emotional arenas: 'on any given day, a paramedic can expect to be a lifesaver and a death worker, sometimes within an hour of each other' (Boyle and Healy, 2003, p. 261). EMTs need to 'change face' (Bolton, 2001) from call to call and perform 'dual-sided' (Filstad, 2010, p. 372) or 'double-faced' emotion management (Tracy and Tracy, 1998, p. 407;

Scott and Myers, 2005, p. 76) – managing patients or/and their relatives as well as their own emotions simultaneously.

When retreating to 'back regions' (Goffman, 1959), EMTs informally practise 'other emotional management' (Thoits, 1996; Poder, 2010). Here they process tough experiences by talking through episodes when needed. In other work, I have developed the notion of 'communities of relief' to describe these informal modes of mental and emotional coping amongst the male EMTs (Kyed, 2014; Kyed, 2016). This collective caring practice is interesting as it differs from a persistent image of men as 'emotionally inarticulate' (Seidler, 1992, 2007; Lupton, 1998, p. 113).

In the remaining part of this chapter, I will focus on the ways in which male EMTs practise emotional competence in ambulance work, and how they use social-emotional competence discursively. I will use this as a yardstick to measure EMT competence in general and to carve out symbolically favoured and, simultaneously, marginalized social positions within the occupational field. Second, I turn towards the occupational backstage area where social participation and sociability are used as both a measure and validation of personal and professional trustworthiness. The seemingly informal and mundane sociability in and around the emergency department has important implications for the ongoing negotiations of social status, recognition and attributions of personal trustworthiness amongst the EMTs.

Socio-emotional Competences in the Ambulance

> In the ambulance, John examines patient a little further, mostly for the sake of the patient record; there isn't much that he can do […] John is impressively adept at making conversation with the elderly man. Like many other older patients, this older male wants to know what an EMT actually is. He asks John if he is a physician. 'No, I'm not, I'm just Falckman.[1] But we can also do stuff nowadays.' 'Yes, yes, I'm sure you can', the older man answers. Then John empathetically asks the patient what he did when he was in the labour market. The older man starts talking far and wide about his work life and his family for the remaining part of the drive to the hospital. It seems that he completely forgets about his pain, and John can quietly complete the patient record and check the patient's values [heart rate, blood pressure, etc.], interrupted only by a few new questions when the patient's narrative stops every now and then.
> (Field notes, Dept. South Ville, 16 August 2012)

Ambulance work is full of heroic and spectacular cultural symbolism, and EMTs have specialist skills which save lives from time to time. According to some studies, quasi-medical skills and heroic dispositions are used discursively to construct masculine self-identities (Palmer, 1983; Tracy and Scott, 2006). Surprisingly, however, male EMTs in Denmark usually reject the culturally available hyper-masculine heroic image. The EMTs do indeed display pride of their increasingly specialist quasi-medical prehospital skills in their day-to-day work. However, when offered an opportunity to position themselves in conversations, the male EMTs hardly ever adopt the stereotypical 'heroic saviour model' of masculinity.

During interviews or conversations in the field, many EMTs seek to position themselves as emotionally proficient. This is, for instance, evident in an interview with the experienced Basic EMT, Kaj, with 25 years of tenure. He argues that emotional support and their mere calm presence are often *the* most important aspects of the treatment they provide:

> ... Things are not always as critical as they are made up to be – It is often wound up, and then we have lots of instruments out and measure and so on. And sometimes people almost get more stressed or wound up by that – I think many of us old-timers just go out and test the water. I had an incident yesterday where we were out and picked up a 20-year-old girl with convulsions. They [the family] had just returned from 14 days' holiday. She was otherwise healthy, [but] had a congenital heart defect. But we get contact with her. She was not aware of what had happened at all.... But subsequently her mother thanks us and says: 'what calmness you preserved when you arrived. You just sat down on the floor and looked at the girl, and got her to open her eyes.' But we kept calm and just put a hand on her and talked to the family. Then the girl actually walked out into the ambulance without even knowing it. She got more and more clear, but she didn't know what she was doing [...] But 80% ... of the help is that we just turn up. That we just arrive and put our hand on people and calm them down.
> (Interview, Kaj Hansen, Basic EMT)

Kaj positions himself according to his abilities at mobilizing emotional energy through caregiving for the patient, control of his own emotions and control of the emotions of the relatives. Interestingly, Kaj is also simultaneously 'doing' emotionality and seniority in this extract; he is simultaneously positioning himself in relation to emotional competences and in relation to experience – due to his experience, he knows how to test the water and prevent the situation from becoming overly agitated. This emotional and empathetic positioning practice echoes a key point in Mareen Boyle's (2002, p. 137) study of Australian EMTs. Boyle finds that several of the older EMTs in Australia position themselves against younger and more technically oriented EMTs – 'the techno-kids' – who are more focused on performing their technical and intellectual skills rather than their abilities related to patient care. A similar tension between a caring rationality and a technical-vocational rationality is evident in my empirical material. However, in my material, the age dimension is less clear-cut. Both relatively young and experienced EMTs are expressing concern with the socio-emotional skills of newly recruited EMTs.

One morning after a plenum at the ambulance station, a male EMT in his late twenties subsequently turned to me and said:

Our job is to be out and help people, and hold the hands of the old ladies etc. This, in here, is something else entirely. And here [at the morning plenum] is often just some chit chat that is pulled over our heads; you just sit and nod and say yes, yes. Because out there [points outside the station]; we find the solutions ourselves.

(Field notes, St. South Ville, 9 July 2010)

Here, the young EMT simultaneously positions himself and his colleagues according to androgynous nexuses of empathy/care and assertiveness (pace Illouz 2008). This positioning practice is evident in several instances in my data material.

The following is an excerpt from an interview with Henrik, a relatively new EMT with four years of tenure. He explains what he sees as the exemplary characteristics of a good EMT.

[An EMT must] be able to act around other people, test the water when you get out to patients and judge what they need … are they [the patients] people who can take a joke … or are they people who require a totally neutral style, where you just do what you should do and no more. Being able to go in and judge that, that's for me the hallmark of an EMT. There are lots of people who have no sense of propriety, they just wade in and say the wrong things at the wrong times …

(Interview Henrik, Basic EMT)

Henrik's idealization of abilities to read social situations and 'test the water' – social awareness (Goleman, 2006) – is common amongst the male EMTs. He also draws clear symbolic boundaries towards colleagues who lack these skills. This issue of symbolic marginalization due to lacking social skills will be discussed later in this chapter. During the interview, I also asked Henrik if he could describe a colleague he thought of as an ideal EMT. He answered that:

… there was one in my former department, who I think of as a kind of a role model. He was a bit of a joker in a quiet way. He was always good for a joke. When he was out with patients, his main goal was to bring a smile on their faces. And he did. He could wade into people in an impressive way. He possessed a sense of care for humans which allowed him to get away with many things. He could go to a patient that felt really bad, and he could make a small remark that would make them relax, smile and feel comfortable. They would feel that things were under control. Help is on its way and we don't need to be afraid. The mentality he had and displayed, though he said a lot of shit but it was in a good way. Many are over overstrung. But Arne, his entire charisma when going out to people, that's really how I want to be. He just created such peace about him. Some of the comments he made could offhand be perceived as inappropriate, but he just had a way of saying it, and the words fell at the right time, it provided a positive experience. It is important to me. Human skills are the most important for an EMT.

(Interview, Henrik Frandsen, Basic EMT)

It is very common for the EMTs to stress socio-emotional skills when describing what it means to be a good EMT, and the majority of EMTs mentioned these as the *most* important vocational skill. Henrik describes a skilled and sensitive joker as his role model. Joking is extremely important for the EMTs. They use it to ease patients, as Henrik describes here, but they also constantly use humour between themselves to relieve tension (Kyed, 2014). Often, the humoristic style is quite tough and dark. But there are always fine and deeply situated lines between what is funny and what is inappropriate, and colleagues who balance these fine lines in a skilful manner are culturally honoured.

One day during field work I asked Casper, another young EMT of around 30 years of age, what, in his opinion, characterizes a good EMT. He responded that 'You're a "service organ". You can always learn the technical stuff, but you must be able to be kind, understanding and be able to talk to people.' I asked him if it is something you learn, as part of the craft, or if it is a personal capacity:

> Yes and no. It is also to do with what people have done before. It may well be more qualifying that you have been a hairdresser rather than having transported patients in the army, though some think it may make them an obvious candidate.
>
> (Field notes, Dept. South Ville, 15 August 2012)

It was argued earlier that ambulance work involves a mixture of craftsmanship, care work and quasi-medical work. Here, Casper clearly positions ambulance work as fundamentally service work. In doing so, he emphasizes a self-identity as service worker. Casper also recites a widespread perception of technical skills as 'something that can be learned', as opposed to socio-emotional skills which are considered a matter of personality and hence more difficult to learn. His remark that training as a hairdresser may be more qualifying than having transported patients in the army is clearly also a way of manifesting not only the value of social and interactional skills in ambulance work, but also the legitimacy of females within the occupation. An increasing number of females are entering the ambulance service in Denmark, but the occupation is still vastly male-dominated with only 10–15 per cent female EMTs. Not only does Casper's statement speak against the value of military experience, the former hallmark for new recruits, it also idealizes a more sensitive and gender-egalitarian hegemonic masculine position.

People Work and the Commitment to Make Every Patient Feel Good

Several of the EMTs emphasize how they are making an effort to give all patients the same meticulous and decent treatment, no matter their social position.

But in order to succeed in this, the EMTs must sometimes engage in a little cognitive work and 'deep acting' in the beginning. One very experienced EMT with 26 years of tenure explains, for instance:

> We have many calls downtown, fights, and in socially deprived areas where chances are that you meet a suicide attempt or a socially deprived someone, that you have to handle some way or another. You might think 'that drunk pig lying in his own vomit', but sometimes, if you put your medical gloves on and just abstract from it, then in some cases there's a really funny man and a funny story behind it. Once you start to talk with them, and get them to relax a little then, in some cases the wife left them or [they may explain] I have done this or that in my life. 'What the hell; have you been a lawyer!? And now you're here?' 'That's life; have a talk about it'.
>
> (Interview, Simon, EMT)

Throughout the interview, Simon speaks eagerly about ambulance psychology; he is particularly interested in neurolinguistic programming (NLP). It is indeed possible to read this interview extract as an example of NLP at work. Simon argues that his ability to reframe the situation cognitively will enable him to engage better with the patient, but also to enjoy the situation and perhaps learn something about the complexities of human biographies. Simon is probably the most emotionally reflexive and emotionally conscious of the EMTs I interviewed. At several points in the interview, he talks at length about how he uses different psychological techniques and careful choices of words to (re)frame situations in order to get the patients – and relatives – to relax and calm down.

Henrik, who in the example above talked about empathic humour and capabilities to test the water as hallmarks of a good EMT, also talks empathetically about 'people work':

> It's human fates we're driving with and it is our job to sit there and give them the best possible trip, because it is not pleasant to lie in such a car. And if the patient is a little insecure to begin with, if they are going to get examined for something, then it's a distressing situation, and it is our job to make it safe for them. Make them feel comfortable in our care. For someone who feels bad mentally it may be [enough] just to put a hand on their shoulder and say some well-meaning words to them. Then they'll feel good, or better, by knowing that there is someone who sees me as a human being.
>
> (Interview, Henrik Frandsen, Basic EMT)

Both of these examples demonstrate the dominant ideals about care in the occupation. Once again, the mere physical presence, emotional goodwill and capacity to connect with people from any walk of life is emphasized not only as important, but as an obligation towards people in a critical and emotionally disturbing situation.

'I Don't Understand How He Got In'

Socio-emotional skills are not only used as markers of professional distinction and symbolic capital (Bourdieu, 1984). Ideals of socio-emotional skills also pose normative constraints to the vocational identity formation. The normativity of empathic skills also becomes evident when EMTs find their colleagues' socio-emotional performativities deficient. My empirical material contains several examples of EMTs drawing symbolic boundaries between themselves and colleagues who, in their view, lack socio-emotional skills. On one occasion, an interesting symbolic boundary is made during an ambulance trip. The paramedic, Michael, and the EMT, Mikkel, are talking about a female colleague, Åse, who is known to be polemical in her approach to patients:

MIKKEL: It's funny she says that she likes to go on calls to drunken people; she's often very offensive and rude towards them.

MICHAEL: I've sometimes curled my toes with embarrassment when we're out to patients together. I don't want to feel that way. I think it's OK to say something to your partner when they are like that. I would like for them to do so, if they think I am creating an unpleasant tone when dealing with patients.

(Field notes, Dept. North Ville, 8 May 2012)

In this situation, the two male EMTs are negotiating, or perhaps rather establishing, consensus on proper norms of sympathetic conduct around patients. Interestingly, the colleague who is considered morally unacceptable in this situation is a female colleague whose behaviour is known to be quite rugged and in many ways too conventionally masculine.

On another occasion during an interview, Henrik draws a symbolic boundary towards a colleague who, in Henrik's opinion, lacks socio-emotional skills:

I went to EMT school with someone; I didn't understand how he got in [to the ambulance service]. He was very, very clever and very, very theoretical … [But] I would like to be a fly on the wall when he was in an ambulance; I could not imagine him sitting with people […] he lacked much. He possessed all the theoretical skills; he could well go all the way to paramedic. But it doesn't help if you don't have the human characteristics.

(Interview Henrik Frandsen, Basic EMT)

Henrik is not specific about the nature of the human skills this particular colleague lacks, but I think he is arguing that the colleague is insufficiently skilled in being intimate with the patients. This quote also illustrates tension, not only between two men with different occupational habituses before entering the ambulance service, but also between the combination of two sets of competences that are both recognized as increasingly important in the ambulance service. Henrik was a trained waiter, while the colleague he is talking about has a background in technical engineering. The colleague in question does not have previous professional experience, or 'natural' skills, in interacting with people and coding the subtle signs they give off. Therefore, despite being recognized as extremely intellectually and technically skilled, he is positioned as incompetent at operating an ambulance.

Sociability and Social Competences outside the Ambulance

So far, I have demonstrated how socio-emotional skills are considered important for the interaction when dealing with patients. In the remaining part of this chapter I will focus on how socio-emotional skills are also vital in order to pass as a trustworthy colleague in a 'sharp-end' occupation. Trust and trustworthiness are particularly crucial in a dangerous profession such as ambulance work, where the EMTs are in an interdependent safety relation; the personal safety of the EMT is often in the hands of their colleague. Moreover, if one EMT acts negligently, they may harm their colleague (Kyed, 2014). Hence, the EMTs need to learn how and whom to trust. Consequently, demands for social skills are not only confined to the onstage performance of the EMT.

In one of the foundational texts of trust research, Robert D. Putnam argues that all well-functioning cooperative relationships entail mutual trust; 'trust lubricates cooporation', while 'ongoing social relations can generate incentives for trustworthiness' (Putnam 1993, p. 171ff.). Strong appreciation of homosocial intimacy exists amongst the EMTs, and it is probably closely related to their interdependent safety relation in as well as out of the field. Another cultural, but related, implication of this interdependence is that lack of social 'savoir faire' is normatively sanctioned:

> If it's a 'sharp task', and someone really puts their foot in their mouth, then it's talked about afterwards. Then people may well talk behind his back: 'Now listen to this: he just didn't fucking do that; what a twit'. And if it's really glaring, you may take hold of him and say, 'Listen, that just wasn't OK. If we need to go on a run together again, you don't do that.'
>
> (Interview, Mads Green, EMT)

Colleagues with social competences and 'savoir faire' are easier to trust because their social practice confirms that they understand and master the premises of the interaction within the community of practice. Hence, they are easy to read and predictable, which is crucial in emergency situations where the EMT's social and professional relationships are severely tested. Colleagues with social competences understand and master 'the language of hint' (Goffman, 1967, p. 30). This is especially crucial when the collaboration takes place under pressure. However, people who fail to perform according to the normative scripts or do not master 'the language of hint' risk stigmatization and marginalization within their community of practice. They risk being spoken badly about. This serves a double social function within the community of practice. First, the gossip serves as an informal warning about a colleague who may not be completely safe or reliable under pressure. Second, it is a reminder to others, especially newcomers within the community, that they should be careful not to make the same mistake.

Social competences and sociability are thus important in the 'back stage regions' (Goffman, 1959). Whereas the target and audience front of stage are the patient, and sometimes their relatives, the audience backstage is the co-worker. EMTs use behaviour in the 'backstage region' to (re)produce social bonds and confirm trustworthiness. Life at an ambulance station is characterized by a high level of 'intimate sociality' amongst the EMTs (see also Chetkovich, 1997, p. 26; Ericson, 2011, pp. 155–172; Robinson and Hockey, 2011, pp. 107–116). The intimate social, physical and emotional interactions lead to a feeling that they know each other 'in and out', as several EMTs phrase it. They often describe the community as a family, and a common (heteronormative) statement amongst the male veterans is that 'they almost know their colleagues better than their wives'.

Moreover, the interdependency of the EMTs outside the station naturally influences the culture and the social interaction at the station. Elaborating on Mary Douglas and Claude Levi-Strauss, the American folklorist Robert S. McCarl (1984) describes the dinner at a fire station as 'a microcosm of the day-to-day canon of technique performance' of the work. By participating actively in everyday activities, such as cooking, the firefighter confirms his collegial solidarity and contributes to the maintenance of the community at the station as a 'home-away-from-home' (McCarl, 1984, pp. 394–395). Following McCarl's concept of a 'microcosm of the day-to-day canon of technique performance', I suggest that it is possible to understand cooking, inspection of the ambulance and its equipment as well as other minor daily activities as 'low-risk arenas' where one colleague can evaluate the other colleague's credibility before they find themselves in sharp situations where the safety of one EMT depends on his co-worker's behaviour. The formation of trust is dependent on situations that are easy to interpret (Luhmann, 1999, p. 87). Hence, if you cannot rely on a colleague in one context, it is likely that you cannot in other contexts. This is reflected in many EMTs' emphasis on a basic 'participation ethos'. In an interview, the experienced Basic EMT Georg Larsen, with more than 40 years of tenure, highlights that a good colleague is:

> a person who takes part in the daily life. When we're checking the ambulance every morning, he participates. He's got that, and I've got this and that. And if he's done with it, then we go on [together] with the rest until the ambulance is finished ... it's a team.

Reciprocity and team spirit are also confirmed and reproduced through constant participation in the ongoing small and trivial social activities at work. When I asked another EMT what earns recognition amongst paramedics, he answered along a similar line that 'it's very much the social stuff, because we spend so much time together. It's one's other family. That's a third of your time you spend together.'

MK: You say social, it is about being sociable or what?
JEPPE: Yes, definitely. And don't be the one who gets into the couch, even if you have been on calls most of the day, when dinner is cooked, and [that] you participate in taking the dishes and things like that. That's really important for us on day shifts. You will soon end up in bad standing, if you laze around.

(Interview, Jeppe Larsen, EMT)

In his well-known book *Men and Masculinities*, Stephen M. Whitehead argues that 'trust comes with gendered scripts', and that 'trust is highly problematic for men and masculinities, for before one can trust, one must let go of fear and of a desire to control' (2002, p. 170f.). My data seem to confirm Whitehead's first point, but not the second. Tight social and normative control is a premise for the strong bonds and high generalized level of trust amongst the male EMTs I studied. Participation and cooperation in all tasks of everyday life are essential for the social integration of an EMT. The fundamental interdependence between the EMTs, especially in emergency situations, creates a widespread 'norm of reciprocity' and 'generalized reciprocity', which is essential for the production of mutual trust and social cohesion (Putnam, 1993, 2000). This norm is imperative; EMTs who violate it are at risk of social marginalization in their community of practice. Hence, through the informality of everyday life, they demonstrate that they are trustworthy; there is correspondence between what they say and what they do (Luhmann, 1999, p. 81).

Emotional Capitalism and New Modes of Marginalization?

Marginalization is a social process that takes place at all social levels. Taking socio-emotional skills as its point of departure, and complying with Connell and Messerschmidt's emphasis on studying configurations of masculinity empirically at different societal levels (Connell and Messerschmidt, 2005; Messerschmidt, 2016), this chapter has focused on the mundane dialectics of domination and marginalization at a *local* level – within a specific occupational community of practice. Mundane local processes of discursive domination and marginalization are not only interesting because they occur in all social groups, but also because they reveal something about the relative impact of, or links to, the regional and global cultures to which they are related.

The empirical analysis of emotional labour in a traditional and strongly male-dominated occupation has demonstrated how emotional labour and socio-emotional skills are increasingly mobilized as key elements in constructing desired subject positions. At the same time, these elements also cause EMTs with perceived socio-emotional deficits to be symbolically marginalized amongst male EMTs. However, masculinities are often constructed in relation to different and contradictory masculine positions (Edley and Wetherell, 1999; Whitehead, 2002). Dominant masculinity amongst male EMTs today is indeed a complex and multidimensional configuration that is associated with trustworthiness and an ability to remain cool-headed and rational and to 'hurry slowly' even in the most chaotic situations (Kyed, 2014). But, interestingly, dominant masculinity is also closely associated with genuinely empathic and caring action towards patients.

It is important to state that not all male EMTs in my study share this new sensitive emotional practice. The emotional habitus of some of the older EMTs in particular does not correspond with the new dominant emotional and sensitive masculinity practice demonstrated in this chapter. Nevertheless, my data material indicates that discourses and ideals of socio-emotional skills are nowadays dominant not only amongst the EMTs but throughout the entire organization. Hence, any lack of these skills entails marginalized symbolic and discursive positions amongst the EMTs in their everyday work life.

This strong positioning through empathy and care contradicts previous studies of masculinities in ambulance work. Earlier studies of male EMTs have emphasized that the occupational demand for public emotional labour and care can be threatening to the self-identity of male EMTs and their desired technical and heroic masculinity (Palmer, 1983; Tracy and Scott, 2006). The ETMs in my study express ambivalent attitudes towards the associated heroic image of their occupation; on the one hand they often explicitly disassociate themselves with the public image as heroes. On the other hand, their use of quasi-medical technical skills to help people in need is also an important resource in their identity practice (Kyed, 2014).

Several reasons probably explain why many of the male EMTs in Denmark construct masculinity so clearly around caring and empathetic performativities. I thus will end this chapter with a short discussion of what I see as three of the most important foundations for these 'new' and more socio-emotional masculinity practices. First, EMTs are employed – structurally positioned – in an occupation that is conventionally masculine. Prehospital work is loaded with masculine symbolism and EMTs are often positioned in the general public and by the media as some of the heroes of everyday life (Kyed, 2014). This provides them with 'masculine capital' which enables them to display conventionally feminized ideals without risking their overall masculine accountability (de Visser *et al.*, 2009). Hence, displays of socio-emotional competence – e.g. knowing when and how to be cool and caring respectively – only cause them to appear more competent as EMTs and more multifaceted and rounded as men. Moreover, from a critical feminist perspective, we may even read several of the emotional accounts of the male EMTs in this chapter as practices of emotional heroism and 'masculinisation of emotional labour' (Lewis and Simpson, 2007, pp. 7–11; Simpson, 2014, pp. 128–130).

Second, but relatedly, male EMTs in Denmark live and act in a Scandinavian context where gender equality regimes are relatively dominant; the cultural gender binaries are also relatively more blurred compared to the situation in other national contexts. Bloksgaard *et al.*'s (2015) recent study of male ideals across class positions in contemporary Denmark, for instance, shows that 'the most valuable and legitimate form of masculinity in a contemporary Danish context is a man who is multifaceted and displays different dimensions, among these an emotional side'. This corresponds very well with the complex socio-emotional positions (cool, rational and dynamic *and* team oriented, empathetic and caring) between which male EMTs alternate symbolically as well as practically (Kyed, 2014).

Finally, a more structural explanation to the male EMT's socio-emotional normativity probably also applies. As argued in the introduction to this chapter, contemporary Western societies are characterized by the twin dynamics of emotional capitalism and an ever-expanding therapeutic culture distributing vast amounts of socio-emotional discourses, scripts and increasingly androgynous perceptions of socio-emotional competence (Illouz, 2008). As my study demonstrates, this is also evident amongst the male EMTs. While the dominant socio-emotional scripts of emotional capitalism seem to be expanding the range of men's legitimate emotional and caring practices, other forms of conventional but less emotionally articulate masculinities are simultaneously being marginalized. This chapter has demonstrated how symbolic marginalization is practised subtly but continuously in talks about ambulance work and colleagues. Further studies need to explore how gendered marginalization and exclusion based on socio-emotional competences is (re)produced in other areas and other levels of the post-industrial economy.

Acknowledgement

I would like to thank the Danish Health and Safety Research Fund for financing the PhD research on which most of this article is based. I would also like to thank The Danish Council for Independent Research for the postdoctoral grant (grant-ID: DFF – 4003-00140B), which has financed the time spent on the re-analysis of the data used in this chapter.

Note

1 Falck is the name of the company John works for. Falck has been operating ambulances in most of Denmark for generations, and is, nowadays, a cultural institution in Denmark, and in Danish everyday language (Kyed 2014).

References

Alvesson, M. (1998). Gender relations and identity at work: A case study of masculinities and femininities in an advertising agency. *Human Relations* 51(8): 969–1005.

Adkins, L. (2001). Cultural feminization: 'Money, sex and power' for women, *Signs* 26(3): 669–695.

Anderson, E. (2009). *Inclusive Masculinities: The Changing Nature of Masculinity*. London: Routledge.

Brandth, B. and Kvande, E. (1998). Masculinity and child care: The reconstruction of fathering, *The Sociological Review* 46(2): 293–313.

Bolton, S. (2001). Changing faces: Nurses as emotional jugglers, *Sociology of Health and Illness* 23(1): 85–100.

Bolton, S. (2004). *Emotion management in the workplace*. Basingstoke: Palgrave Macmillan.

Bourdieu, Pierre (1984). *Distinction: A Social Critique of Judgement of Taste*. Cambridge, MA: Harvard University Press.

Boscagli, M. (1992/3). 'A moving story': Masculine tears and the humanity of televised emotion, *Discourse* 15(2), 64–79.

Boyle, M. V. (2002). 'Sailing twixt scylla and charybdis': Negotiating multiple organisational masculinities, *Women in Management Review, 17*(3/4): 131–141.

Boyle, M. V. and Healy, J. (2003). Balancing mysterium and onus: Doing spiritual work within an emotion-laden organizational context, *Organization* 10(2): 351–373.

Chetkovich, C. A. (1997). *Real Heat: Gender and Race in the Urban Fire Service*. New Brunswick: Rutgers University Press.

Connell, R. W. (2005). *Masculinities* (2nd edition.). Cambridge: Polity Press.

Connell, R. W. and Messerschmidt, J. W. (2005). Hegemonic masculinity: Rethinking the concept, *Gender and Society*, 19: 829–859.

Davies, B. and Harré, R. (1990). Positioning: The discursive production of selves, *Journal for the Theory of Social Behaviour* 20(1): 43–63.

De Visser, R. O., Smith, J. A. and McDonnell, E. J. (2009). 'That's not masculine': Masculine capital and health-related behaviour, *Journal of Health Psychology* 14(7): 1047–1058.

Edley, N. and Wetherell, M. (1997). Jockeying for position: The construction of masculine identities. *Discourse and Society* 8(2): 203–217.

Edley, N. and Wetherell, M. (1999). Imagined futures: Young men's talk about fatherhood and domestic life, *British Journal of Social Psychology* 38(2): 181–194.

Edley, N. (2001). Analysing masculinity: Interpretive repertoires, ideological dilemmas and subject positions. In M. Wetherell, S. Taylor and S. Yated (eds), *Discourse as Data: A Guide for Analysis,* pp. 189–228. Buckingham: Open University Press.

Ericson, M. (2011). *Nära inpå: Maskulinitet, intimitet och gemenskap i brandmäns arbetslag*. PhD diss., Department of Sociology: University of Gothenburg.

Filstad, C. (2010). Learning to be a competent paramedic: Emotional management in emotional work, *International Journal of Work Organisation and Emotion 3*(4): 368–383.

Fineman, S. (1993). *Emotion in Organizations*. London: Sage Publications.

Furedi, F. (2004). *Therapy Culture: Cultivating Vulnerability in an Uncertain Age*. London: Routledge.

Goffman, E. (1959). *The Presentation of Self in Everyday Life*. Harmondsworth: Penguin.

Goffman, E. (1967). *Interaction Ritual: Essays in Face-to-Face Behavior*. New York: Pantheon Books.

Goleman, D. (1995). *Emotional Intelligence: Why It Can Matter More than IQ*. London: Bloomsbury Publishing.

Goleman, D. (1998). *Working with Emotional Intelligence*. London: Bloomsbury.

Goleman, D. (2006). *Social Intelligence: The New Science of Human Relationships*. London: Bloomsbury.

Grossman, B. (2012). The feminised service sector: From micro to macro analysis, *Work Organisation, Labour and Globalisation* 6(1): 63–79.

Hall, E. J. (1993). Waitering/waitressing: Engendering the work of table servers, *Gender and Society* 7(3): 329–346.

Hammarén, N. and Johansson, T. (2014). Homosociality in between power and intimacy, *SAGE Open* 4(1), 2158244013518057.

Harding, T. (2007). The construction of men who are nurses as gay, *Journal of Advanced Nursing* 60(6): 636–644.

Harding, T., North, N. and Perkins, R. (2008). Sexualizing men's touch: Male nurses and the use of intimate touch in clinical practice. *Research and Theory for Nursing Practice: An International Journal* 22(2): 88–102.

Hochschild, A. R. (2003). *The Managed Heart: Commercialization of Human Feeling.* [2nd edition]. Berkeley: University of California Press.

Husso, M. and Hirvonen, H. (2012). Gendered agency and emotions in the field of care work, *Gender, Work and Organization* 19: 29–51. doi:10.1111/j.1468-0432.2011.00565.x

Illouz, E. (1997). Who will care for the caretaker's daughter? Toward a sociology of happiness in the era of reflexive modernity, *Theory, Culture and Society 14*(4): 31–66.

Illouz, E. (2007). *Cold Intimacies: The Making of Emotional Capitalism.* Cambridge: Polity.

Illouz, E. (2008). *Saving the Modern Soul: Therapy, Emotions, and the Culture of Self-Help.* Berkeley: University of California Press.

Johansson, T. and Klinth, R. (2008). Caring fathers: The ideology of gender equality and masculine positions, *Men and Masculinities* 11(1): 42–62.

Kyed, M. (2014). John Wayne and Tarzan no longer work here: An Ethnographic tale of masculinity, safety and 'EMT-ship' [John Wayne og Tarzan arbejder her ikke længere: En etnografisk fortælling om maskulinitet, sikkerhed og 'redderskab']. PhD diss, Department of Sociology and Social Work: Aalborg University.

Kyed, M. (2016). Masculinity, Emotions and 'Communities of Relief' among Male Emergency Medical Technicians. In M. Ericson and U. Mellström (eds) *Gender, Emergency Work and the Rescue Services: Contested Terrains and Challenges*, Aldershot: Ashgate.

Lave, J. and Wenger, E. (1991). *Situated Learning: Legitimate Peripheral Participation* Cambridge: Cambridge University Press.

Leidner, R. (1993). *Fast Food, Fast Talk: Service Work and the Routinization of Everyday Life.* Berkeley, CA: University of California Press.

Lewis, P. and Simpson, R. (2007). Gender and emotions: Introduction. In P. Lewis and R. Simpson (eds) *Gendering Emotions in Organizations,* pp. 1–15. Basingstoke: Palgrave Macmillan.

Lloyd, C. and Payne, J. (2009). 'Full of sound and fury, signifying nothing' interrogating new skill concepts in service work – the view from two UK call centres, *Work, Employment and Society 23*(4): 617–634.

Lindsay, C. and McQuaid, R. W. (2004). Avoiding the 'McJobs': Unemployed job seekers and attitudes to service work, *Work, Employment and Society 18*(2): 297–319.

Luhmann, N. (1999). *Tillid: En mekanisme til reduktion af social kompleksitet.* København: Hans Reitzels Forlag.

Lupton, B. (2000). 'Maintaining Masculinity: Men who do Women's Work', *British Journal of Management* 11: 33–48.

Lupton, B. (2006). Explaining men's entry into female-concentrated occupations: Issues of masculinity and social class, *Gender, Work and Organization, 13*(2): 103–128.

Madsen, O. J. (2014). *The Therapeutic Turn: How Psychology Altered Western Culture.* New York: Routledge.

McCarl, R. S. (1984). 'You've come a long way and now this is your retirement': An analysis of performance in firefighting culture, *The Journal of American Folklore, 97*(386): 393–422.

McDowell, L. (2003). *Redundant Masculinities? Employment Change and White Working Class Youth.* Malden, MA: Blackwell Pub.

McDowell, L. (2009). *Working Bodies: Interactive Service Employment and Workplace Identities*. Chichester, UK: Wiley-Blackwell.

Messerschmidt, J. W. (2016). *Masculinities in the Making – From the Local to the Global*. London; New York: Rowman and Littlefield.

Nayak, A. (2006). Displaced masculinities: Chavs, youth and class in the post-industrial city, *Sociology, 40*(5): 813–831.

Nickson, D., Warhurst, C., Commander, J., Hurrell, S. A. and Cullen, A. M. (2012). Soft skills and employability: Evidence from UK retail, *Economic and Industrial Democracy* 33(1): 65–84.

Nixon, D. (2006). 'I just like working with my hands': Employment aspirations and the meaning of work for low-skilled unemployed men in Britain's service economy, *Journal of Education and Work* 19(2): 201–217.

Nixon, D. (2009). 'I can't put a smiley face on': Working-class masculinity, emotional labour and service work in the 'New Economy', *Gender, Work and Organization* 16(3), 300–322.

Palmer, C. E. (1983). 'Trauma junkies' and street work, *Journal of Contemporary Ethnography* 12(2), 162–183.

Poder, P. (2010). Når medarbejdere håndterer hinandens følelser: Om betydningen af kollegers 'other emotion management' for deres identitetsarbejde, *Tidsskrift for Arbejdsliv, 12*(3): 72–86.

Putnam, R. D. (1993). *Making Democracy Work*. Princeton: Princeton University Press.

Putnam, R. D. (2000). *Bowling Alone*. New York: Simon and Schuster.

Robinson, V. and Hockey, J. L. (2011). *Masculinities in Transition*. Basingstoke, UK: Palgrave Macmillan.

Rose, N. (1989). *Governing the Soul: Technologies of Human Subjectivity*. London: Free Association.

Scott, C. W. and Myers, K. K. (2005). The socialization of emotion: Learning emotion management at the fire station. *Journal of Applied Communication Research, 33*(1): 67–92.

Scott, M. B. and Lyman, S. M. (1968). Accounts. *American Sociological Review*, 33(1): 46–62.

Seidler, V. J. (1992). *Men, Sex and Relationships: Writings from 'Achilles heel'*. London: Routledge.

Seidler, V. J. (2007). Masculinities, bodies, and emotional life, *Men and Masculinities*, 10(1): 9–21.

Simpson, R. (2009). *Men in Caring Occupations: Doing Gender Differently*. Basingstoke, UK: Palgrave Macmillan.

Simpson, R. (2014). Relations, emotions and differences: re-gendering emotional labour in the context of men doing care. In R. J. Burke and D. A. Major (eds) *Gender in Organizations: Are Men Allies or Adversaries to Women's Career Advancement?* pp. 118–132. Cheltenham: Edward Elgar Publishing.

Thoits, P. A. (1996). Managing the emotions of others. *Symbolic Interaction, 19*(2): 85–109.

Tracy, S. J., and Scott, C. (2006). Sexuality, masculinity, and taint management among firefighters and correctional officers, *Management Communication Quarterly* 20(1): 6–38.

Tracy, S. J. and Tracy, K. (1998). Emotion labor at 911: A case study and theoretical critique. *Journal of Applied Communication Research*, 26, 390–411.

Wetherell, M. and Edley, N. (1999). Negotiating hegemonic masculinity: Imaginary positions and psycho-discursive practices, *Feminism and Psychology*, 9(3): 335–356.

Whitehead, S. M. (2002). *Men and Masculinities: Key Themes and New Direction.* Cambridge: Polity Press.

Widding Isaksen, L. (2002). Masculine dignity and the dirty body, *NORA*, 10(3): 137–46.

Williams, C. (1989). *Gender Differences at Work*. Berkeley, CA: University of California Press.

Witz, A., Warhurst, C. and Nickson, D. (2003). The labour of aesthetics and the aesthetics of organization, *Organization*, 10(1), 33–54.

6 Male Migrant Workers and the Negotiation of 'Marginalized' Masculinities in Urban China

Xiaodong Lin

Introduction

Recent years have witnessed growing debate on integration and social inequalities as a result of the expanding scale of rural–urban migration in China. It is seen as a major social phenomenon in contemporary Chinese society. At the same time, it has raised a range of interconnecting issues in relation to the issue of marginalization, such as exclusion, inequality and social justice. The chapter aims to address an underdeveloped field of inquiry, exploring the lives of a group of socially marginalized men – male migrant workers. The chapter examines the rural men's narratives of their migrating experience in urban China, with particular reference to their gendered experiences and practices in relation to their familial lives. In so doing, it sets out to respond critically to public representations of migrant workers as 'marginalized' others in the discourse of modernization, marked by progress and development. In turn, the chapter contributes to an understanding of marginalization in the context of rural migrating men as both social exclusion and symbolic otherness, within the context of the reconfiguration of the relation between tradition and modernity at a time of rapid, globally inflected change.

The 'Marginalization' of Male Migrant Workers in China

'Reform and opening up' since the late 1970s in China has triggered a series of debates on economic development and transformation in different areas of society, as a result of the globally and locally based transition from a 'planned economy' to a 'market economy'. Rural–urban labour migration is one of the most-discussed social transformations. There are currently more than 260 million migrant workers living and working in urban cities in China. People tend to move from poor areas, located mainly in the north, west and inland regions to the more economically developed south, east and coastal areas, such as Guangdong, Shanghai and Zhejiang. At the same time, it is suggested that the number could be underestimated, as there is still a large number of informal workers who have yet to register with the local authorities and there are about 200 million workers who are potential migrants. On the one hand, rural–urban migration contributes surplus labour to urban development; while on the other hand, it has enabled people from rural areas to leave their rural household so as to generate income and thus address their experience of poverty. However, the issue of rural–urban migration also highlights the material conditions of inequality and the attendant social marginalization resulting from economic reforms.

In recent years, critical discussions have emerged about the neo-liberal process operating within China (Ong, 1997; Nonini, 2008). Amongst these discussions, there is much public anxiety about the transformation of the self within the context of rapid modernization, including asking who are the neo-liberal winners and losers. Ong's (2006) work argues that neo-liberalism in Asia encourages the self-enterprising subject. The discourse of free choice and self-enterprising activities has generated new social norms and behaviours in people's everyday lives. At the same time, it has transformed ordinary people's understanding of their self-identity towards a 'responsible' neo-liberal subject in different aspects of their lives (Liu, 2011; Zhang and Ong, 2015). Other research has suggested an alternative and incoherent formation regarding modernization with Chinese characteristics (Rofel, 2007; Yan, 2003). In particular, rural–urban migrant men have been seen as modernization losers due to their lack of 'suzhi', reinforced by the institutional governance of rural/urban division to manage population movement. One of the institutional constraints that has contributed to social marginalization is China's household registration system, known as *Hukou*.

The *Hukou* system (household registration system) has been central in debates on internal migration. In particular, its impact on rural–urban labour migration has been identified through social stratification patterns and the classification of 'peasant workers' who are positioned as the modernization losers of this institutional system, implemented by the central government's economic development policy. Research studies have acknowledged that the social classification, stratification and inequity of rural migrants in the cities fundamentally results from the household registration they hold, as well as other institutional barriers relating to *Hukou* (i.e. the different benefits available to the agricultural/non-agricultural household registrations) at the state level (Solinger, 1995, 1999; Xiang, 2007; Knight and Song, 1999, 2005). More importantly, the discourse of post-Mao modernization and rural/urban divisions have strengthened the ideological formation of the dichotomy of the urban and the rural, which has gained new meaning in relation to the associated concepts of the 'modern' and the 'traditional'. Such a geographical dichotomy is also accompanied by unequal power relations that are seen to have intensified since the introduction of the government's uneven regional development policy, as well as imaginary differences of space existing amongst urban residents and migrant men. What is significant is the explanation of such geographical differences, as a result of economic modernization, in helping to construct dominant images of male migrant workers' masculinity through media representation of them as 'dysfunctional others' in their move from rural villages to cities. Migrant workers are discursively portrayed as 'disadvantaged', particularly due to lack of education in terms of improving the 'quality' (*suzhi*) of their lives that would enable them to participate in the modernization project. *Suzhi*, according to Yan (2003, p. 494),

> refers to the somewhat ephemeral qualities of civility, self-discipline, and modernity ... [*suzhi*] marks a sense and sensibility of the self's value in the market economy ... it is often used in the negative by the post-Mao state and educational elites to point to the lack of quality of the Chinese labouring masses.

The values of self-progress and development in China have positioned migrant workers in general as 'marginalized', due to their lack of education credentials and economic capital that are considered to be essential for a 'neo-liberal' subject. This chapter focuses upon male migrant workers' negotiation of ascribed notions of marginalization as they actively develop other ways of being in their move from rural to urban spaces, marked by loss, disorientation and loneliness as well as excitement, freedom and urban desire. In addressing these (dis)located/relocated men, the chapter builds on recent feminist studies of female migrant workers in China.

Gender, Masculinity and Social Identities in China

My study is informed by a theoretical synthesis of early structuralist understandings of migrant workers as a new sector of the working class, and a late modern framework with particular reference to individual self-identities and identity formation (Lawler, 2013; Skeggs, 1997). Such an analytical approach has been productive in light of the shift from early theorization on oppression to more recent debates on individualized empowerment within a late-modernity framework (Giddens, 1992; Beck and Beck-Gernsheim, 1995) with the focus on self-identity formation particularly informative in theorizing migrants' shifting identities. This is particularly important within a context in which (rural–urban) migrants in China are being portrayed as a 'marginalized' sector of the working class.

Western theorization of identity, advocated by the 'reflexive modernisation' thesis (Giddens, 1992; Beck and Beck-Gernsheim, 1995), has informed a critical understanding of men's gender identities, particularly focusing on the issue of individualization and the self. It has provided a productive interpretation of the meanings of gender as a result of socio-cultural changes. The 'do-it-yourself' identity focuses on the transformation of identity formation from being *given* to a self-making entity that emphasizes issues of *choices* and individual lifestyles. Beck and Beck-Gernsheim (1995) suggest individual interests rather than inherited family responsibilities have become the primary driving force for decision making. Such a late-modernity framework (Giddens, 1992) has suggested that individualization has led to alternative lifestyles and intimate relations, reflected in debates on gender, sexuality and desire in contemporary society. In other words, individual reflexivity has transformed intimate relations, which have broken away from traditional institutions, such as the family. Hence, women are seen as late-modernity 'winners' being able to pursue individual empowerment, given their personal choice and reflexivity.

Meanwhile, feminist Bourdieusian class analysis (see Skeggs, 1997; Lawler, 2004; Reay, 2004) has provided a critical theoretical framework in engaging with the notion of the reflexive self. In deploying Bourdieu's (1989) metaphors of capitals, Skeggs' (1997) critical examination of women's social location and subjectivities suggests that the women in her research are not the originators in producing their identities as they do not occupy the economic and cultural conditions that would enable them to construct what she refers to as a middle-class notion of self-identity. It is through 'the nexus of structures, power relations and capital transfers which produce frameworks of representation and values which establish what it is to be a white working-class woman' (Skeggs 1997, p. 160). What is important in her study is the acknowledgement of the dominant value of 'respectability' the working-class women engage with in the making of their self-identities. She suggests that working-class women operate within a different trajectory to middle-class women in constructing their subjectivities. As she maintains, there are limitations that constrain them in how they 'deploy many constructive and creative strategies to generate a sense of themselves with value' (Skeggs, 1997, p. 162) within the dominant discursive ideology, operating within British society. In this process, a particular culture of working-class women has been revealed in negotiating various subjectivities, which are developed within the context of close relations with others and more public social relations rather than an individualistic project. Her argument in terms of the theorization of the self provides a profound criticism of the project of the self as a 'western bourgeois project' (Skeggs, 1997, p. 163). More specifically, my research project endorses Skeggs' (2014) argument regarding the expression of local values beyond value set by neo-liberalism.

Such a Bourdieusian class perspective provides analytical space to broaden the possibility of presumed fixed social subjects. More specifically, it has opened up a broader discussion about structure and agency, in order to critically understand the 'marginalization' of migrant men's masculinities in the process of migration. Their relocation to the city has challenged the existing gender order within the rural household. Thus, feminist Bourdieusian class analysis, represented by Skeggs and other critical feminist class analysis (also see Reay *et al.*, 2009; Lawler, 2004), offers a productive analytical lens to understand the changing lives and the meanings of masculinity for male migrant workers in a globally inflected, fast-changing society in China.

Negotiating 'Marginalized' Masculinities

Media representation of male migrant workers has described them as experiencing a dislocating sense of loss in a new migrating gender order that involves the feminization of work and the dislocation of gender roles as a result of migration. This is particularly relevant in the context of my research location where service-based and textile manufacturing industries dominate the local economy. The chapter presents findings from my ongoing qualitative research on rural–urban migrant men in China. In the study, a life history approach illustrates that the construction of identity is an ongoing process in relation to the movement of rural men into urban spaces. Through a gender lens with a particular focus on the negotiation of their gendered subjectivities in relation to the family and workplace, the chapter highlights the men's active negotiations in the process of identity formation. It has enabled me to move away from an overly structuralist perspective on the social stratification and integration of Chinese (male) migrant workers with a sole focus on their class marginalization, to an investigation of the dynamic interplay between structure and agency in producing a broader understanding of their identity formation. More specifically, in the context of their ascribed position as marginalized male, the productiveness of exploring the intersection of class and masculinity through their active negotiation of their masculine identity, as workers, fathers, husbands/partners and sons, as illustrated below.

Gender Obligations and the Practice of a 'Capable' Man

The notion of marginality is not limited to migrant men's material conditions, such as their social economic status as urban working-class men. For example, for many male peasant workers in my study, traditional family values were incorporated within their accounts, and served as an important cultural resource for them to negotiate their ascribed 'marginal' masculinity status. For them, family expectations, such as carrying on the family name, had become a burden when they encountered the difficulty of living and working in the city due to their subordinated working-class position. Such a traditional ideology affected unmarried young male peasant workers in particular. In traditional Chinese ideology, the worst offence against filial duty is not having any progeny, according to Confucianism (Fei, 2008). Their parents and extended families placed much pressure on them to get married as soon as they reached the age of late 20s/early 30s. Many of my participants were single. For example, Xiao Mao, aged 36 when I interviewed him, revealed his frustration at being single and the pressure he was facing from his family. Within this context, it may be argued that his status as single challenged the heteronormative patriarchal order that the migrant men had internalized. He felt embarrassed at not being able to fulfil his responsibility: being a married son with an established new family.

XIAO MAO: My parents said there should be an order to get married within the family. As I am the oldest son, I should be the first. Relatives keep asking and introducing girls to me. Once or twice is fine. It is quite embarrassing when they ask too many times. They asked my parents: 'Your son is quite capable; why doesn't he quickly find a wife? Urge him to marry and give birth to a grandchild for you.'

INTERVIEWER: What do your parents say?
XIAO MAO: They were embarrassed, too. After all, they live in the same village … it is inevitable that people 'zhi zhi dian dian' [gossip].

Xiao Mao's narrative regarding his feeling of embarrassment revealed the issue of face (*mian zi* or *lian* in Chinese) and its role as a central attribute in the formation of masculine identity. His emotional feeling of embarrassment can be located specifically within the heteronormative cultural context within which he lives out being a son. Within Chinese culture, the concept of face (see also Qi, 2011) is deployed to highlight that individual identity is relational, as it indicates an individual's prestige and respectability from other people's perceptions of them (Ho, 1976; Jia, 1997).

Many migrant men as sons are developing different strategies of playing out their filial responsibility that differs from traditional practices of their parents' generation. For example, providing a better material life, such as sending money home, building a house for their parents and other family members, has gained significant symbolic meaning of displaying oneself as a filial and capable son. For example, Ah Fu spoke of his being able to demonstrate his way of being a filial son by sending money home.

AH FU: They [parents] ask me not to blow money away and should save the money for my marriage in the future.
INTERVIEWER: Do you send your salary to your parents?
AH FU: I keep 200 yuan [20 British pounds] for daily expenses and send the rest of the money to my parents…. They [my parents] asked me not to send money home as they said it's expensive to live outside. They said they will save the money for my marriage … I am happy that I can send money back home because they have been supporting me for nearly 20 years. It is time for me to repay them…. If I were them, I should have got married and have a child and let them enjoy 'Tian Lun Zhi Le' [family happiness with extended generations living together].

More specifically, the migrant men were actively reworking the meaning of being a 'filial' son. The men were aware that their need to reinvent the meaning of what it means to be a 'good son' was breaking a long tradition that they had witnessed in their early lives, which had been lived out by their fathers, uncles and grandfathers. Sometimes, it was a challenge for them to find a way to become a 'filial son' within current material conditions, as a member of a new urban working class, who were experiencing low wages and poor working conditions with little security. Of particular importance in the men's narratives, their gender identities, constructed in the process of such daily interactions within familial relations, have served as an important lens to understand the formation of emerging subjectivities in the city. For migrant men, such as Ah Fu, their break with the past is accompanied by the continuity of intergenerational gendered practices. As he reported, Ah Fu's parents were worried about whether he would have enough money for his future marriage. Hence, they saved the money Ah Fu sent to them to enable him to marry, so that he could carry out the traditional obligation as 'the man in the family' to pass on the family name. The migrant men's narratives suggest a tension between the structural constrains of family life and their active agented practices (with brotherly non-kin relationships and female colleagues) and the development of alternative filial practices in their everyday lives.

Becoming a 'Capable' Subject

Contemporary Chinese modernization in terms of economic prosperity is seen as making profound changes in people's everyday lives. This is reflected in the migrant men's articulation of what they consider as being capable within the dominant discourse of 'suzhi', as I have indicated above. For the migrant young men in my research, the appreciation of urban modern life is having a major impact on the development of their self-identification in the workplace. They have also developed a unique sense of what they would like to be in the future. In their life history narratives, such sense of aspiration was governed by the interweaving of both the discourse of 'suzhi' and cultural values of traditional gender expectations, such as being/becoming a filial son, explored above. For Burke (2006, p. 720): 'Discourses constrain and create the kinds of spaces we live in and the ways we give meaning to our experiences. They shape our aspirations and world views and are interlinked with competing sets of cultural practices.'

Unlike their parents' generation, which has a strong commitment to rural agricultural work, the younger generation of migrant men had little commitment to returning to their home towns. Rather, they were in the process of thinking through alternative ways of achieving and performing their capability as young men.

INTERVIEWER: What do you want to do in the future?
JIANG XI: I wish I can run my own business.
INTERVIEWER: What kind of business?
JIANG XI: I haven't thought about it. Working in the factory does not have much 'benshi' [capability]. We just do the same job again and again for other people, like part of the machine. They can fire you anytime. Doing business is more 'you chuxi' [promising] ... I wish I could make a lot of money.
XIAO WU: ... People have more prospect working in the sales department. People like us don't have much opportunity to 'biao xian' [perform/demonstrate] ... I would really like to have a try to work as a 'gen dan' [following up order and communicating with clients]. I am not afraid of suffering a bit of hardship outside.... At least I can learn something useful.
INTERVIEWER: What would you like to learn?
XIAO WU: Doing business.

Both at home or at work, in private or in public, a sense of 'achievement' was governing the migrant men's desire to become a man with 'nengli'. It seemed that an urban lifestyle has enabled the migrant men to develop an aspiration for upward mobility. However, for them, the notion of aspiration for upward mobility was more complex. Tomba (2009, p. 597) points to the obstacles of preventing rural young men from becoming upwardly mobile in the city, noting that:

> the trajectory and patterns of upward social mobility in China are shaped not only by the marketization of social relations, but also by policies that explicitly facilitate access to resources and wealth accumulation among the members of a new group of educated youth and professionals.

Yan (2008) argues that in her research on migrant women, they experience extreme exploitation in the market economy while, at the same time, they are offered a mirage of success and progression as they migrate from rural areas to the cities. She maintains that there is a wide disconnection between the rural women's imagination of seeing migration as a journey in search of a new identity, thus fulfilling their expectation of 'accumulating suzhi [human quality]' in the modern space, and their materially lived experiences of working in the city. As she argues, they are 'trapped as modern subjects in a space in, but not of, the culture of modernity' (Yan 2008, p. 46). For the men in my research, the meanings of upward mobility contain specific cultural meanings that they articulated. They were aware of their material marginalization compared to their established urban counterparts. However, their narratives of looking after their fellow villagers illustrate the generational specificities of innovative cultural strategies in negotiating their sense of masculinity, as they deployed traditional gender relations operating within their rural families, such as father–son relations, as a means of overcoming the official ascription of them as 'marginalized' men.

WU XIONG: ... working on our own in the city, you have to be able to 'chi ku' [bear hardship].... You don't have parents to rely on. When you are away from home, you have to rely your 'laoxiang' [fellow villagers].

YANG HUI (45-year-old): There was always 'laoxiang' asking me to introduce jobs to them a couple of years ago. Even now, as factories need workers, they can easily find a job elsewhere, but people still prefer their children to work here with me or asking me to find them a job.

INTERVIEWER: Why?

YANG HUI: It is good to have someone who can look after you like a family. At the end of the day, you are working outside, if you know 'shou ren' [familiar person], it is easier to work here.

Wu Xiong and Yang Hui's accounts illustrate the importance of a 'laoxiang' network amongst migrant workers. For men in particular, their role as a father/brother figure has been played out in a setting where social contacts and qualification have been central in the process of modernization (Lin and Mac an

Ghaill, 2013). For them, hard-working and non-kin familial social relationships have been their response to the public representation of migrant workers, that is, on the issue of 'lack' with reference to the dominant discourse of 'suzhi'. For many young migrant men, to be able to bear hardship has become a distinctive characteristic of demonstrating their ability. More specifically, the practice of 'bearing hardship', or 'chi ku' (eat bitterness) in their own words, illustrates the role of traditional gender values in the making of progressive subjects.

More recently in the summer of 2015, I revisited the field to interview a younger generation of migrant workers, as young fathers. I found that traditional familial practices were working together with neo-liberal ideology, which emphasizes the 'enterprising' self. This is particularly relevant in China where a large number of the population are active in the stock market and investment for a better life. Interestingly, within this context, Yang Dong, a 23-year-old man working at a delivery company, discussed his investment in a property. Rather than emphasizing the buying of property as a way of self-investment, he claimed it demonstrated his responsibility as a good father.

YANG DONG: What I am thinking now is that I am young, but I don't have any 'benshi'… I can only use my labour. I would like to use the money I earn from my labour to buy a property … at least when you are getting older, like when you are in your 40s and 50s, you can tell people that you own a property. Buying other things, such as stock share is not practical. You don't know what will happen in the future. You might end up losing everything and have nothing to leave for your children. Owning a property means that it belongs to me and I can pass on to my children.

INTERVIEWER: So, the reason to buy a property is for your child's future?

YANG DONG: Definitely for my child … my family have property in the village. Both of us (my wife and I) are happy to rent [in the city].… There is a new development for a residential area near my hometown. So I have asked my father to keep an eye on it. I prepare to buy a property … a property for my child. I have only one child. It is not a big burden to afford the mortgage as long as I don't have to make the first payment (deposit).

INTERVIEWER: Who will make the first payment?

YANG DONG: My parents.… When I first came to work, I sent money home. My father said they don't need money and asked me to spend it on my son. Now we just give them some money when we go home. They said they would save it for me in case we need the money in the future. I talked to them before saying we were thinking to buy a house. And they would like to help to make the first payment.… People like us won't be able to afford a house without our parents' help.

Yang Dong's account of buying a property illustrated his negotiation as a good father and as a neo-liberal subject. For him, the continuity of traditional familial practices, such as the circle of 'filial piety' and receiving support from his parents, illustrated their material marginality as a working-class migrant worker in the city. At the same time, such practices of 'parent–child' relations strongly illustrate the tradition of filial responsibility. This strong bond between parents and their children continues to exist within modern Chinese society and, for Yang Dong, serves to demonstrate the enactment of his masculinity identity as a responsible son and young father.

Of importance, my study also suggests that these men deployed different strategies in reworking their performance of capability, in order to develop their masculine identities in the process of migration that is officially marked by a notion of marginalization. Neo-liberal ideology is impacting upon late modern subjects' lives through globally inflected modernization projects at a local level (Mac an Ghaill and Haywood, 2007). For example, becoming capable has become a central theme underpinning these migrant subjects' everyday lives. This can be achieved and displayed through different locally based strategies and negotiated through diverse practices. Although rural–urban migration has created a highly visible class division between migrant working-class and urban middle-class sectors of the population (Pun and Chan, 2008), a theorization of the new urban marginalized men is still underdeveloped that this collection aims to address.

Conclusion

The chapter critically engages with the concept of 'marginality' in attempting to explore Chinese male (rural–urban) migrant workers' negotiation of (modern) masculinities. Although we cannot generalize from their experiences, as a result of carrying out a small-scale qualitative research project, the chapter illustrates an alternative account of how the concept of 'marginality' has been negotiated within the context of the migrant men's mobility. Connell maintains the importance of such accounts, in exploring the meanings of masculinities from the global South:

> There is a rich archive of accounts and analyses of masculinity from around the global South, in a variety of genres. These provide an important foundation for post-colonial thinking about masculinities. The formation of masculinities needs to be considered on a historical terrain including worldwide processes of conquest and social disruption, the building of colonial societies and a global economy, and post-independence globalization.
>
> (2014, p. 217)

With reference to Chinese economic modernization, it is important to explore emerging alternative meanings of 'marginality'. The understanding of marginality in relation to the migrant men's material conditions as an urban working class does not constrain the active negotiation of deploying various local cultural resources in performing their familial roles as sons and fathers.

Rural–urban migration has been a major socio-economic phenomenon in China's modernization process as a global rising power. Through the study of their narratives regarding the ways the migrant men seek resources to make sense of their social positioning and self-identity formation, the chapter highlights the rural–urban migrant men's gendered identity through the negotiation of 'nengli' (capability) in different domains of their social lives. Therefore, it provides an insight into understanding different ways of making sense of their masculine identities that are often neglected within the dominant discourse of 'suzhi' (quality) in China, where migrant workers are perceived as marginalized in the process of modernization, marked by progress, economic development and self-responsibility.

The above study suggests the importance of synthesizing the cultural domain of traditional familial values and the dominant economic ideology of neo-liberalism in order to understand identity formation in the context of changing family life as a result of migration. Through engagement with traditional cultural values, such as filial piety, as an important resource for migrant men's identity formation, the chapter critically applies Western analytical frameworks, such as 'Bourdieusian class analysis', to address the intersection of different forms of power illustrated in the men's narratives. Thus, I argue for the need to hold on to the productive tension between materialist and post-structuralist accounts of these men's migrating experiences.

Writing from within a Western location, there is a danger of reinscribing a common-sense view that the above narrative is evidence of East Asian societies simply reproducing Western models of globalization and late-modernity sex/gender politics. The chapter addresses the cultural specificity of contemporary Chinese society, with particular reference to local (national) cultural values, such as filial piety and heteronormativity. More specifically, deploying a comparative perspective to frame the conceptual and empirical questions addressed here, will enable us to be sensitive to the epistemological gaps in research on the next generation of 'marginalized' men both locally and globally, as illustrated throughout this edited collection.

Acknowledgement

Some of the data in the chapter are drawn from my recent study funded by the British Academy (SG142139). Many thanks for their financial support in enabling me to carry out my fieldwork in China.

Reference

Beck, U. and Beck-Gernsheim, E. (1995) *The Normal Chaos of Love*. Cambridge: Polity.
Burke, P. J. (2006) Men accessing education: gendered aspirations, *British Educational Research Journal* 32(5): 719–33.
Connell, R. (2014) Margin becoming centre: for a world-centred rethinking of masculinities, *NORMA International Journal for Masculinity Studies* 19 (4): 217–231.
Fei, H.-T. (2008) *Peasant Life in China*. London: Hesperides Press.
Giddens, A. (1992) *The Transformation of Intimacy: Sexuality, Love, and Eroticism in Modern Societies*. Cambridge: Polity Press.

Ho, D. Y.-F. (1976) On the concept of face, *American Journal of Sociology* 81: 867–884.

Jia, W. (1997) Facework as a Chinese conflict-preventive mechanism – a cultural/discourse analysis, *Intercultural Communication Studies* VII-1997–8: 43–58.

Knight, J. and Song, L. (1999) *The Rural-Urban Divide: Economic Disparities and Interaction in China*. Oxford: Oxford University Press.

Knight, J. and Song, L. (2005) *Towards a Labour Market in China*. Oxford: Oxford University Press.

Lawler, S. (2004) Rules of engagement: habitus, class and resistance. In L. Adkins and B. Skeggs (eds) *Feminism after Bourdieu*. Oxford: Blackwell.

Lawler, S. (2013) *Identity: Sociological Perspectives* (2nd). Cambridge: Polity.

Lin, X. and Mac an Ghaill, M. (2013) Chinese male peasant workers and shifting masculine identities in urban workspaces, *Gender, Work and Organization* 20(5): 498–511.

Liu, F. (2011) *Urban Youth in China: Modernity, the Internet and the Self*. Oxon: Routledge.

Mac an Ghaill, M. and Haywood, C. (2007) *Gender, Culture and Society: Contemporary Femininities and Masculinities*. Basingstoke: Palgrave Macmillan.

Nonini, D. M. (2008) Is China becoming neoliberal? *Critique of Anthropology* 28(2): 145–76.

Ong, A. (1997) Chinese modernities: narratives of nation and of capitalism. In A. Ong and D. M. Nonini (eds) *Ungrounded Empires: The Cultural Politics of Modern Chinese Transnationalism*. London: Routledge.

Pun, N. and Chan, C. K.-C. (2008) The subsumption of class discourse in China, *Boundary 2.* 35 (2): 75–91.

Qi, X. (2011) Face: A Chinese concept in a global sociology, *Journal of Sociology* 47(3): 279–296.

Reay, D. (2004) Gendering Bourdieu's concept of capitals? Emotional capital, women and social class. In L. Adkins and B. Skeggs (eds) *Feminism after Bourdieu*. Oxford: Blackwell.

Reay, D., Crozier, G. and Clayton, J. (2009) Strangers in paradise: Working class students in elite universities, *Sociology* 43(6): 1103–1121.

Rofel, L. (2007) *Desiring China: Experiments in Neoliberalism, Sexuality, and Public Culture*. Durham, NC: Duke University Press.

Skeggs, B. (1997) *Formations of Class and Gender: Becoming Respectable*. London: Sage.

Skeggs, B. (2014) Values beyond value? Is anything beyond the logic of capital? *British Journal of Sociology* 65(1): 1–20.

Solinger, Dorothy J. (1995) The floating population in the cities: chances for assimilation? In D. S. Davisect (ed.) *Urban Spaces in Contemporary China*. Cambridge: CUP.

Solinger, D. J. (1999) *Contesting Citizenship in Urban China: Peasant Migrants, the State, and the Logic of the Market*. Berkeley, CA: University of California Press.

Tomba, L. (2009) Of quality, harmony, and community: Civilization and the middle class in urban China, *Position* 17(3): 591–616.

Xiang, B. (2007) How far are the left-behind left behind? A preliminary study in rural China population, *Space and Place* 13: 179–91.

Yan, H. (2008) *New Masters, New Servants: Migration, Development, and Women Workers in China*. Durham, NC: Duke University Press.

Zhang, L. and Ong, A. (2015) *Privatizing China: Socialism from Afar*. NY: Cornell University Press.

Part III
Marginalization, Bodies and Identity

7 Derailed Self-constructions

Marginalization and Self-construction in Young Boys' Accounts of Well-being

Niels Ulrik Sørensen and Jens Christian Nielsen

Introduction

This chapter focuses on the construction of self amongst a group of young boys in Denmark who have had experience with eating disorders, self-harm, loneliness and other manifestations of a lack of well-being. At first glance, these manifestations of a lack of well-being seem rather distinct and incomparable, but they have in common the fact that the young boys who have had these experiences say that they are due to personal faults and imperfections. In other words, they are related to problematizing thematizations of the self. In this chapter, we investigate these problematizing thematizations and explore the ways that young boys understand and experience the self, and how they link this self to their lack of well-being. As will become apparent, fear of marginalization seems to be an important part of this connection: The young boys are struggling to live up to expectations in an increasingly individualized and competitive society, and their fear of being lost and excluded seems to have a destabilizing effect on their well-being. The young boys in this chapter are not socially excluded in terms of being outside 'mainstream society' (Schiffer and Schatz, 2008), rather their marginalization is that of insiders, who feel that their insider position is fragile and on the verge of collapsing, which is why they are struggling all they can to avoid being excluded and marginalized.

The chapter presents a post-structuralism-inspired perspective of young boys' construction of self, lack of well-being and how experiences of marginalization are related to that. On the one hand, this perspective implies that self-construction is seen as something that is embedded in and conditional on social and cultural notions and norms of gender, class, age, etc. On the other hand, it implies that the young boys are attributed the capacity to work on and change these notions and norms through citing practices, which must, however, be culturally identifiable and acceptable, if the young boys are to achieve social inclusion (Wetherell and Potter, 1992; Søndergaard, 1996, 2005, 2014). By this, the chapter also deals with the boundaries between what is culturally identifiable and acceptable and what is not, e.g. what is on the inside and on the outside of social and cultural perceptions and norms regarding the construction of self, and the implications it has for young boys to be positioned on either side of these boundaries (Kofoed, 2003; Staunæs, 2004). Though the majority of the young boys discussed in this chapter are students or have jobs and lead seemingly conventional lives, the majority of the chapter is about the self-construction processes that take place while the young boys manoeuvre and rework the boundaries in order to maintain a culturally identifiable and acceptable self. This paradox is vital to the marginalization presented in the chapter, which occurs in a society where notions of normality are becoming narrower, and a culturally identifiable and acceptable self is becoming increasingly difficult to meet. In other words, the chapter deals with a marginalization that is occurring in a society where the space of alterity is increasing to such an extent that more and more young people are struggling to keep it at bay.

A considerable amount of research explores how young people manage the increased demands on self-construction in today's individualized and competitive societies. However, whereas most of this research focuses on the connections between the increased demands on self-construction within specific social or cultural fields and specific manifestations of a lack of well-being, e.g. experiences of social exclusion related to an increasingly individualized educational system (Murning, 2013; Hutters and Sørensen, 2015) or negative body perceptions in an increasingly aestheticized youth culture (Johansson, 1997; Sørensen, 2008), this chapter explores the implications of the increased demands on self-construction for young boys' lack of well-being, and how this is related to their experiences of marginalization in a broader sense. The chapter does not focus on the relationship between self-construction and a lack of well-being within a particular social or cultural field. Instead, we define self-construction as a field of its own and explore the relationship between this field and various forms of a lack of well-being, which are characterized by their problematizing thematizations of the self. To this end, the chapter explores different situations and contexts in the young boys' lives, which appear to be crucial for the relationship between their self-construction and their lack of well-being.

Though the young boys in this chapter exhibit a high degree of fear and vulnerability, and thus appear far away from traditional notions of hegemonic or dominant masculinity (Connell, 1995), they do not seem to assume subordinate masculinity positions. As will become apparent, their vulnerability and fearfulness seem to function as a constant impetus for them to work and struggle to succeed with their self-construction; something that involves a great deal of self-determination and goal-orientation, which are some of the main characteristics in hegemonic or dominant masculinities. Therefore, what may be associated with a subordinate masculinity position can also be linked to more dominant masculinity positions. In this sense, the chapter is not only about young boys who are struggling all they can to avoid being excluded and marginalized, it is also about young boys whose struggle is taking place in a field of tension between dominant and subordinate masculinity positions.

Disposition

Individualization and self-construction are two key concepts in the chapter. In the first section, we provide an outline of our understanding of these concepts and how they have been used in empirical studies within youth research. Section 2 describes and discusses the methodological approach adopted in the study, which is followed, in Section 3, by a presentation of our analyses, which is divided into three sub-sections: 'To create/find yourself'; 'In the shadow of perfection'; and 'The fight against an imperfect self'. Each section deals with an important part of the young boys' self-construction processes and the implications it has for the young boys' well-being. In the final discussion, we summarize the major analytical findings and discuss their wider relevance for the young boys' experiences of marginalization.

Individualization and Self-construction

Since the introduction of Erikson's identity theory (Erikson, 1968; Kroger, 2007), youth research has been concerned with questions regarding young people's formation of identity. In recent decades, this preoccupation has gained additional currency with the emergence of a number of agenda-setting social science theories, which have turned the self into a prism through which current societal changes are viewed. This is seen not least in modernity theory, which has developed a long series of concepts about the construction of self, e.g. *self-identity* (Giddens, 1991) and *do-it-yourself biography* (Beck and Beck-Gernsheim, 2002), which are seen as expressions of a particular development that is considered central in contemporary society, i.e. *Individualization*. According to modernity theory, individualization revolves around the idea that social and cultural positions and communities which until now have been identity forming (gender, sexuality, ethnicity, class, age, etc.), are dissolving, the result being that people today are *culturally liberated* and can create their own selves (Ziehe, 1991). Modernity theory describes self-construction as one of the primary purposes of being – and an enormous challenge, not least because contemporary society is thought to be characterized by changeability and fragmentation, whereby the conditions of existence are being continuously altered. It is against this background of continuous change that the individual must construct his or her self (Sennett, 1998; Bauman, 1999).

As in many other Western societies, individualization has also left its mark on the Scandinavian societies, which are characterized by an increasing emphasis on the individual's capacity to perform and compete. Whereas Anglo-Saxon scholars focus on the increasing impact of neo-liberalism (Shildrick *et al.*, 2012), Pedersen (2011) argues that the Nordic welfare states have been transformed into *competition states* in which good breeding, democracy and community, so crucial in the welfare states, have been replaced by an emphasis on the individual's responsibility for her own life and her freedom to realize her own needs. According to Willig (2013), this contributes to the creation of societies in which there is not only a constant demand for self-optimization and self-discipline, but also high levels of self-criticism: You are the master of your own destiny, and if something goes wrong, you are also the one to blame. However, scholars argue that not everybody is equally likely to succeed or fail. Though the individual's capacity to construct herself is the centre of attention in individualized societies, even in the relatively equal Scandinavian societies, people have different preconditions for constructing themselves (Rasborg, 2013). How this manifests itself and the consequences it has for different young people has been a recurring theme in empirical studies within Nordic youth research in the last decade.

In the area of Youth Studies, research has been inspired by post-structuralist thinking – another agenda-setting theoretical trend, which, like modernity theory, focuses on the social and cultural processes through which groups and individuals are constructed as selves (Foucault, 1991; Butler, 1993; Søndergaard 1996, 2005). Here, normative ideals of gender, sexuality, ethnicity, class and age, etc., are considered to have a continuous effect in societies characterized by individualization – and there is a strong focus on researching the potential limitations these ideals may place on the self-construction of groups and individuals. It is argued that individuals risk becoming marginalized and abject, e.g. expelled as non-subjects, if they construct themselves in ways that stray too far from the ideal (Butler, 1990, 1993). At the same time, it is emphasized that normative ideals are being constantly transformed through individuals' and groups' *citations* of socially and culturally identifiable subject positions, which accordingly are meant to contain a performative potential (Davies and Harré, 1990). This duality has not least been apparent in a number of empirical studies on school life and subjectivity which, amongst other things, have focused on how young people construct their selves through the gender, class, sexuality and ethnicity positions available to them in various school and home-town contexts (Armbjörnsson, 2004; Staunæs, 2004; Cawood, 2007; Gilliam, 2009; Fangen *et al.*, 2010). The studies demonstrate the continued influence of these positions on young people's self-construction; but at the same time, they demonstrate that young people actively interpret the positions by, amongst other things, combining them in new ways thereby challenging some of the limitations that the positions place on their self-construction.

The educational arena is also the setting for a number of studies, which are inspired by modernity theory, amongst others, and investigate how education is increasingly exerting its influence on an arena in which young people are required to take positions and make choices which have a bearing on their future – who they are, and who they could become (Katznelson, 2004; Pless, 2014). An important point in these studies is that the young people meet an individualized logic and rhetoric in the educational system. Though emphasizing free choice, this is not portrayed as a liberating process, but on the contrary as an institutionally embedded mechanism which entails relatively narrow options and a lack of variation and opportunities to deviate, which, to a large extent reproduces social and cultural power structures and inequalities (Illeris *et al.*, 2009).

The fact that individualization does not necessarily expand diversity amongst young people seems also to be a consistent finding in youth research concerning lifestyle and youth culture (Johansson, 1997, 2006; Sørensen, 2008), which focuses on, amongst other things, the aestheticization of the self, resulting from the increasing demand for individuals to create their selves. In this way, individualization is linked to an increased preoccupation with self-promotion and bodily self-presentation, which blurs certain boundaries between female/male, homosexual/heterosexual, etc., but which, at the same time, is considered to represent a progression towards ever greater inflexibility and narrower ideals regarding the body and the exterior, which creates new demands regarding positioning as well as new forms of exclusion (Andreasson and Johansson, 2014). This is tied to a lack of well-being for ever greater numbers of young people, who experience it as a pressure to construct themselves in relation to the narrower ideals of the body and the exterior, reflective of the times. Many young people respond to this lack of well-being with self-directed behaviour in the form of eating disorders, self-harm and self-loathing, etc., which is partly explained by the fact that the young people, due to the prevailing logic of individualization, feel responsible for their personal triumphs and failures (Nielsen et al., 2010; Sørensen et al., 2011; Due et al., 2015).

Empirical studies within youth research portray young people's self-construction as a field of tension subject to individualizing forces which, on the one hand, emphasize the young people's opportunities to construct themselves, while on the other, do not provide them with much room to do so, partly because well-known categories such as gender, class and ethnicity continue to have an influence on the building blocks available to young people, and partly because of the spread of new normative ideals, which also regulate their self-construction. At the same time, youth research shows how young people in different situations and contexts reinterpret and displace the positions available to them, which contributes to the renewal and change of the room in which their self-construction occurs. However, even though the individualized self-construction does contain some degree of freedom, young people are not free to avoid it as it has become compulsory for all young people – no matter what conditions they have for managing it. This definitely seems to be the case for the young boys in this chapter, who are caught up in painful self-construction processes and are driven by a fear of marginalization, which they are struggling to avoid.

Methodology

The empirical basis for the chapter is qualitative interviews which were conducted with 19 young boys aged between 15 and 24 years old. These boys find themselves in a grey area in that while they have problems, the intensity and extent of which appear to be a cause for alarm, they do not appear to be so severe that their entire lives are dominated by a lack of well-being. The young boys were selected from a large, quantitative study of young people's well-being and lack of well-being (Nielsen et al., 2010) on the basis of their answers which indicated that they had experienced a serious lack of well-being in certain areas in their lives, while they seemed to be thriving in other areas.

In the study, the 19 young boys stated that they had had experiences with bullying, loneliness, self-harming behaviour or problems with body image and their appearance. Amongst other factors, the latter was based on whether the boys had stated in the questionnaire that they were unhappy with their body, had starved themselves, felt guilty about eating and/or had harmed themselves. However, none of the young boys had received a clinical diagnosis, and when they were asked to evaluate their lives as a whole – for instance their self-confidence, their popularity, etc. – their answers were largely positive, indicating that they had a relatively positive image of themselves and their well-being, even though they were affected by problems and issues which were linked to problematic thematizations of the self.

At the time of the interviews, the 19 young boys lived all across Denmark – in the capital area as well as in provincial towns and villages. One was in primary school, four were in high school, three were in vocational school, one was attending an adult education centre, three were going to university, three were enrolled at other further education institutions, three were employed and one was unemployed. Therefore, the interviewees represented a broad mix of young boys in different life situations and with different family backgrounds and social environments. The boys were not selected to reflect a representative sample of the young boys in the quantitative study with the kinds of lack of well-being in question. They were chosen because each could provide a different perspective on being a young boy with experiences of a lack of well-being related to a problematizing thematization of the self. Thus, we selected the young boys to obtain a varied and nuanced insight into the life situations, positions and narratives etc. that characterize young boys who have had these kinds of experiences regarding a lack of well-being.

We set out to frame the interviews in such a way as to give the young boys' experiences and subjective perspectives the greatest space possible. Therefore, we stressed to them that the interview was focused on their current situations in life, and on young people's lives in the broadest sense. After this, we read some of their answers from the questionnaire survey which were the reason for their selection. We were very careful, however, not to position the young boys too specifically with regard to these answers – for example, we did not say to them, 'I'd like to talk to you about being lonely' – but rather used formulations such as 'I see that around six months ago, you answered that you often felt lonely. This is one of the things we'd like to talk to you about'. Our underlying message was that, e.g. loneliness could be a subject for discussion if they chose to pursue it during the interview, but that our primary interest was to hear how they were doing in general, and how they perceived their youth etc. in a wider sense. This reticent approach was adopted because we did not want to impose a lack of well-being and marginalization on the boys if they did not experience or identify with it themselves. It was important for us that they were able to define their own situation, which then became the focus of the interviews.

The young boys were interviewed individually in semi-structured interviews (Haavind, 2000; Fog and Kvale, 1995) which were organized around six overall themes, which made it possible for them to talk about self-construction and a lack of well-being in relation to different situations and contexts in their lives. The themes were: (1) Important choices and control of life; (2) Present challenges and difficult life-phases; (3) Friends, partners and network; (4) Family; (5) Future; and finally, (6) Perceptions of 'a good youth life'. During the interviews, we let the young boys concretize the themes in that the incidents and thoughts etc. that they found relevant to talk about directed the course of the interview. Gender and masculinity were not included as themes unless the young boys found them relevant to mention as we did not want to systematically 'gender' the manifestations of a lack of well-being. Though some of the interviewed young boys had experienced a lack of well-being in one form or another (e.g. starving themselves, self-harm, etc.) that were mostly associated with girls and were, therefore, gendered to a certain extent, they did not bring up the subject of gender or masculinity during the interviews. Though compromising norms of gender and masculinity may have contributed to their fear of marginalization, this was not articulated during the interviews. As will become apparent, the boys connected their fear of marginalization to many other factors, which we have emphasized in our analysis.

In the analysis, we have attempted to identify *internal correlations* (Haavind, 2000) in the young boys' accounts of the themes, i.e. the connections that the young boys themselves establish between different phenomena and subjects when they talk about a lack of well-being, challenges and networks etc. during the interviews. In particular, we focused on the internal connections they make between a lack of well-being and self-construction, i.e. the subjective meanings they ascribe to these phenomena, and the interplay between them. Furthermore, we sought to determine how these meanings relate to marginalization and how this is experienced (Andenæs, 2000).

In line with a post-structuralist analysis strategy, the interpretations, perspectives and logics produced by the young boys in the interviews are understood as citations of cultural notions and norms which apply in the young boys' society (Butler, 1990, 1993). The connections between self-construction and a lack of well-being which the young boys identify in the interviews are, thus, understood less as cultural expressions of an inner subjectivity amongst these young boys, and more as the young boys' assuming positions within the culture – i.e. as cultural actions through which they create such subjectivity (Wetherell and Potter, 1992). These cultural actions can be more or less culturally normative, i.e. they replicate cultural understandings and expectations to a greater or lesser extent. One of the aims of our analysis was to explore the relationship between normative and non-normative citations: What are the expectations of self-construction? What happens when an individual fails to meet these expectations? And how is this related to a lack of well-being? Furthermore, the analysis attempts to determine when the characteristics of the informants approach the boundaries of what is culturally identifiable and acceptable, what it means to approach these boundaries and how it is related to experiences of marginalization (Staunæs, 2004).

In our analysis, we focus on two self-construction axes which have emerged in the young boys' accounts of a lack of well-being. Each axis can be thought of as a line between two points, which constitute different versions of the same aspect of the self with self-construction entailing movement along this line from one point to the other. The first axis is described in the section 'To create/find yourself' and connects the points *What I am* and *What I can be*. In this case, movement is made to make a decision regarding education, which all of the young boys see as crucial for realizing self-construction. The other axis is explored in the sections: 'In the shadow of perfection', and 'The fight against an imperfect self'. This axis runs between the points *My imperfect self* and *Perfect normality*. Here the focus is on the significance of the notion of perfection for the boys' self-construction, and how they struggle in different ways to live up to this notion. As will become apparent, not being able to move along the lines of the two axes is associated with fear of marginalization.

To Create/Find Yourself

During the interviews, we asked the young boys to describe what they considered to be the greatest current challenge in their lives. The majority of the answers were concerned with making what were considered to be important decisions regarding their future. As described by Illeris *et al.* (2009), amongst others, the young boys in this study felt that having to make such choices is an unavoidable condition of a young person's life. However, even the young boys who on the surface seemed to master this condition described these choices as onerous and complicated because, to a large extent, they put both their current and future selves on the line. When asked what the biggest challenge in his life was, 22-year-old apprentice floor fitter Stephan, who has a lower middle-class background, answered as follows:

S: All these educations. You see, I'm 22 now and I have to start a new [education]. And deciding which path to take for the rest of your life is bloody difficult. But this is what you have to do.
I: What could help you decide what you want to do?
S: Well … I don't know. It's a big problem for me.

Stephan's future is uncertain, but will be created by the decisions he must make. The decision about which education to take seems to be particularly important. He has made a choice, but the idea that it is 'for the rest of your life' seems overwhelming, and he does not seem to be sure that a career as a floor fitter is the right choice, but he has absolutely no idea how to make the right choice. Stephan has already made a number of decisions regarding his education – he started several vocational courses, but did not finish any of them. The number of potential educations seems enormous, and Stephan does know how to navigate his way through all the options. He seems to be caught in a decision process that he cannot manage, but at the same time cannot escape. And he is not alone in this.

The interviews are full of accounts of crises connected with educational choices which the young boys see as decisive for their future. 23-year-old Anders – a university student with a middle-class background – tells us that he 'almost broke down' when he realized that he had made the wrong decisions regarding his education:

A: Well, I think I was very good at suppressing it, but it probably wasn't very smart. Well, I guess that's also why I think it hit me a little hard when I found out that it didn't really work out with my studies.
I: How did it hit you hard? In what way?
A: Well, I almost broke down in tears [said with a small grin]. And it was actually quite strange because I haven't experienced that so often. It happened one evening when I was talking to my girlfriend.... In fact, it was probably because I admitted to myself that it wasn't going very well.

As the choice of education is thought to be decisive for one's future, the boys consider making the right choice to be extremely important and failing to make the correct decision is associated with great anxiety. For a long time, Anders had pushed away a nagging feeling that something was wrong. However, in the end he had to acknowledge 'that it wasn't going very well' with his studies. Though he talks lightly about his breakdown, acknowledging that he had made the wrong educational choice clearly was not easy for him, probably because it meant that he had to make a new decision and that his future was at stake. At the time of the interview, Anders had gone through this process and had decided to take the same education as his father, although:

> That has not been the primary reason [for my choice]. It is certainly not anything I was aware of. Because in fact ... I do not know if I was embarrassed, but when I found out that I was to study the same as my father, I probably thought it was a bit annoying. Or not annoying, but there are so many [young people] who do not break with their social inheritance.... Not that it's a negative social inheritance.... But I think that it is something that I have found out myself.

According to Anders, at first, he was not 'aware' that he had decided to do the same education as his father, and when he found out, he was not pleased. On the contrary, it made him 'annoyed', as an educational choice, which can be interpreted as a reproduction of parents' education, family tradition etc. clearly doesn't have the same legitimacy as a choice based on his own interests and aspirations. This is something that we observe in most of the interviews with the young boys: They tend to strive for educational choices that are based on their own interests and aspirations. In this way, it is not only their future which is at stake when they are faced with choices about their education; the present also features as an essential element, because the lives that they are supposed to create for themselves are supposed to be based on the selves that they are here and now. Therefore, problems related to choosing educations and experiencing crises and breakdowns are not only related to uncertainty about how their lives will be in the future, but also to uncertainty about what and who they are here and now, and the pressure they experience in their attempts to define themselves.

The young boys seem to share the idea that they can construct themselves and their future through their choice of education as well as other important decisions made during youth; something which seems to represent a big challenge for them, not least because they feel that they have to build the foundations upon which the building will rest. Important decisions, thus, entail a double orientation towards the self, which is seen as something that must be simultaneously found and created in relation to these decisions. Therefore, the choices function as intermediaries between what the young boys are, and what they can become. Since both of these poles appear to be unknown, to some extent, the young boys are not completely clear about who they are, or who they can become.

This lack of certainty and clarity is experienced as something defective and dysfunctional and is associated with crises and breakdowns, which must be rectified and eliminated. They desire control over who they are and who they can be, along with whatever choices this may lead them to make. In other words, the ideal is to make choices which move them in a straight line from a current self to a potential self, and to avoid wrong decisions or detours, which are perceived as crisis situations, to be avoided or resolved as soon as possible. In this orientation towards certainty and clarity, there seems to be an assumption that one will not necessarily become someone; that you may be or become nothing which, on the face of it, seems to indicate a realization of the individualized self-construction outlined by modernity theory in which nothing exists, but the self which is created through the choices made by the individual, etc. (Giddens, 1991; Beck and Beck-Gernsheim, 2002). At the same time, though, there is a notion that you may end up becoming no one if you are unable to make the necessary decisions and construct yourself.

A consistent theme in post-structuralism is the identity paradigm in the modern era with its production of naturalized (gendered, sexualized and racialized, etc.) subject positions, which brushed away and concealed the fact that identity is the result of construction processes involving power and subjugation, etc. (Foucault, 1991; Søndergaard, 2005). However, for the young boys in this chapter, the constructionist aspects of their identities appear obvious: They do not perceive their selves as natural or given, but rather as something that they must endeavour to construct. However, although they feel that it is up to them to construct their own selves, they do not feel that they can choose to ignore this. On the contrary, actively constructing themselves seems crucial to gaining acknowledgement and inclusion in today's individualized competition state (Pedersen, 2011; Willig, 2013). The young boys, therefore, see it as their job to construct themselves, which seems to involve defining two solid and clear points, and to move along a line between them. One point consists of *what I am*, and the other of *what I could be*, and the line between the points involves educational and other important choices, which ensure a progression between *what I am* and *what I could be* – the first axis of our analysis.

The young boys do not talk of power or subjugation in relation to educational choices – they talk about the difficulties in choosing between the many different studies. However, in the competition state, where having a good education is considered decisive for one's ability to manage one's life, they hardly have the freedom to go without an education. Outside the education system, there does not seem to be any obtainable identity (Sørensen *et al.*, 2013). Not getting an education appears as a subjective no man's land (Søndergaard, 1996; Kofoed, 2003; Staunæs, 2004). Therefore, if an individual is on the fringe of the education system, he is also on the fringe of no man's land. In other words, the position of 'uneducated' seems to be a non-position for the young boys in the chapter: If one is uneducated, one has moved to a place where it seems terribly difficult to effect self-construction.

In the Shadow of Perfection

The other self-construction axis we have identified in our analysis is not concerned with having to make a particular decision, which is crucial for a future self, it is about a broader and more diffuse experience of not being able to measure up to other young people, and about the effort involved in achieving their level. Despite the fact that some of the young boys talk about vulnerable or problematic siblings and classmates, siblings are often lauded as incarnations of good young lives, i.e. as young people who live the kind of life that the young boys would also like to live. Siblings perform excellently in the arenas of youth life and their futures look bright and promising. As a rule, the level is considered to be so high that young boys abandon any hope of attaining it. At the same time, the accounts show that they, nonetheless, place themselves and their own lives on a scale that is determined by the lives of their siblings and classmates, although this is rarely to their advantage. In the following quote, 22-year-old Lasse, a student at an adult education centre, who comes from a middle-class background, is describing a situation in which he had to ask his family for help:

L: I think it was really lovely that I was given so much help. Because I thought: 'OK, maybe it's not so bad to ask for help after all'. It was because I've got siblings, and all three of them do fantastically well, so I just sit and think, 'How can I ever live up to that?' And right now, for example, when I see my brother's apartment, it is always gleaming white and scary. And I just sit there and think, he's handling studying medicine, in good time, and doing amazingly well. You can't compare yourself to that. That's really something to live up to.
I: Is it something you think about?
L: Yeah, I do, for sure. I think it's very subconscious. Because I want to show that I can also do well myself. I think it's like that for the majority of younger siblings – they want to show that they can do well themselves.

The success of Lasse's siblings clearly puts the weight of expectation on Lasse. On the one hand, it sets a standard, but it is one that he rejects that he has to live up to ('You can't compare yourself to that'). On the other hand, he clearly wants to live up to it ('How can I ever live up to that?'/'Because I want to show that I can also do well myself.'). Lasse also assumes that the desire to live up to older brothers and sisters is a widespread feeling amongst younger siblings. However, for 23-year-old Gustav who comes from a middle-class background and is a student at a teacher training college, it is his relationship with his younger brother that causes problems:

> You see, my little brother, he is really exceptional. He's a really annoying type, who doesn't have to study; he's just good at everything. All kinds of sports, you know. A really annoying type, you know. And my parents are well aware that he's good at all these things, and it doesn't come as easily for me, for example exams and things. I have to study. I can't just come up with the perfect solutions. ... I'm lucky once in a while and do it, and other times I am not so lucky, and they know it – so they are like a bit more ... well, I do not know whether to say that they are happy that I have come this far or something like that. But I only got this far, because I've worked hard for it.

Gustav recognizes that he is doing well at times, but it does not really count, as it is mostly a matter of hard work and luck. Not like his younger brother, who seemingly glides effortlessly through life and masters everything to perfection. Whereas Gustav is a hard worker, the little brother is exceptional. Even though Gustav uses his little brother as a yardstick, he has given up hope of ever living up to him. Furthermore, according to Gustav, this is also how his parents view the situation; they know very well that his little brother is talented whereas everything is more difficult for Gustav. Although he doubts that they are relieved – or 'happy' – that he has come as far as he has, he does not completely reject that it might be the case as they know that he has had to work hard for everything that he has achieved.

Even though Lasse and Gustav do not feel that they can live up to the ideal standards of perfection, which are represented by their siblings, they do not question these standards. Perfection is not considered some distant goal that very few achieve. Though Gustav describes his perfect brother as exceptional, he is far from the only perfect sibling or classmate in the young boys' narratives. Perfection almost seems to be the norm and, therefore, constitutes a reference point for young boys' self-construction, which consequently is not only about clarifying the points *this is what I am*, and *this is what I could be*, in relation to educational decisions. Self-construction is also drawn out between two points, the content of which has, to a large extent, already been filled in: *my imperfect self* and *perfect normality*. But where the choice of education represents a well-defined link between *what I am* and *what I can be*, it seems harder to identify a clear link between *my imperfect self* and *perfect normality*, which appear as two relatively unconnected points, even though they help to substantiate each other's meaning, *the imperfect self* thereby gaining significance through comparison with *perfect normality*. *My imperfect self* appears almost as a shadow self, i.e. a self that does not have its own qualities or intrinsic values, but instead exists primarily as a pale reflection of *perfect normality*.

There does not seem to be a great deal of identity available to the young boys outside *perfect normality*. Perfection delineates a field of possible, perfect positions or subjectifications, but outside this field only non-positions are apparently to be found. Therefore, the border between the perfect and the imperfect is also a border between subjectivity and non-subjectivity – and everything outside this has the character of an identity no man's land. As Lasse and Gustav and the other boys in the study tend not to feel perfect, they experience a risk of ending up in this identity no man's land. Though neither of them are socially excluded in terms of being outside 'mainstream society' (Schiffer and Schatz, 2008), they experience a constant fear of falling into a space of alterity. This is the fear of marginalization that an individual feels when they think that they are never good enough or worthy of being inside, which is why they can always be legitimately rejected and pushed out. In other words, this is the fear of marginalization that an individual feels when they are on the border, neither inside nor outside, and have to constantly prove that they are good enough and worthy of inclusion. Since the young boys see themselves as being responsible for constructing themselves, they have tried various strategies to improve themselves in order to obtain legitimate access to *perfect normality*, with its field of attractive subject positions (Rose, 1999). However, not all of them have been successful to the same degree.

The Fight against an Imperfect Self

The young boys' *imperfect selves* appear, to some extent, to be a kind of reservoir for diverse, problematic relationships and events in their lives, which they have collected and made into a part of their selves, and which are, therefore, made into objects for a large range of strategies for helping them to transcend imperfection, and to move themselves as far along towards *perfect normality* as possible. The strategies revolve in different ways around optimizing their selves in order to lift themselves out of life situations, behaviours and emotional issues etc. in which they feel trapped. They may feel that they perform inadequately in school, and talk about applying different strategies to improve their performances, or they may think that they are too introverted and make plans to become more extroverted. However, quite a few of their strategies focus on their bodies, which they consider to be imperfect and which must be improved in order to make them feel content about themselves. According to Rune – a 20-year-old unskilled worker who comes from a middle-class background – everything he does must have a bodily purpose. When asked about drinking alcohol at parties etc. he said the following:

R: It doesn't really appeal to me because it … I don't know, it just seems like, you know, shallow drinking. It seems a bit unimportant. Well, I do not

I: really know what the goal should be. I just think that I'm the type that … it must have a purpose whatever I do, otherwise I won't bother, you know. Everything simply must have a purpose. The food I eat simply must have a purpose … otherwise I might as well not eat it all, no. So, it's not just that I eat it, just because I'm hungry. It's more like, it must have a purpose.
I: So, in relation to food, what does that mean?
R: Well, I'm careful to combine calories and carbohydrates in the right way. There are a few pieces on the Internet by me. I have also written a couple of paragraphs for youth sites. [X site] has a paragraph by me – a complete diet plan, an eight-page chapter on carbohydrates, calories, the various fatty acids, muscle building, fat reduction, etc.
I: Okay. Have you ever counted calories?
R: Yes, I do that often. I always have an idea of what it is. I can't say that I weigh it accurately, but I have a fairly good idea of how many calories and carbohydrates and proteins there are in everything.

Rune states that he does not do anything without a 'purpose'. Even though he does not define purpose clearly in the quote, the examples he gives clearly illustrate that his notion of purposefulness is related to building up his body in accordance with well-defined and rather narrow notions of the ideal physical appearance and physical health. He has acquired considerable expertise on building muscle, reducing fat and losing weight etc., which he not only applies in his own body-building processes, but also shares with other young people on internet sites. Thus, his approach to body building is knowledge-based and rational, but he is clearly also very passionate about it. The relationship between diet and body building clearly takes up an important space in his life, and it contributes to defining what and who he is. However, in order to achieve his own well-defined – and rather narrow – notion of purposeful body building, he has to display considerable self-discipline over his physical behaviour and is at continuous risk of ending up in situations where his physical behaviour might transgress this notion of purposefulness and thus enter a field characterized by purposelessness.

Quite a few of the young boys find themselves in such a situation from time to time. When they are unable to eat or exercise according to their well-defined and rather narrow standards for one reason or another, they often become miserable and feel bad about themselves. For three weeks, 23-year-old Jamil, who is a pharmacy student from a middle-class background, was too busy studying for his exams to exercise; something which he did not feel good about at all:

J: It really means a lot to me and, you know, I really haven't exercised for three weeks since I started studying, you know, for my exams, and I have had a bad conscience, like, every day. It's like every time I came home and I had to sit down and study, I just thought: I could actually do some exercise, and I kept thinking that, but then I just told myself that there was no time for that … [I am not addicted] to exercise, but on the other hand I actually think that I cannot be without it for a long period of time any more. Those three weeks when I was studying for my exams were like hell; I had no time for my girlfriend or exercising or any of the other things that go on in my life.

Studying for exams apparently is not a good excuse for not exercising. Jamil feels that he has to exercise regardless of his exams, but for three weeks he was unable to do so, which gave him a bad conscience. Jamil was caught in a cross-pressure between managing his body and managing his exams. He clearly did not want to drop either of the activities, so choosing to focus on his exams at the expense of his exercise made him feel bad about himself, and not just slightly annoyed or guilty – he describes the three weeks when he did not manage his body through exercise as 'hell'. Like Rune, Jamil seems to associate certain body construction processes with meaning or purposefulness, so that life without these body construction processes loses meaning and purposefulness. And like Rune, the body construction processes Jamil associates with meaning and purposefulness involve considerable self-discipline, without which life apparently loses meaning and purpose. As his life from time to time prevents him from practising this self-discipline, it is continuously on the verge of seeming meaningless and without purpose, which is all the more reason to strive for self-discipline and self-control – the markers of meaning and purpose.

23-year-old Nikolaj, who is a university student from a middle-class family, knows all about this. For a long time, he strived for self-discipline and self-control in most aspects of his life – his body, emotions and school, etc. However, eventually he found that he had lost control over his attempt for self-control, so now he is applying a number of alternative strategies that are helping him contain and counteract his attempt for self-control:

N: I think I have become a bit dependent on the idea of having control over it, I mean self-control. It is very important to me, self-control, but you know.... And you can say that for someone with a very strong urge to control himself it could be a big problem. But for me it has slowly become ... it has changed through ... I have been to a convent a couple of times after high school through a religious practice. Through reading, psychology, meditation and stuff, the desire to have complete self-control slowly has ... developed in another direction, where you learn to set free ... to set yourself free in a way, where you don't put too much effort into it.... So it becomes willpower instead of ... in the beginning it was a kind of self-repression.

Nikolaj makes use of a number of alternative strategies to contain and counteract his attempt for self-control, which he now defines as 'self-repression'. For a long time, he attended a meditation course and, at the time of the interview, he was still doing yoga on a regular basis. These strategies are supposed to set him free from his self-control attempt thereby converting his self-repression to willpower. However, it is a comprehensive process that involves continuous therapeutic and mental work and engagement, which seems to intervene drastically in his life. Giving up his self-disciplining and self-controlling self-optimization strategies, thus, seems to involve other forms of self-disciplining and self-controlling strategies. However, Nikolaj associates these forms of self-disciplining and self-controlling strategies with building up his willpower rather than repressing himself, which makes a huge difference for him. Nikolaj is an exception. The other young boys in the study do not apply counter strategies to contain their self-optimization strategies – as is the case with Rune and Jamil; they struggle to follow them. But his narrative illustrates that there is a fine line between self-optimization, on the one hand, and self-curtailment and even self-undermining on the other. The young boys' strategies may improve some aspects of their selves, but may curtail or undermine others.

Nowhere is self-undermining more manifest than in the self-harm practices to which some of the boys resort. Even though, on the face of it, these practices can be hard to link to self-optimization, the young boys ascribe a range of characteristics to self-harming which resemble other self-optimization strategies. Despite the fact that the psychological literature emphasizes that young people are seldom able to put words to their self-harming behaviour (e.g. Møhl, 2006), the self-harming informants in this study, to some extent, articulate their self-harming behaviour as an intervention in an inadequate self, which can help to build up this self. This is the case with Brian, who is 25, unemployed and comes from a working-class background. He considers his self-harm to be self-punishment:

> I did it to punish myself, because I had failed, because I wasn't good enough ... I smashed my own knuckles.... It was supposed to hurt and bleed.... It was my punishment, and then the pain could leave my body together with the blood.

Brian describes his self-harm as a form of re-socialization: it was about teaching himself a lesson because he was not good enough, and for a moment, as the pain left his body with the blood, he not only felt better, but also like a better person. However, though he kept doing it for years, these effects were short-lived: 'I don't know why I kept doing it because it never worked. It didn't make me feel better', he says.

Self-harming practices, like the other self-optimization strategies, intervene in the self, which is simultaneously built up, undermined and as a consequence undergoes fragmentation and, therefore, leads down roads which seem contradictory and unpredictable. The young boys' self-optimization strategies intervene in their selves, which for better or worse change character due to the self-constructions, producing a continuous need to adjust their self-optimization strategies. However, this can be rather difficult – the young boys may be trapped in particular self-optimization strategies, even though they feel the need to change strategies perhaps because the self, which is the result of self-optimization strategies, is rarely well defined or clear-cut. The strategy can work and not work at the same time; some things get better, others worse. One aspect may become perfect, while another may move further away from perfection. Yet with perfection as a generalized demand made on the self, the result seems to be that young boys – despite their self-optimization strategies – struggle to gain access to *perfect normality* with its attractive field of subject positions. They are not completely marginalized – they are on the border. Though they are not in the field of *perfect normality*, they are not in the identity no man's land either, although they are in constant fear of being left there, devoid of identity, marginalized; a fear that seems to be a constant driver in their self-construction processes. They can always do more, and if they do not, it is 'like hell' as Jamil put it above.

Discussion

This chapter has explored self-construction processes amongst young boys in Denmark who have had experience with eating disorders, self-harm, loneliness and other manifestations of a lack of well-being, which are related to problematizing thematizations of the self. Though the majority of the young boys in the chapter are students or have jobs and lead seemingly conventional lives, the chapter, like the others in this book, has been about marginalization; the kind of marginalization that occurs when someone thinks they will never be good enough or worthy of being inside, so that they can always be legitimately rejected and pushed out. Thus, it has been about the marginalization that occurs when you are on the border, neither inside nor outside, and constantly have to prove that you are good enough and worthy of inclusion.

In the chapter, we have seen how the young boys are struggling to be included and to avoid marginalization: They are struggling to choose the right education, to achieve the right body image, live up to seemingly perfect siblings and classmates, etc. We have seen that the young boys' notion of normality is so narrow that marginalization is considered a constant threat. In the chapter, this situation is analysed against the background of individualization and an increasing neoliberal influence in the Nordic welfare states. The young boys feel tremendous responsibility for constructing themselves, and they feel guilty and ashamed when they do not succeed. Guilt, shame and fear of marginalization seem to be constant travelling companions in the young boys' self-construction processes.

We have zoomed in on two self-construction axes. Each axis consists of a line drawn between two points that constitute different versions of the same aspect of the self. Self-construction is about moving along the line, from one point to the other. In the young boys' accounts, education emerges as a primary driving force in the movement from one point to another, and the choice of education is considered crucial for which self you can construct. At the same time, educational choice contains an inherent duality; even though education should move them from an existing self to a new self, choosing an education which is unconnected to the existing self is not considered possible. This makes the choice of education a significant challenge because it is assumed that they are able to identify the aspects of their existing selves to be taken as a starting point when they choose an education around which to build themselves. However, the young boys are rarely able to do this, not least because they doubt that their selves contain anything of relevance to the selves they would like to build.

The young boys consider their selves to be largely inadequate, and the strategies they apply to self-construction are, therefore, concerned with optimizing those aspects of the self that are felt to be especially lacking – be it physical appearance, educational performance or something else. At times, their self-optimization strategies have the desired effect on these aspects of the self. However, we have seen how Nikolaj's attempts at self-control led to self-repression. Self-optimization, thus, goes hand in hand with a self-destruction. At the very same moment that one aspect is built up, another may be broken down. Thus, *normal perfection* – which to a large extent represents the yardstick for a successful construction of self – inevitably slips through the young boys' fingers. While they imagine that siblings, classmates and all manner of other young people fuse effortlessly with the self-aspects associated with this normative ideal of the self, they experience it as an insurmountable task.

On the one hand, they seem to be *culturally liberated*, as modernity theory (e.g. Ziehe, 1991) advocates: self-construction is thus less about realizing the potentials of a self they are already holders of, than about building up a totally new and radically different self. On the other hand, as outlined by post-structuralist theories (e.g. Butler, 1993), there seems to be an abundance of constraints on the self that they have to build. In other words, it is not a case of a self that the young boys are free to assemble. On the contrary, they appear to be extremely preoccupied with positioning themselves adequately in relation to these constraints. However, when they doubt their own abilities to carry out such positioning, positions which break with these constraints likewise show up in their accounts as some kind of image of what they can expect if they do not develop such abilities.

In this sense, the young boys' accounts are about boundary problems. They take place in a border region between a legitimate and a non-legitimate positioning field, which is likewise a border region between what it is to be someone and what it is to be nothing. And the young boys' self-construction endeavours are about avoiding being left in the non-legitimate field and entering the legitimate field. Yet, in order to enter this field, they must meet a series of criteria, which prevents them from passing through border control. As such, the young boys stay in the border region constantly struggling to get access to the field of *normal perfection*, but without gaining real access, which results in guilt and shame due to a perceived failure to master an apparently elementary, basic condition of *culturally liberated* youth experience: the ability to construct yourself in relation to the ideal of *normal perfection*. As a consequence, they have the feeling of being on the verge of marginalization, always at risk of ending up in the identity no man's land, which tends to make them struggle even harder to cross the border to normal perfection.

It can be hard to find evidence of what would be characterized, in a post-structuralist perspective, as a subversive citing of the dominant subject positions (Butler, 1990). On the contrary, young boys seem to do everything to undertake a normative citing, letting criticism shower down on them when it does not succeed, while to a large extent letting the ideal of *normal perfection* escape criticism. At the same time, however, one can also interpret the young boys' accounts as a demonstration of the pain and misfortune which may be closely associated with this ideal. *Normal perfection*, therefore, comes to be linked with a fear of marginalization which may be the result of an individualized and competition-oriented society (Illeris *et al.*, 2011; Pedersen, 2011), where identity must be constructed, but where the standards are so high that one is constantly on the verge of being excluded as a nobody.

The young boys' accounts seem to be free of any criticism or problematizing of the social and cultural relations which frame their lives. Instead, the young boys direct their criticism and problematizing reflections at themselves (Willig, 2013). However, we have heard about the importance of getting a good education, and we have seen that coming from a less privileged background may be a barrier to meeting this demand (Stephan), whereas having parents with higher education may provide an implicit advantage (Anders). We have also heard about the importance of managing and balancing conflicting demands, and how difficult and painful it may be (Gustav, Jamil), and if you are unable to do it, you may end up imposing this pain on yourself, like Brian, who is unemployed and comes from a less privileged background. This may, therefore, lead one to ask whether, for instance, Stephan and Brian, who have working-class backgrounds, constitute particularly marginalized border figures amongst the youths in the analysis, who all find themselves in a border region. In other words, it is possible to argue that there are some class-related barriers inherent in the young boys' accounts, which are not addressed directly, but which are decisive for whether the young boys are able to handle their self-construction (Skeggs, 2004; Rasborg, 2013).

The relatively narrow focus in the accounts of the self and self-construction can, on the one hand, be seen as an expression of the individualization of society and culture which is typical of the times (e.g. Beck and Beck-Gernsheim, 2002). On the other hand, it can also be understood as a characteristic of the young boys who have been selected to be interviewed. To a large extent, these young boys have had problems to do with a lack of well-being in their lives whereby the self is ascribed a more or less central role. Therefore, they may be considered a biased sample of young boys with a pronounced orientation towards the self. Nonetheless, youth research shows that the idea that a young person is responsible for constructing themselves has gained wide recognition amongst young boys in late modern society (Illeris *et al.*, 2009), just as several investigations have documented the fact that self-oriented problems connected to a lack of well-being are still more widespread amongst young people (Ottosen *et al.*, 2010; Due *et al.*, 2015). This may be an indication that the pain and misfortune that we have seen above – and the fear of marginalization – could be a relatively widespread phenomenon amongst contemporary youth.

In this process, something may also happen to the construction of gender and masculinity. Though the young boys in the chapter do not talk explicitly about these issues, the question is whether they are examples of a new kind of masculinity that transgresses the well-known distinction between dominant and subordinate masculinities: On the one hand, the young boys seem vulnerable and fearful and, thus, victims of an increasingly individualized and competitive society. But their victimization is double-edged: Their vulnerability and fearfulness seem to be a constant impetus for them to work and struggle even harder to succeed with their self-construction; something which involves a great amount of self-determination and goal-orientation, which are the main ingredients in constructions of dominant masculinities. In this sense, what may be associated with a subordinate masculine position may constitute a bridge to a more dominant masculine position. In other words: In a society where notions of normality are becoming narrower and the fear of marginalization is becoming more and more pronounced, vulnerability and fearfulness may no longer be the antithesis of dominant masculinities. If one is not destroyed by one's vulnerability and fearfulness, it may bring one closer to a dominant masculine position.

References

Andenæs, A. (2000) Generalisering. Om ringvirkninger og gjenbruk av resultater fra en kvalitativ undersøkelse. In H. Haavind (ed.) *Kjønn og fortolkende metode. Metodiske muligheter i kvalitativ* forskning, pp. 287–321. Oslo: Gyldendal Akademisk.

Andreasson, J. and Johansson, T. (2014) *The Global Gym. Gender, Health and Pedagogies*. London: Palgrave Macmillan.

Armbjörnsson, F. (2004) *I en klass för sig – genus, klass och sexualitet bland gymnasietjejer*. Stockholm: Ordfront.

Bauman, Z. (1999) *Liquid Modernity*. London: Polity Press.

Beck, U. and Beck-Gernsheim, E. (2002) *Individualization*. London: SAGE Publications Ltd.

Butler, J. (1990) *Gender Trouble. Feminism and Subversion of Identity*. New York: Routledge.

Butler, J. (1993) *Bodies that Matter. On the Discursive Limits of 'Sex'*. New York: Routledge.

Cawood, S. H. (2007) *Velkommen til pussyland: Unge positionerer sig i et seksualiseret medielandskab*. PhD diss., Danish School of Education.

Connell, R. W. (1995) *Masculinities*. Cambridge: Polity Press.

Davies, B. and Harré, R. (1990) Positioning and the discursive production of selves, *Journal for the Theory of Social Behaviour* 20(1): 43–63.

Due, P., Diderichsen, F., Meilstrup, C., Nordentoft, M., Obel, C. and Sandbæk. A. (2015) *Børn og unges mentale helbred Forekomst af psykiske symptomer og lidelser og mulige forebyggelsesindsatser*. Copenhagen: Vidensråd for forebyggelse.

Erikson, E. H. (1968) *Identity: Youth and Crisis*. New York: Norton.

Fangen, K., Fossan, K. and Mohn, F. A. (eds) (2010) *Inclusion and Exclusion of Young Adult Immigrants: Barriers and Bridges*. Surrey: Ashgate.

Fog, J. and Kvale, S. (eds) (1995) *Artikler om interviews*. Aarhus: Center for kvalitativ metodeudvikling, Psykologisk Institut, Aarhus Universitet.

Foucault, M. (1991) *The History of Sexuality Vol. 1. An Introduction*. USA: Penguin Books.

Giddens, A. (1991) *Modernity and Self-Identity: Self and Society in the Late Modern Age.* Stanford: Stanford University Press.
Gilliam, L. (2009) *De umulige børn og det ordentlige menneske – identitet, ballade og muslimske fællesskaber blandt etniske minoritetsbørn.* Aarhus: Aarhus Universitetsforlag.
Haavind, H. (2000) På jakt etter kjønnede betydninger. In H. Haavind (ed.) *Kjønn og fortolkende metode. Metodiske muligheter i kvalitativ* forskning. Oslo: Gyldendal Akademisk. *Kön och tolkning. Metodiske möjligheter i kvalitativ forskning*, pp. 7–59. Oslo: Gyldendal Norsk Forlag.
Hutters, C. and Sørensen, N. U. (2015) Eksamensangst – et voksende problem I konkurrencesamfundet. In H. Hvass (ed.) *Eksamensangst. Et problem vi skal løse i fællesskab.* Frederiksberg: Samfundslitteratur.
Illeris, K., Katznelson, N., Nielsen, J. C., Simonsen, B. and Sørensen, N. U. (2009) *Ungdomsliv. Mellem individualisering og standardisering.* Frederiksberg: Samfundslitteratur.
Johansson, T. (1997) *Den skulpterade kroppen. Gymkultur, friskvård och estetik.* Stockholm: Carlssons Bokförlag.
Johansson, T. (2006) *The Transformation of Intimacy. Gender and Sexuality in Contemporary Youth Culture.* Aldershot: Ashgate.
Katznelson, N. (2004) *Udsatte unge, aktivering og uddannelse – Dømt til individualisering.* PhD diss., Roskilde University.
Kofoed, J. (2003) *Elevpli. Inklusion-eksklusionsprocesser blandt børn i skolen.* PhD diss., Danish University of Education.
Kroger, J. (2007) *Identity Development. Adolescence through Adulthood.* London: SAGE Publications.
Møhl, B. (2006) *At skære smerten bort – en bog om cutting og anden selvskadende adfærd.* Copenhagen: PsykiatriFondens Forlag.
Murning, S. (2013) *Social differentiering og mobilitet i gymnasiet. Kulturel praksis, sociale positioner og mulighed for inklusion.* PhD diss. Aarhus University.
Nielsen, J. C., Sørensen, N. U. and Osmec, M. N. (2010) *Når det er svært at være ung i DK – unges trivsel og mistrivsel i tal.* Copenhagen: Center for Ungdomsforskning, Aarhus Universitet.
Ottosen, M. H., Andersen, D., Nielsen, L. P., Lausten, M. and Stage, S. (2010) *Børn og unge i Danmark. Velfærd og trivsel 2010.* Copenhagen: SFI – Det Nationale Forskningscenter for Velfærd.
Pedersen, O. K. (2011) *Konkurrencestaten.* Copenhagen: Hans Reitzels Forlag.
Pless, M. (2014) Stories from the margins of the educational system, *Journal of Youth Studies* 17(2): 236–251.
Rasborg, K. (2013) Individualisering og social differentiering i den refleksive modernitet. *Dansk Sociologi* nr. 4/24: 9–35.
Rose, N. (1999) *Governing the Soul: The Shaping of the Private Self.* London: Routledge.
Schiffer, K. and Schatz, E. (2008) *Marginalization, Social Inclusion and Health: Experiences Based on the Work of Correlation – European Network Social Inclusion and Health.* Amsterdam: Correlation Network.
Sennett, R. (1998) *The Corrosion of Character. The Personal Consequences of Work in the New Capitalism.* New York: Norton.
Shildrick, T., MacDonald, R., Webster, C. and Garthwaite, K. (2012) *Poverty and Insecurity: Life in Low-Pay, No-Pay Britain.* Bristol: Policy Press.
Skeggs, B. (2004) *Class, Self, Culture.* London: Routledge.

Staunæs, D. (2004) *Køn, etnicitet og skoleliv*. Frederiksberg: Forlaget Samfundslitteratur.
Søndergaard, D. M. (1996) *Tegnet på kroppen. Køn: Koder og konstruktioner blandt unge voksne i akademia*. Copenhagen: Museum Tusculanum.
Søndergaard, D. M. (2005) Making sense of gender, age, power and disciplinary position: intersecting discourses in the academy, *Feminism and Psychology* 15(2): 189–208.
Søndergaard, D. M. (2014) Social exclusion anxiety: Bullying and the enactment of exclusion amongst children at school. In R. M. Schott, and D. M. Søndergaard (eds) *School Bullying: New Theories in Context*, pp. 47–80. Cambridge: Cambridge University Press.
Sørensen, N. U. (2008) Where the ordinary ends and the extreme begins: Aesthetics and masculinities among young men. In T. Schilhab, M. Juelskjær and T. Moser (eds) *Learning Bodies*, pp. 131–162. Copenhagen: Danish School of Education Press.
Sørensen, N. U., Grubb, A., Madsen, I. W. and Nielsen, J. C. (2011) *Når det er svært at være ung i DK. Unges beretninger om mistrivsel og ungdomsliv*. Copenhagen: Center for Ungdomsforskning, Aarhus Universitet.
Sørensen, Niels U., Hutters, C., Katznelson, N. and Juul, T. M. (2013) *Unges motivation og læring. 12 eksperter om motivationskrisen i uddannelsessystemet*. Copenhagen: Hans Reitzels Forlag.
Wetherell, M. and Potter, J. (1992) *Mapping the Language of Racism*. New York: Columbia University Press.
Willig, R. (2013) *Kritikkens U-vending*. Copenhagen: Hans Reitzels Forlag.
Ziehe, T. (1991) *Zeitvergleiche. Jugend in kulturellen Modernisierungen*. Weinheim: Juventa.

8 Doped Manhood

Negotiating Fitness Doping and Masculinity in an Online Community

Jesper Andreasson and Thomas Johansson

In different sporting venues, the notion of masculinity has followed the imagery of athleticism like a cultural ally for centuries (Guttmann, 1991; Kimmel, 1996; Messner, 1992; Mosse, 1996). Through the mimicking of physically demanding practices performed by older men and idols, young men have been said to internalize normative masculine values through sport. In addition, devoting time to strengthening the body, building muscles and projecting an attitude of domination has historically been related to violence, warfare and the building of nations, thus implying an interest in cultivating what Mosse (1996) describes as 'the masculine stereotype'. The cultural history of contemporary gym and fitness culture makes no exception from this kind of cultural narrative (Budd, 1997; Denham, 2008). Klein (1993), for example, who conducted one of the first bodybuilding studies in the early 1990s, describes bodybuilding as a predominantly masculine preoccupation. He also describes homophobia, hyper-masculinity and the use of performance- and image-enhancing drugs (PED) as institutionalized phenomena in this kind of physical culture (Locks and Richardson, 2012; McGrath and Chananie-Hill, 2009).

The relationship between PED use and gender is complex. The usual position, in the literature, is that the main trigger for its use is men's desire to gain muscle mass and to construct a masculine identity (Dimeo, 2007; Parkinson and Evans, 2006; Sas-Nowosielski, 2006; McCreary and Sasse, 2000; Andreasson and Johansson, 2014). Looking at previous research on gender and doping one can see that the use also has been understood as an outcome of a search for a competitive edge within sport, as risk taking, as an integral feature of hegemonic masculinity, and thus as an expression of some kind of societal over-conformity when it comes to the construction of masculinity (Andreasson, 2013; Monaghan, 1999, 2012; Thualagant, 2012). At the same time, however, PED use has also been analysed in terms of deviance and marginalization. It has been connected to mixed abuse, crime, violence and the margins of society (DuRant *et al.*, 1995; Lentillon-Kaestner and Ohl, 2011). Existing images of PED users are often quite judgemental, and the use has also been understood as an expression of a marginalized, uncertain and outdated masculinity (Bach, 2005: Klein, 1993).

Internationally, official regimes and public health organizations conduct fairly comprehensive anti-doping measures. As a consequence, numerous 'new' ways to learn about and access these types of drug have emerged. This is not least the case in Sweden where legislation does not simply forbid the possession and distribution of doping substances – as it does, for example, in many other European countries – but also the presence of these substances in the body. This development, combined with technological development in recent decades, has resulted in the emergence of new ways of accessing and discussing PED. Social media and different internet forums, for example, have become part of a new self-help culture in which people can anonymously approach these subjects, discuss their experience of using them and minimize the possibility of encounters with the police. What we see today is the development of new doping trajectories that sanction acceptable and unacceptable masculinities. As expressed by Monaghan (2012), there is a gap between PED users' actions and societal expectations. Within this gap, we will suggest that it is possible for PED users to renegotiate their practice in relation to possible health warnings, legal sanctions and, of course in terms of gender, as they formulate a rationale for their practice.

In this chapter, we will focus on this emerging complexity in the understanding of PED use and gender. Empirically, we will focus on PED users' narratives found on a Swedish online community called Flashback. We aim to explore how participants in this community learn about and negotiate the meanings of PED use and how such negotiations can be understood in terms of gender, masculinity and marginalization processes. Furthermore, we are interested in exploring how PED use and online fitness communities sometimes challenge dominant regimes of masculinity and gender equality, and also how the positionality of the marginal and central must be understood as dynamic, contradictory, mutable and contextual. We are interested in questions such as: What kinds of understanding of PED use are manifested in the online community and how is the practice related to current legislation and official government policy? We are also interested in the kinds of symbolic language regarding drug use that are developed within the community, and how its use is continuously negotiated in terms of different notions of masculinity.

Subcultures, Marginalization and Mainstreaming

In the chapter, we will explore the dynamic interplay between 'accepted' and legitimate identities and alternative or even 'deviant' identities in terms of hegemonic and marginalized masculinity. Connell's (1995) understanding of marginalization situates and positions masculinities within a gender theory framework configured by hegemonic masculinity. Thus, marginalized masculinities are often referred to as 'outcasts', or as Cheng (1999, p. 295) expresses it, as those men who have a 'disadvantaged unequal membership'. Thus, in many ways, marginalized masculinities are located in relation to a masculinity that holds a cultural privilege. Dahl-Michelson and Nyheim (2014) develop the notion of marginalized masculinities as not only those that could not meet hegemonic standards, but also did not operate or make sense of their identities through hegemonic gender norms. As we will see, there is a dynamic interplay between dominant ideals of masculinity in society at large, and more specific and subcultural ideals nurtured in certain social and cultural contexts. Bodybuilding culture may, for example, foster *protest masculinity*, that is, a marginal masculinity involving antisocial activities. Another way of looking at this could be to use the concept of *hypermasculinity*, which can be described as a strong exaggeration of certain stereotypical male qualities, such as the emphasis on muscular strength, aggression, sexual virility and the subordination of women (Mosher and Sirkin, 1984; DeReef, 2006). At the same time, within the subculture, these positions or identities can in fact be combined with a desire to fit in to the dominant masculinity (McDowell, Rootham and Hardgrove, 2014). Analytically, it is this ambivalence, and the dynamic and complex interplay of protest and dominance, as well as hypermasculinity and hegemonic masculinity, that we focus on in this chapter on doped masculinities in an online community. In addition, we will also discuss the role of digital media when it comes to shaping and questioning the experience of marginalization.

We will use the concept of subculture in order to investigate how particular masculinities are created through social interaction within the online community. More specifically, we will look closer at the interplay between subcultures and the mainstreaming of certain body ideals and practices. According to Fornäs (1995, p. 112):

> One problem with earlier subcultural studies was their exclusive focus on homologies, on the ways in which subcultural styles fitted together into homogeneous totalities. This has to be counteracted by an attendance to the inner differences, tensions and contradictions within subcultures and groups, which newer studies of social relations show as an increasingly important element in late modern lifestyles and life forms.

Becoming a member of and joining an online community, for example, involves aspects of both identity construction and learning (Wenger, 1998). We suggest that such a process of learning also affects the individuals' understanding of the self and maybe more specifically the notion of masculinity being idealized (Becker, 1953). As individuals gain knowledge and discuss theories about how to reach desired goals, they increasingly become integrated in the community. As a consequence, some people will then choose to take drugs, thus challenging the dominant norms and values in mainstream society, and at the same creating their own spaces of alterity. Analysing an online community can thus give insight into the ways in which a particular subculture can create a space in which members simultaneously can feel elevated and marginalized. Following the discussion of subcultures as contradictory and ambivalent social constructions, we will also look deeper into how the PED users' perceptions of themselves adhere to different and sometimes even conflictual gender ideals.

Fieldwork on the Internet

The chapter is based on 'written accounts resulting from fieldwork studying the cultures and communities that emerge from online computer-mediated or

Internet-based communications' (Kozinets, 2010, 58). We have sampled discussions posted on an online forum and community called Flashback. This platform is hosted in Sweden and, although there are occasional contributors from other Nordic countries, the postings are mainly in Swedish. At the same time, there are many possible sites and online communities to be found across the world in which criminalized and marginalized activities, such as PED use, are discussed and promoted (see, for example, Smith and Stewart, 2012).

On Flashback, one can read that this is 'Sweden's largest forum for freedom of expression, opinion, and independent thinking' (Flashback, n.d.). Anyone with an internet connection can read different postings and learn from other community members' experiences. A person can also create an account and, with a fictive username, start up different threads and discussions with other members. Discussions basically concern just about anything, including sport, sex, home, culture, travel and more. But, due to the fact that the forum facilitates the expression of opinions anonymously, many discussions concern prohibited activities. One popular theme is drugs, with PED representing a subcategory.

Although the use of usernames precludes the confirmation of gender and other kinds of demographic information about community members, the postings analysed are apparently dominated by men. As stated earlier, in previous research the use of PED has also been considered a highly gendered activity. Analysing postings on Flashback gives us not only access to different discussions on PED, it also enables us to analyse how this practice is understood and negotiated in terms of masculinity within the community. In conducting our online ethnography, we have been inspired by Kozinets (2010) who developed a specifically designed method for studying different online forums and communities, that is, 'netnography'. Our analytic focus is on different text extracts published on Flashback, taking the perspective that these extracts and the ensuing discussions can be viewed as cultural manifestations through which the understanding of a particular activity is constantly negotiated (Kozinets, 2010; Porter, 1997).

In our sampling of postings, we initially focused on the contents of two main themes connected with discussions on PED. The first theme was named 'Doping substances', and the second 'Course reports'. At the time of analysis, these themes consisted of 107 and 1,741 threads (sub-themed discussions), respectively – threads in which understandings of different kinds of PED were negotiated and reports on personal courses recited. As suggested by Kozinets (2010), data collection in netnography does not happen in isolation from data analysis. In our fieldwork, we have tried to understand the reasoning of community members, and to read different postings from the perspective that they are rich sources of cultural information. Our sampling of postings and discussions has then been distinguished by an intertwining of analytical relevance, and the richness, heterogeneity and interactivity manifested amongst participants as they engaged in different discussions within the community. Put differently: In the selection of quotes we have aimed to capture narratives in which PED use is discussed dynamically within this community and how these discussions can be understood both in terms of dominant and marginalized conceptions of masculinity.

Although community members on Flashback can use fictive usernames, and most likely are aware that their postings will be stored and transmitted, some aspects of this study call for an extended ethical concern (Walther, 2002). This chapter focuses on postings in which community members discuss and sometimes promote a criminalized activity. This means that the quotations we have chosen for our analysis could have legal repercussions, if the authorities were to locate the particular IP address of a community member. In this sense, it is a highly marginalized community that is in focus.

To protect the identity of community members quoted we took the following measures. First, we created fictitious usernames for all of the participants. Second, we translated the postings, which are originally in Swedish, into English, making it more difficult to use available search engine technology in order to track down specific postings and community members. Third, in our sampling of postings we were careful not to focus on particularly sensitive information. This means that information of a personal character, such as the mentioning of a specific gym, person or the home town of a community member, has been left out (Hsiung, 2000).

The remainder of this chapter is structured as follows. First, we will explain how PED use is discussed on Flashback, trying to present the kind of community being the unit of analysis and also situating the community in relation to, for example, current legislation and popular perceptions on drug use in Swedish society. Consequently, we will here present the texture of the community, discussing it in terms of how a marginal position is gradually embraced and legitimized. Then we will zoom in on the practice and the kind of symbolic language that is developed within the community and connected to the practice. Finally, we will analyse how the drug use practice is understood and negotiated in terms of different notions of masculinity and how idealized masculinities, when re-contextualized, are seen as marginal and vice versa. Following this line of thought and structure in the chapter, we will we suggest that it also becomes possible to examine how the drug use practice is related to dominant regimes of masculinity and ideals of gender equality within mainstream society.

(Re)Negotiating PED

The subject of the pros and cons of PED use is popular on Flashback and attracts lively debate. These kinds of discussions are highly relevant for many reasons. First, they are important if we want to understand how different members negotiate and understand the use of PED. Second, such an understanding could clarify the different ways in which different members relate to PED and how dominant perspectives on PED use are formed and, sometimes, challenged within the community. Third, they constitute significant empirical material that could be analysed in relation to Swedish legislation and official state policy.

The section on Flashback entitled 'Course reports' contains extensive discussions about PED. Often, a seeming novice who expresses a desire to learn more about the practice initiates these discussions. In one posting, for example, a member explains that he has been doing strength training for a while, without reaching his desired goals. He is thinking about starting a course of steroids in order to further boost his muscular development. He is a little hesitant, however, regarding the possible side effects. He reaches out for some advice on what to do, and gets the following answer:

> Let me tell you, I was in your situation when I was about 18 years old. I never had a drink, I trained seriously without using steroids and I followed a healthy diet, but I wanted to get results faster. I did not want to wait. But I waited anyway. For one year I waited and built a better foundation to start with. So now I have been on steroids since I was 19, and today I am 20 years old. It is the best thing I've ever done. During this year I have grown enormously – I've gained at least 10 kg of muscle mass. About my decision to start using at the young age of 19? Well, actually I'm really happy with it, and I feel 100 times better than before. I look forward to every new day. But also, if you want to start using, only do it if you can accept that there may be side effects and be aware that it's easy to get stuck, never wanting to get off the juice again.
>
> (WaitOrNot)

WaitOrNot quickly adopts the role of the experienced user. He also describes his personal process of deciding to engage in drug use. In addition, he also presents a complete chart of his own courses of steroids and lets readers know what to do and expect, and how to avoid potential side effects. In the same thread, several other community members describe their similar PED use trajectories. Altogether, these postings articulate a process of learning about the practice and a way to understand it. Information is distributed and testimonies given. Different variables, such as age, strength-training history, drug experience, health, bodybuilding goals and possible side effects are integrated into the narratives. Consequently, this information represents quite a comprehensive platform that new members can take advantage of when deciding whether to engage in PED use. What we also have here is narratives by young men (novices), to some extent feeling physically marginal to the cultural hegemonic ideal, seeking ways to become part of it. Sought for is a key to transition from the marginal to the hegemonic body ideal, albeit through illegal means. Many of the Flashback postings are also definitely encouraging when discussing the ways to complete such a transition. But there are also critical and dissuasive opinions, such as the following:

> There are plenty of negative aspects of steroids that people do not seem so eager to talk about openly. As it is, I really believe that you should not start with steroids when you're, like, 18 or 20. This is a decision that has to

mature over time. You have to mature both physically and mentally. A teenager is not mature! I will always argue for this statement. One of my best friends is an old bodybuilding profile today. He started using steroids when he was 16. Today, at nearly 30, his system is totally fucked up. He gets problems with asthma and other things when he is off the steroids. He only gets horny at odd times, and more. He really regrets that he started so early.

(NoSteroids)

Although Flashback is considered a highly liberal forum with few limitations as to the type of subjects and practices that can be discussed, it is not a homogenous enterprise. Community members do not always agree with one another, and when it comes to the use of PED many different positions are explored and developed. At the same time, the dominant attitude towards PED, as expressed on Flashback, appears to be clearly encouraging, or at least cautiously favourable. As a consequence, when NoSteroids posts his critical view of PED use, other members are quick to counter this narrative, formulating vocabularies of motive and trying to legitimize the practice (Monaghan, 2012). For example, some postings dismiss him, describing his bodybuilding friend with problems as a person who probably started without knowing what he was doing, and is therefore an uninformed and ignorant user. Others talk about health and the importance of using lower dosages and taking longer breaks between steroid courses. This is clearly an issue that community members find relevant. While potential health risks associated with the practice are acknowledged, they are also presented adjacent to advice regarding how to recognize and deal with them. What is taking place here is a critical discussion and social diffusion of knowledge regarding PED use. Furthermore, through this socially constituted process within the community the marginal position, the experience of being a man who uses PED in order to build muscles, is legitimized and somewhat also idolized. Knowledge on PED use then becomes a resource within the community through which a marginal position is questioned.

In the postings, members discuss PED and analyse different kinds of substances in terms of bodily expectations and possible side effects. These discussions can thus be understood as part of an ethno-pharmacological culture through which the instrumental use of PED is partly normalized and rationalized within the community (Monaghan, 1999, 2002). Through the different threads, members can read and learn from each other. The knowledge being shared is also presented in association with a medical discourse. In developing their arguments and theories about how best to use the drugs, the community members ignore the ethical aspects of this use, focusing instead on how different substances affect the body. In this way, the understanding of the practice is constructed as if it belongs, at least partly, to a health-promoting agenda and is thus quite the opposite of official Swedish policy, which is often described as having a less knowledgeable foundation. This is obvious in the quotation below in which one community member tries to explain his views on Swedish legislation against PED and government policy.

> Regarding doping substances, I think that Swedish government policy is idiotic. Certainly it is true that many people commit violent crimes due to the use of steroids, but on the other hand there are also many who manage their bodybuilding hobby in an exemplary fashion. Doping should clearly be legal (I'm talking about hobby doping; obviously I don't defend cheating in competitions). The doping ban is a consequence of the government's feministic hatred of men. Smash the state!
>
> (Legalise)

Certainly, there is not much identification with a political agenda of gender equality built into this posting. Instead, the use of PED is understood as a viable path to secure manhood, and a way to construct a hyper-masculine body. Above, the understanding of the practice is detached from how it may be used in organized sport in order to cheat, and is instead connected to a more neo-liberal, individualistic ideology. Also, in many postings the right to choose what to do with your own body is asserted as a rationale for the practice. This rationale is thus formulated in relation to perceived changes in society and to the meanings of manhood and a gender-equal society. What we are witnessing here is the construction of an alternative and subcultural understanding of masculinity and a response to the experience of being condemned by (feminist) representatives of mainstream society (Sykes and Matza, 1957).

Clearly there is an awareness of the risks attached to PED use being expressed within the community. The choice of using PED is constantly being negotiated by different members; in these discussions, different positions are adopted as regards the understanding of the practice. For some members, it seems to be mainly understood as a possible way to boost muscular masculinity, while others are more careful in their approach, trying to problematize the practice in relation to age, maturity, goals, risks, health and more. One thing clearly being negotiated by different members within the community is also how the practice can be understood in terms of body ideals, gender and masculinity. This will be further developed in the two following sections.

PED and the Genetic Max

Like many other communities, Flashback can be understood as part of a culture with its own ways of talking about and understanding particular activities. Using different illicit substances while building up a solid body can thus be understood as the construction of a subcultural affiliation in which a symbolic language game and specific terminology are developed. One term often used when discussing PED, body ideals and muscular development is the 'genetic max'.

> Certainly it is reasonable to assume that we all have a genetic max, but the problem is to determine what that max is, for each individual. We all have different preconditions. If we look at testosterone production, for example: it varies quite a lot between different individuals. Then, in addition to the

testo, there are a hell of a lot of other factors that will affect how easily you can gain muscles (thyroid hormones, growth hormones, insulin). Your age is also a factor. It must be really hard to tell if someone reached their genetic max, when there are so many factors. One can always try to change something when it comes to training, nutrition, rest, etc.

(Mr.Testo)

The relationship between PED use and the genetic max is complicated. Sometimes the term genetic max is understood as a means to reach bodily goals that exceed a person's genetic max, and sometimes it is more about using PED in order to reach the max. The conceptual discussions about the genetic max can therefore be understood as a mixture of conceptions of physical potential and masculine fantasies, sometimes dramatic, about what is humanly possible to achieve (Locks and Richardson, 2012). This becomes evident in the posting below in which a member describes the expectations he had on his first course of steroids:

'No Guts, No Glory'.

Mission accomplished! It's time to get real! Be great or be nothing! I am so fucking powered up now. It will surely be interesting to see how things turn out at the gym. While working out clean, I have already managed to increase the number of reps on some exercises, despite my diet, so there will probably be like a swelling explosion with the juice [PED] in my system!

(FirstInjection)

Clearly PED is understood here as a symbol of a rite of passage (Gennep, 2004), enhancing different features of masculinity. The expectations of bodily possibilities 'with juice in the system' are high. This kind of approach, in which PED is viewed as something of a miracle cure, expected to give visible results in a matter of days, is expressed in a number of threads. Most often, the discussions are connected to ideas about reaching one's genetic max, being transformed into a new and better self and becoming more of a man. Furthermore, when it comes to postings regarding the possible ways to achieve one's genetic max without using PED, the views are quite pessimistic. This becomes evident in the posting below where a community member explains what he thinks of natural bodybuilding.

All these 'natty' [natural] bodybuilders have given people a distorted image of what is possible to achieve in a natural way. Natural bodybuilding is just something shitty that the industry created in order to sell us a bunch of crap. 'Oh look, he is natural.' 'If I only buy the same protein drinks as him, and follow the advice he presents in his blog, then I can also be like him!' The truth is that steroids are used on the 'natural' bodybuilding scene. Another thing: I don't understand the logic of those who are constantly saying 'I think he is clean just because his physique can be reached by natural means.' […] It's also worth checking out the time it takes for all these 'natties' to reach their maximum natural potential. It doesn't take two to three years to reach one's genetic max; it takes a fucking lifetime, and in the meantime, you have to have experience and knowledge.

On Flashback, there are quite a few postings in which the use of PED is rationalized in different ways. PED is obviously an intrinsic part of this online culture: there are even members who discuss ways to use PED to change the basic conditions of the human body, to exceed the limits of human genes and reach the genetic max. In this sense, we are witnessing the construction of a transformable masculinity and the development of strong ideas about scientifically engineered 'super-bodies' (see also Bakhtin, 1984; Pitts, 2003). This kind of narrative is also strengthened by the sceptical perspective put forward regarding the chances of getting results from natural bodybuilding. The natural bodybuilder is seen as more or less a moral fantasy – a 'fitness cream puff' who sells useless products for financial gain.

Making Manhood and Notions of Masculinity

From the different postings on Flashback it is obvious that the (anticipated) effects of PED are largely connected to the notion of masculinity. Below, one community member explicitly tries to situate his PED use in relation to manhood, career and sexual virility.

> I have experienced really good effects. I have become extremely focused – more of a man. At work, yeah, when I talk, people shut up and show respect. Since my goal in life is to dope myself as much as possible, to achieve as much as possible, I have always seen my job as a parenthetical detail – something you just have to do until you arrive at your real job, the gym. So I've never really invested in pursuing a career. But still, I speak more in front of people. I have become more sincere and upright. I give and take more […] not to mention the insane sex drive you get on testo – makes women think you are from Planet Porno.
>
> (HeMan)

The posting above vividly captures an understanding of PED that involves an anticipated process of transformation. The PED use is basically connected to adjectives describing the self as becoming more of something, such as 'focused', 'ambitious', 'muscular' and 'virile'. Other posters describe how they have developed greater interest in furthering their education, performing at the top of their class in university and more. Despite the occasional mention of other, negative consequences, these qualities are basically described as being desired. They are connected to the construction of a dominant, muscular and self-assured (hyper) masculinity. It is a rational and performance-oriented masculinity that emerges in the postings. This masculine position is further developed below, where a community member constructs a hypothetical experiment while simultaneously trying to develop his ideas on the limit-pushing potential of PED.

> Think about this: Wouldn't it be fun to conduct this experiment. Joe works as an officer and his brother works at Lindex [Swedish women's lingerie chain], selling women's underwear. You sneak some oestrogen into Joe's coffee and give his brother testo instead. You do this for a couple of months. Talk about different results! What do you think would happen? Yeah, I think I know. In this way we would play out the extremes against each other, to see what really happens, within a particular profession. Testo could be EXTREMELY beneficial. Ha, ha, yeah, and it would be fun to see the outcome. The total ruin! From officer to army bitch! Ha, ha. I guess that the other military boys wouldn't have to pay for porn mags any more. And the brother would probably be reported for sexual harassment at Lindex, found by the surveillance monitors jerking off, while watching the women trying on lingerie in the changing rooms.
>
> (TheProfessor)

It is obvious that the use of PED works as a powerful symbol of an expected transformation and construction of masculinity. Although not all of the features that result are desired, the outcomes of PED use clearly relate to a masculine and heterosexual stereotype. Aggressiveness and dominance (or the lack thereof), sexual virility and callous sexual attitudes towards women are constructed as part of a hyper-masculine identity, fuelled with testosterone. However, while many of the postings seem to rationalize PED use, constructing it as a masculinity booster or anchor, there are also narratives in which its use is understood as an activity that puts aspects of manhood at risk. This is exemplified in the posting below.

> I actually think it's hard to get anywhere in your career, if we're talking about more qualified jobs. If I were an employer I would probably hesitate before employing a guy who was too big and had obvious side effects of steroids. Imagine that nice office, and a guy who just wears GASP clothing, as regular shirts don't fit. Hmmm. After all, my experience from different workplaces is that there's a lot of bullshit said behind the backs of people who look like they're doped.
>
> (TheEmployer)

In the posting above, the use of PED is understood in quite a pessimistic way when related to career advancement. It exemplifies the negotiation between a muscular and dominant hyper-masculinity and what are perceived to be other important aspects of manhood. The doped body, that is the dominant and intimidating body, is here seen as something of a threat to employability and the imagery of the breadwinner. Although PED use is mainly discussed in positive terms on Flashback, it is not always understood as a winning concept. Clearly, the understanding of the practice is situated and somehow shifting. This becomes abundantly clear below, where a young single dad, after asking for advice regarding the risk of losing custody if he were to be caught by the police, tries to explain his perspective on life, drugs and fatherhood.

> The thing is that I didn't seek out family life. I thought that I would be with my girlfriend for life, that we would get our education and live the life of a child-free couple. Then came the news that she was pregnant, and she wanted to keep it, and my whole world collapsed. I played along for a year. After two years I began to question my life situation on a daily basis. Then I left my family after 2.5 years. Now, I want to start a new life. The plan is to move, get a degree, focus on my training and start a course of steroids. Basically, I want to do what I want, before I start a family (I was 22 when I became a father). Am I selfish leaving my child? Yes, but what about mothers who give birth to a child against the man's will and think it's going to work?
>
> (DaddyNo)

The above posting attracted a lot of interest. DaddyNo did not, however, get many comments about custody issues as he had initially hoped. Instead, several members condemned DaddyNo's line of reasoning. To be clear: the discussion on Flashback is mainly encouraging when it comes to PED use, but this is obviously not the case when the use is situated as in DaddyNo's story. Instead, DaddyNo was strongly advised not to use drugs. Several community members become clearly irritated, calling him 'immature' and 'self-centred' and 'an idiot with no character'. He is instructed to rethink his priorities in life and to take responsibility for his actions. One community member summarizes the advice contained in the thread by saying: 'Be a man and take care of your child. I know what it means to grow up without a father and I would never expose my own child to that.' Clearly, there are different notions of masculinity being juggled in this discussion of PED and PED use. The masculine body, the dominant man, the employee, the breadwinner and, particularly, the responsible and mature father are all integrated into the negotiation of manhood and steroids. The masculinities constructed in the postings are thus understood slightly differently, depending on situation and how the (potential) PED use is contextualized by the community members.

PED, Subcultural Practices and Mainstreaming

The Internet community studied in this chapter can be read as an example of a transformational process in which ordinary rules and regulations are questioned and partly put out of play. What is studied here is a process of deregulation and de-normalization in which the notion of masculinity and the acceptance of certain forms of drug use is extended and expanded considerably. This process of normalization and acceptance of drug use within the community is constructed in alliance with neo-liberal attitudes and the cult of the individual, making it possible to transgress and challenge norms and regulations (Foucault, 1994; Miller and Rose, 2008). These processes are, of course, also connected to a more general discussion of how neo-liberal discourses have penetrated our way of thinking about individual freedom and health (Rich and Evans, 2013). Certainly, the gym and fitness industry, and the practices carried out in these contexts, fits nicely into a neo-liberal world view, in which people are considered individually responsible for their own body and health. In some ways, the striving for the perfect body even makes it logically necessary, for instance, to challenge legislation on PED and to develop subcultural norms and values. And in the Internet community studied in this chapter, people can find extensive knowledge about and substantial support for the necessity of using certain means, and certain illicit drugs, to achieve their goals.

In the different postings, we can see how different body ideals and notions of masculinity are pitted against each other, and how a marginalized masculinity and identity in the subcultural context is sometimes regarded as a dominant and hegemonic ideal. In some postings, it also appears obvious how pride in one's physical transformation, the attainment of an idealized masculinity and the symbolically loaded language expressing high expectations, can turn rapidly into something perceived as shameful behaviour when the circumstances are laid out in a problematic way (Sparkes, Batey and Owen, 2012). The notion of masculinity attached to the understanding of PED use, as it is expressed here within the community, should be understood as a scattered and uncertain construction. Within the community, it is most evoked to counter and challenge reductive representations put forward by Swedish official policy and media, for example (Mogensen, 2011). This form of protest masculinity, however, is not always idealized within the community. Masculinity here is, for example, constructed in the intersection between a muscular masculinity and ideas about the employable man and the responsible father. When one member expresses a desire to be an absent father and to simultaneously focus on training and muscle development with the help of PED, it is met with strong condemnation. Fatherhood and maturity are apparently understood as superior masculine ideals. Consequently, abdicating one's role as father and leaving an innocent child behind is not legitimate in the search for freedom and a muscular masculinity.

Many of the behaviours and bodily appearances constructed within this subculture could be regarded as signs of marginalization – of a marginal masculinity in society at large. However, what we find here is an interesting relationship between hegemonic and marginalized hyper-masculinities. In the world of the bodybuilder, the marginal masculinity in certain senses becomes dominant. In one sense, achieving a muscular and well-trained body is regarded as a core aspect of masculinity within the community. In another sense, however, the practice – the trajectory – leading to such a hyper-masculine body is also challenged by other highly valued masculine ideals. What makes this even more complex today is a trend towards the normalization of the hard-core muscle culture cultivated in the fitness and bodybuilding context, leading to changes in attitudes towards drugs, hyper-bodies and protest masculinity in society at large. To a certain extent, we are now seeing hyper-masculinity becoming normalized and brought into mainstream culture. If we look at the film industry and its celebration of muscular masculinity, this becomes obvious. Over time, bodybuilding culture has moved from being an extreme subculture to being integrated into the mainstream, feeding into contemporary masculine ideals and creating a new bodily ethos.

References

Andreasson, J. (2013) Between beauty and performance: Towards a sociological understanding of trajectories to drug use in a gym and bodybuilding context, *Scandinavian Sport Studies Forum* 4: 60–90.

Andreasson, J. and Johansson, T. (2014) *The Global Gym. Gender, Health and Pedagogies*. Houndmills: Palgrave Macmillan.

Bach, A. R. (2005) *Mænd och muskler. En bog om stryketæning og anabole steroider [Men and muscles. A book about weight lifting and anabolic steroids]*. Copenhagen: Tiderna skifter.

Bakhtin, M. (1984) *Rabelais and His World*. Bloomington: Indiana University Press.

Becker, H. S. (1953) Becoming a marihuana user, *American Journal of Sociology* 59(3): 235–242.

Budd, M. A. (1997) *The Sculpture Machine. Physical Culture and Body Politics in the Age of Empire*. London: Macmillan Press.

Cheng, C. (1999) Marginalized masculinities and hegemonic masculinity: An Introduction, *Journal of Men's Studies* 7: 295–315.

Connell, R. W. (1995) *Masculinities*. Cambridge: Polity Press.

Dahl-Michelson, T. and Solbrække, K. N. (2014) When bodies matter: significance of the body in gender constructions in physiotherapy education, *Gender and Education* 26(6): 672–687.

Denham, B. E. (2008) Masculinities in hardcore bodybuilding, *Men and Masculinities*, 11(2): 234–242.

DeReef, J. F. (2006) The relationship between African self-consciousness, cultural misorientation, hypermasculinity, and rap music preference, *Journal of African American Studies* 9(4): 45–60.

Dimeo, P. (2007) *A History of Drug Use in Sport 1876–1976. Beyond Good and Evil*. London; New York: Routledge.

DuRant, R., Escobedo, L. G. and Heath, G. W. (1995) Anabolic-steroid use, strength training, and multiple drug use among adolescents in the United States, *Pediatrics* 96: 23–29.

Flashback. n.d. Flashback forum [website]. Retrieved from www.flashback.org/

Foucault, M. (1994) *Power. Essential Works of Foucault 1954–1984. Volume 3.* Harmondsworth: Penguin Books.

Fornäs, J. (1995) *Cultural Theory and Late Modernity*. London. Sage.

Gennep, A. V. (2004) *The Rites of Passage*. London: Routledge. (1st ed., 1960)

Guttmann, A. (1991) *Women's Sports. A History*. New York: Columbia University Press.

Hsiung, R. C. (2000) The best of both worlds. An online self-help group hosted by a mental health professional, *Cyber Psychology and Behavior* 3(6): 935–950.

Kimmel, M. (1996) *Manhood in America. A Cultural History.* New York: The Free Press.
Klein, A. (1993) *Little Big Men. Bodybuilding, Subculture and Gender Construction.* New York: State University of New York Press.
Kozinets, R. V. (2010) *Netnography. Doing Ethnographic Research Online.* London: SAGE Publications.
Lentillon-Kaestner, V. and Ohl, F. (2011) Can we measure accurately the prevalence of doping? *Scandinavian Journal of Medicine and Science in Sport* 21: 132–132.
Locks, A. and Richardson, N. (eds). (2012) *Critical Readings in Bodybuilding.* New York: Routledge.
McCreary, D. and Sasse, D. (2000) An exploration of the drive for muscularity in adolescent boys and girls, *Journal of American College Health* 48(6): 297–304.
McDowell, L., Rootham, E. and Hardgrove, A. (2014) Precarious work, protest masculinity and communal regulation: South Asian young men in Luton, UK, *Work, Employment and Society*, Online January 2014.
McGrath, S. A. and Chananie-Hill, R. (2009) 'Big freaky-looking women'. Normalizing gender transgression through bodybuilding, *Sociology of Sport Journal*, 26: 235–254.
Messner, M. A. (1992) *Power at Play. Sports and the Problem of Masculinity.* Boston: Beacon Press.
Miller, P. and Rose, N. (2008) *Governing the Present. Administering Economic, Social and Personal Life.* Cambridge: Polity Press.
Mogensen, K. (2011) *Body Punk. En afhandling om mandlige kropsbyggere og kroppens betydninger i lyset av antidoping kampagner [Body Punk. A Thesis on Male Bodybuilders and the Meanings of the Body in the Light of Anti-Doping Campaigns].* Roskilde: Roskilde Universitetscenter.
Monaghan, L. F. (1999) Challenging medicine? Bodybuilding, drugs and risk, *Sociology of Health and Illness*, 21(6): 707–734.
Monaghan, L. F. (2002) Vocabularies of motive for illicit steroid use among bodybuilders, *Social Science and Medicine*, 55: 695–708.
Monaghan, L. F. (2012) Accounting for Illicit Steroid Use. Bodybuilders' Justifications. In Locks, Adam and Niall Richardson (eds). *Critical Readings in Bodybuilding.* New York: Routledge.
Mosher, D. L. and Serkin, M. (1984) Measuring a macho personality constellation, *Journal of Research in Personality*, 18(2): 150–163.
Mosse, G. (1996) *The Image of Man. The Creation of Modern Masculinity.* New York; Oxford: Oxford University Press.
Parkinson, A. B. and Evans, N. A. (2006) Anabolic androgenic steroids. A survey of 500 users, *Medicine and Science in Sport and Exercise,* 38(4): 644–651.
Pitts, V. (2003) *In the Flesh: The Cultural Politics of Body Modification.* New York: Palgrave Macmillan.
Porter, D. (1997) *Internet Culture.* New York: Routledge.
Rich, E. and Evans. J. (2013) Now I am NObody, see me for who I am. The paradox of performativity, *Gender and Education* 21(1): 1–16.
Sas-Nowosielski, K. (2006) The abuse of anabolic-androgenic steroids by Polish school-aged adolescents, *Biology of Sport* 23(3): 25–35.
Smith, A. C. T. and Stewart, B. (2012) Body perceptions and health behaviors in an online bodybuilding community, *Qualitative Health Research* 22(7): 971–985.
Sparkes, A. C., Batey, J. and Owen, G. J. (2012) The Shame–Pride–Shame of the Muscled Self in Bodybuilding. In A. Locksand and N. Richardson (eds). *Critical Readings in Bodybuilding.* New York: Routledge.

Sykes, G. and Matza, D. (1957) Techniques of neutralization. A theory of delinquency, *American Sociological Review* 22(6): 664–670.

Thualagant, N. (2012) The conceptualization of fitness doping and its limitations, *Sport in Society: Cultures, Commerce, Media, Politics* 15(3): 409–419.

Walther, J. B. (2002) Research ethics in internet-enabled research. Human subjects issues and methodological myopia, *Ethics and Information Technology* 4: 205–216.

Wenger, E. (1998) *Communities of Practice.* Cambridge; New York: Cambridge University Press.

Part IV
Rethinking Marginalization

9 Epistemologies of Difference

Masculinity, Marginalisation and Young British Muslim Men

Mairtin Mac an Ghaill and Chris Haywood

Introduction

In making a contribution to this edited collection, the chapter brings together the concepts of marginalised and masculinities to explore young Muslim men's experience of growing up in Britain. Within a British context, across theoretical, media and policy discourses, until recently, marginalisation was often associated with a vocabulary that was informed by a materialist position which privileged political economy. Discourses of marginalised young men frequently refer to social and economic aspects of their lives. For example, reference to a 'crisis of masculinity' over the last few decades has been explored in terms of the disappearance of the industrial labour market and the accompanying stability of 'jobs for the boys'. What was unstated in this explanation was that the young men were implicitly assumed to be white and working class. Thinking about other categories of difference/oppression, such as gender or ethnicity/race, thus tended to be derivative of structuralist-based class analyses. This materialist analysis associates power with social locations and cultural and economic resources, often where someone either has privilege or doesn't. Within this model, social inequalities accumulate to produce more or less power and dominance. Therefore, as an additive model of social power, the inclusion of an ethnic dimension would suggest a further racial exclusion. Similarly, a reductionist exploration of masculinities was framed within an oppositional couplet that simplistically projected masculinities, defined as social attributes of men, as not femininities. As a result, the combination of an additive model of power and binary forms of gender, sets marginalised masculinities in opposition to hegemonic or privileged masculinities (Connell, 2005).

It is argued here that we need to understand marginalisation that is not simply underpinned by an oppositional dualism and understand the concept of marginalised young men as a political paradox. Conventionally, men are positioned at the centre of patriarchal-based national gender regimes and from a materialist position it is theoretically uncomfortable to position men as oppressed unless they occupy positions of inequality. While a materialist analysis that tracks and measures levels of inequality between groups of men is important, it is crucial that we critically explore who has the power to define what is/is not marginal. It is argued here, that we need to examine discourses of marginality, who authorises them and what is excluded from that authorisation. As indicated in the introduction, Phillips (2006, p. 220) suggests: 'Marginalized masculinities or "outcasts" from the norm are constructed in the productive wake of the ideal, and as the conditions necessary for the ideal's production and "natural" appearance'. This means that state institutions require particular kinds of marginal masculinities, in this case Muslim masculinities, in order to establish and legitimise their claims to authority. Thus, as state policy priorities change, the nature of marginality changes, transforming what we understand as marginalised masculinities. To develop this point further, it is argued that the state depends upon and is actively working to construct and sanction forms of marginality; more recently marginality that is often deemed a threat to social cohesion and national security. While the state instantiates the necessity of risk and fear in order to consolidate its authority, we become increasingly distanced from what this sanctioned marginality means to young Muslim men. Thus, what remains under-explored are the cultural (with a focus on meaning and representation) and psychic dimensions of the young men's lives that may open up questions of emerging subjectivities and identities, as suggested by postcolonial and post-masculinity analyses, which in turn may serve to interrogate the notion of state-authorised marginalised masculinities (Kalra, 2009; Haywood and Mac an Ghaill, 2012).

As outlined below, this chapter, based on a three-year critical ethnography (2008–2011), draws upon this work in focusing on a third generation of young British Muslim men of Pakistani and Bangladeshi heritage, as a classed, ethnocultural and gendered category. Stuart Hall (1996) suggesting a conceptual move away from identity to identification, emphasises the need to examine both how social minorities are positioned by society and how they respond to this positioning. In terms of positioning as a materially marginalised social group, their generation is experiencing increasing neo-liberal-based socio-economic inequalities (in housing, schooling, work and health), pervasive negative visibility across the media and intensified forms of state and institutional monitoring and surveillance (Phoenix, 2004; Davies and Bansel, 2007). In terms of response to the state and wider institutional positioning, for example through education, employment opportunities and their individual self-positioning as multiple subjects, we explore how ethnography enables an alternative representational space for young men who are experiencing specific cultural conditions to provide self-authorised narratives about the complexity of inhabiting subject positions at a time of globally inflected change. What emerges is a complex (ethnographic) narrative, suggesting the need theoretically to rethink established dichotomies operating in this field of inquiry, including global/local, inclusion/exclusion, inside/outside and religious/secular. Thus, we are able to trace a range of fragmented male subjectivities, social trajectories, cultural belonging and their contested meanings around state-sanctioned marginalisation. We do this by exploring a key theme of how are we able to 'know' about the interplay between ethnicity and religion, given the prevalence of state-led representational strategies. We look in particular at the emergence of the transformation of ethnic difference to religious difference and young men's negotiation of the categories of difference.

Alternative Epistemologies: In Search of Knowing Young Muslim Men

One of the challenges of unpacking the experiences of those named as marginal is to enable the research participants to occupy an alternative representational space that provides insightful narratives about the complexity of inhabiting subject positions across public and private spaces. There is a tendency within the academy, government and media to over-generalise about the Muslim diaspora living in Europe and North America. For example, within a North American context, the popular representation of the Muslim is often portrayed as Arab; within a British context the popular representation is often portrayed as South Asian (Jamal, 2008). In reality, the global Muslim diaspora is nationally and ethnically a highly diverse population. Furthermore, our work with a younger generation of Pakistani and Bangladeshi young men in Newcastle, London and Birmingham, makes clear their geographically specific local experiences of growing up in a rapidly changing Britain (Popoviciu and Mac an Ghaill, 2004; Mac an Ghaill and Haywood, 2005). In other words, the young men in this Birmingham-based study inhabit specific lifestyles within a spatial context of diverse social trajectories amongst a changing Muslim diaspora in Britain. Therefore, it is the exploration of the young Muslim men's meaningful experiences that was a key objective of the research design.

During a three-year period, 2008–2011, we have recorded the experiences of 48 Pakistani (30) and Bangladeshi (18) working-class young men, aged 16–21. Twenty-five of the young men's narratives are reported in this chapter. The majority (38) of the young men (20 in this chapter) attended local secondary schools, sixth form colleges and further education colleges. While carrying out empirical work with young people, we were introduced to two young men who were politically involved in the local area. In turn, they introduced us to other young people which subsequently led to further snowballing of other friends, family and community representatives (Patton, 1990). Access was greatly enabled by our being known for our social commitment to the local area, working with families in the local community. Group and life history interviews provided the framework through which to explore a range of critical incidents experienced by these young men. The group interviews were carried out at local community centres and the life history interviews were carried out in a variety of places, including at youth and community organisations and local cafes. These interviews lasted around 45 to 90 minutes and provided insight into growing up, family, schooling, social life and local community. These interviews were supplemented by a range of other research strategies that included observations, informal conversations and interviews with parents and local community representatives (Alvesson and Skoldberg, 2000), as part of a wider critical ethnography on the impact of globally inflected change upon the local formation of diasporic young men's subjectivity and identity (Appadurai, 1991; Harvey, 2003; Ansari, 2004). The data sets from each of the methods was subject to thematic analysis (Braun and Clarke, 2006) that enabled us to explore '... the underlying ideas, constructions, and discourses that shape or inform the semantic content of the data' (Ussher *et al.*, 2013, p. 902). The subsequent analysis was taken back to the young people themselves not simply as a form of 'face validity' but also as a way of exploring the practical and political implications of the findings. All interviews throughout the study were anonymised and the research participants were given pseudonyms as well to protect their confidentiality (Wetherell, 1998).

Beyond Male Folk Devils: The Emerging Figure of the National(ist) Enemy

There is a long (imperial/neo-imperial) history of discarded images of racialized social groups, who are projected across state governance, policymaking and (empiricist) research as a major problem. Currently, the dominant epistemological assumption across state, media and popular culture is that Muslim communities, and more specifically, young Muslims as 'dangerous brown men' are the major threat in and to Britain (Bhattacharya, 2008). Hesse (2000, pp. 11–12) refers to the legacy of imperial themes and assumptions of governance as informing the current 'problematic of British race relations'. At a time of a rapid decline in anti-racist politics and scholarship, austerity Britain is marked by increasingly intense racial divisions visibly exemplified in the re-racialisation of young Muslim men (and women). Kalra (2000, p. 115), drawing upon Hesse's analysis, claims that academic work on British Asian masculinities continues to be located within this race relations discourse. He critiques 'the temporal framing of the British race relations narrative in terms of a post-1945 start'. In sum, the problem of race begins with the arrival of the racialized other in large numbers following the Second World War. In addition, the social implications of this presence are negative primarily because of poor inter-group interaction which can be reduced to a problem of psychological interactions. Currently, the dominant representation of (British) Muslim youth is that of individual and collective identity crisis. Within the context of this crisis, young Muslim men are subject to a state-led project of normalising their masculinity with political and media discourses ascribing to them a highly contradictory masculine identity, in which they are represented as both a major threat to the state (as potential jihadists) and to themselves (as highly vulnerable to terrorist recruitment). The following discussion highlights the contradictions embedded in the current reframing of Bangladeshi and Pakistani men as Muslim:

PARVEZ: I think that black boys were seen in the past as just ordinary bad, like they were called muggers. That was their stereotype and things like being lazy, not working, things like that. But Muslims now are seen as much worse. They have the worst stereotypes ever.

MAIRTIN: So, what would be the main difference?
PARVEZ: Everything, really everything.
MAIRTIN: Such as?
ALI: As always, it's like all mixed up, do you know what I mean? 'Cos, in the past like our dads, our families, got lots of discrimination even though the blacks were seen as the worst ethnics. But then its ... was discrimination cos, they are taking our jobs, or taking our houses, or living off benefits. And now, it's much worse, kind of deeper.
FUROOQ: Like if you hear about a Muslim man in the news, you just know it's going to be some horror story about really threatening Britain.
ALI: Like we were talking the other day, it's not just if you're a Muslim you can't be British, that's the same for black men. But Islam is the worst word in the world for white British people. It sends them mad. They've made up a word, Islamification.
JAVED: That's it. The Muslims are coming to take over Britain. It's crazy. How can we be seen as a threat to them, when they're the ones attacking us?
SHOAIB: A big difference was in the past the black kids were seen as bad just here in Birmingham, London or whatever. But for us, it's like we're like a threat to the whole world.
ALI: The Muslim men have gone global!

The young men were aware that earlier generations of Asians were seen by the state as ideal citizens. At this time, government policy, media and popular culture discourses operated with an oppositional logic that valorised the ascribed cultural unity of the Asian community, with its extended family network and religion as a key positive signifier imagined as providing the necessary support for a younger generation (Lawrence, 1982). In contrast, informed by a discourse of deficit, African-Caribbean young men's projected image as 'folk devils'/'bad boys' was frequently explained in terms of the assumed pathological structure of their family and kinship organisation (Mirza, 1992; Mac an Ghaill, 1990). However, there were contradictory elements in the discursive construction of each minority ethnic group, without which a racial classification could not form a system of knowledge. For example, simultaneously within gender discourses circulating across public institutions, Asians were assumed to be culturally recidivist, with Asian young men positioned as the most sexist, emerging out of the assumed regressive gender/sexual practices of the intensely patriarchal Asian community. At the same time, within the gendered politics of popular culture, Asian young men were ascribed the lowest ethnic masculinity, with terms of abuse – for example, 'Paki' – carrying not simply a racial connotation but at the same moment connoting a gender meaning. Deriving from an imperial legacy of Orientalist discourses, this was part of a wider ascription of institutional processes of feminisation that served to position them as 'non-proper' men (Haywood and Mac an Ghaill, 2003). In other words, currently projected as the major threat to society, possessing a home-produced anti-British ethnicity, the young men were aware of the shift from (the local) feminisation of Asian young men to the young Muslim as (the global) masculine cultural warrior. Furthermore, for them the figure of the British Muslim young man is imagined not simply as a social threat to the state (the latest male folk devils) but as an existential threat to the British nation and its future identity. More specifically, they were aware of the history of the racialized gendered positioning of earlier generations, outlined above, which contrasted with their current ascription as the '(global) bad boys' within schools.

YASIN: You know the police put up these big cameras round here to spy on us. That's one way of doing it and teachers do it in their way. Like we say in a more hidden way, but it's like they're suspicious of us, all the time.

TAREQ: It's true but they do it in their own way. I think they would mostly say they're not racist, not Islamophobic 'cos they probably don't think that we're bombers or terrorists. But they have their own ways of keeping you in a box.

WAQAR: Basically, they see us as trouble. We're the bad boys. I remember in our school earlier on it was the black boys who the teachers picked on most but then it slowly changed and it was us.

M. M: So, what has changed?

WAQAR: My cousins say that Asian pupils used to be seen as really weak, but now Muslims are seen as the strongest, like we're seen as like warriors.

FAROOQ: Yes, it's that, but it's more than that. If you're a Muslim pupil, then they think you're always as a Muslim, whatever you're doing, PE, walking in the playground, coming into the class, everything. They wouldn't think that about a Sikh or a black kid and never about a white kid. We're just marked out.

ALI: Yeah, as trouble makers.

FAROOQ: No. Not necessarily trouble makers. We're seen in a different way than any other group, any other group of pupils. But you're right that most Muslim kids know that if you scratch the surface then white people, teachers, even the good ones, the nice ones, see you in a certain sort of way. You can never escape.

KASHIF: Do you understand? In the past, the word Paki was the stereotype. Now people say Muslims are called terrorists but the real stereotype now is to be called a Muslim. So how are you supposed to behave in school?

JAVED: That is very true.

These young men are part of a de-industrializing city where men's masculinities were embodied through carrying out traditional manufacturing work. Such work was often intrinsically linked to nationhood that in turn is intricately linked to histories of empire and colonialism. This older connection to the global has been reconfigured through the rise of a service-sector economy. In short, the wider restructuring of the global economy, networks of power and capital flows, are creating new forms of marginality for these young men as identifications with older 'British' forms of work are no longer available to a contemporary generation. Although, these young men freed from the structural constraints of traditional labour processes that were often characterised by Fordist organisation, are experiencing underemployment and intermittent education. In short, the traditional resources available to make their masculinities have been subject to global transformations. At present, these young men not only inhabit a location of social and economic marginalisation, the spaces to make traditional hegemonic British identities, are also no longer available to them or the white working class. Their marginalised position also has to be understood within postcolonialism. Theorists, such as Hall (1992), Hesse (2000) and Gilroy (2004), have made available an alternative epistemology in outlining the construction of the racialized 'other' in colonial and postcolonial discourses. Said's (1978) work on Orientalism has been a major critical influence (Spivak, 1988; Young, 1990). Referring to the long-established tradition in Anglo-European scholarship of constructing the Orient as exotic and other, Said (1978, p. xiii) quotes Marx: 'they cannot represent themselves, they must be represented'. Orientalism can be understood as 'a mode of discourse with supporting institutions, vocabulary, scholarship, imagery, doctrines, even colonial bureaucracies and colonial styles …' (ibid., p. 2). The discourse assumes and projects a sense of fundamental difference between a Western occidental 'us' and an Eastern, Asiatic oriental 'them'. The key issue here is that global transformations have made it increasingly difficult to substantiate differences between 'them' and 'us' because the traditional resources through which to make their masculinities are no longer available.

Institutional Re-inscriptions and Re-classifications: Beyond Cultural Containment

Reading through the students' narratives, Avtar Brah's (1996, p. 209) work on diaspora is particularly resonant in a late modern, intensely racially divided Britain. She argues that we are currently located within a *diaspora space*. By this, she means the socially inhabited conditions where the entanglement of identities constructed as 'indigenous' and 'immigrant', national and transnational constitute 'the point at which boundaries of inclusion and exclusion, of belonging and otherness, of "us" and "them" are contested'. The social and cultural specificities of the 'white indigenous' experience of the diaspora space are under-researched. Currently, the Muslim community is caught up as the 'oppositional other' in the British/English reinvention of their collective national identity. Hence, the Muslim's social and economic marginalisation is somewhat in contrast with an unreported assertive English nationalism, involving a forging of a renewed British identity and an accompanying re-racialisation of Muslims that have emerged. For example, as Townsend (2011, p. 1) reports:

> Huge numbers of Britons would support an anti-immigration English nationalist party if it were not associated with violence and fascist imagery, according to the largest survey into identity and extremism conducted in the

UK. A Populus poll found that 48% of the population would consider supporting a new anti-immigration party committed to challenging Islamic extremism, and support policies to make it statutory for all public buildings to fly the flag of St George or the Union flag.... Just over half of the respondents overall – 52% – agreed with the proposition that 'Muslims create problems in the UK'.

Recently, within conditions of socio-economic austerity, increasing inequalities and regional socio-economic disparities, the success of UKIP in local and national elections provides evidence of this emerging new nationalism, as suggested by Townsend. Furthermore, following the murder of Drummer Lee Digby, there has been an increase in anti-Muslim attacks: 'forty percent of Muslim attacks recorded by *Tell Mama UK* [a monitoring group] last year were linked to English Defence League sympathisers' (Shabi, 2013, p. 10). The emergence of this assertive English nationalism provides the most explicit evidence of how different communities within Britain are impelled to live with different social realities. For the young men in this research, the increasing fear of an (imagined) all-pervasive Muslim fundamentalism articulated through English nationalism is central to their experience of marginalisation within the city and wider society.

This mainstream epistemological approach to young British Muslim men, in which the latter's social reality is inverted, has been set out by Shamin Miah (2015, pp. 1–2). He identifies three iconic representational moments, namely the 2001 racial disturbances in northern towns/cities, the events of 9/11 and the bombings in London in July 2005 (7/7) as of central significance in framing public understandings of and national anxiety about 'the nature of Muslim communities in general and young Muslims in particular around the nexus of hyper-masculinity, anti-liberalism and violent extremism'. He maintains that these moments helped reshape:

> state policy away from multi-culturalism and community-cohesion and towards a counter-terrorism agenda based upon a logic which argued that if spatial segregation led to the 2001 civil disturbances then cultural segregation led to violent extremism which culminated in the London bombings.
>
> (Ibid., 2015, p. 2)

For the young men in our study, marginalisation is experienced as an intensified global surveillance, local cultural pathologization and multiple forms of social and racial exclusion of their social lives that operates within this recategorization. Here, they identify the specific ways in which its logic is played out within a schooling arena:

ASIF: My aunt, she moved up North. She said this was seen as a really nice area and all the neighbours respected us. She says suddenly they had all moved away.

YASIN: But you see the news and every time they keep saying Muslims don't want to mix, they want to stay on their own. It's their religion, it's the imams, Sharia law, whatever, forcing us to be separate.

TAHIR: To be fair, there's some sticking together, probably for all ethnic groups when they're been threatened all the time. You see the English Defence League marching and all the white people clapping for them, like a celebration. They want us out.

IFTIKHAR: It's true we're under threat and the police won't protect us, so we have to look after ourselves, our families. But then the media says, all these aggressive Muslim men are doing the bad stuff and threatening white people. You think, where do these people live? What planet?

YASIN: No one would ever think, what's it like for a young Muslim boy growing up with all that fear and prejudice and discrimination and hatred? What's he supposed to do? He's not going to become a terrorist, like they say. But he's really angry, cos he can't even protect his family.

A key issue that emerges here is the question of how does a socially constructed phenomenon, such as religion, become fixed as an apparently stable unitary category. Adopting a postcolonial analysis, we suggest that schools alongside other institutions currently attempt to administer, regulate and reify unstable social categories, such as religion, ethnicity, gender and sexuality (Mirza, 2009). Most particularly, this administration, regulation and reification of the boundaries of these categories is institutionalised through the interrelated social and discursive practices of staffroom, classroom and playground micro-cultures. With young Muslim women, female teachers and Muslim schools, the hijab and the niqab have become symbolic objects, where imagined British identity and values can be 're-stated'. In relation to young men, Muslim masculinity has been an alternative space where the state is attempting to re-claim a safe ethnic identity. Much work remains to be done on the specific late modern dynamics of these processes at the local level of the school.

A major theme that emerges from the students' narratives is the disjuncture between teachers and students in how they mobilise the concept of Muslim. From the students' perspective, this mobilisation consists of students reclaiming the concept of Muslim as a collective self-referent and teachers' racialized ascription of the term 'Muslim' that serves to contain them. Teachers were seen as operating with a highly reductive understanding of religion that assumed a homogenous image of Muslims. In contrast, in the young men's self-representations, reclaiming the concept of Muslim did not necessarily mean an increase in religious identity or behaviour. Most importantly, the research participants illustrate throughout this chapter that the school's institutional attempt to contain young Muslim men by fixing them into a reified singular category of religious identity denies them the social power of self-authorisation.

SHABBIR: I think teachers see a Muslim and straight away think about religion. But most kids in our school are not really very religious. It's just the same like any other group, like the Sikhs. A few are very religious, but most are just ordinary getting on with their lives.

SAJID: Teachers are probably confused by Muslims, cos the media show all these extremists, but Islam is not like other religions, like Christianity, there is no central system governing ordinary Muslims. So it's the opposite to what they think. We're not all brainwashed into acting the same.

ASIF: Sometimes you'd like to explain to a teacher, there's no such thing as *a* Muslim. We're all individuals. But I don't think they'd understand, do you?

A key theme to emerge from our discussion on the notion of containment was its effect on other categories of the young people's lives. For example, they suggested that the teachers in operating with a single category of religion in relation to them had specific gendering effects. It is argued that while institutions operate with a dual notion of masculinity, with young Muslim men being weak and vulnerable to radicalisation and at the same time potential violent extremists, the young men themselves are experiencing alternative forms of gendering.

ABDUL: Yes, definitely, teachers are weird, especially with Muslim girls at school. If teachers saw a Muslim girl with traditional clothes as well as any modern fashion, you would hear them saying, 'Look at her, wearing the fashionable clothes when she's supposed to be a Muslim'. It's like they're the police and they're saying you're supposed to be a traditionalist Muslim girl, why don't you act like one. It's weird, it's like they're offended, so they feel they have to force her back into their stereotype of what a proper Muslim is.

PARVEZ: It's because teachers don't really know Muslims. So, they'll have these strange stereotypes of them being oppressed and forced to wear the veil and all that. It's like we've to act out what they think we are.

ASIF: And then they say, it's those horrible Muslim fathers making their daughters do these things.

AZAM: It was funny at primary [school], the Muslim kids knew that teachers wouldn't ever say, a 'good boy' or 'a very good boy', if you did good at reading or writing. It was weird, it was like if you're a Muslim you're not really a boy, like you're invisible. Why did they do that?

SAJID: You're right. I think even in secondary [school], they talk about men role models, in sport and high jobs, so you become a successful man. But not for Muslim boys. I don't know, it's confusing, very confusing. It's like they must think, if we say anything about growing up, you know to get a good job, or be a good father, that doesn't apply to Muslims, not really. Where do they get this from?

ABDUL: Because we're just Muslims, that's it.

In these young men's accounts, state and institutional discourses of dualistic notions of masculine risk and danger are also experienced through representational space of de-gendering. As Azam and Sajid suggest above, they also experience the institutional application of religious categories as a form of emasculation; in effect, the static categories of religion only allow for specific fixed gender types. Unlike previous research that saw Muslim men negotiating between both traditional patriarchal values and gender equality (Hopkins, 2006), these young men were trying to acquire access to gendered identities that appeared available to their white peers. Thus, the young men maintained that while Muslim female students were over-feminised, young men were de-masculinised. They could not make sense of how teachers were re-inscribing onto their bodies the racial/religious stereotypes that the former assumed were coming out of their bodies, impelled by patriarchal fathers. This institutional regulation of gender operates to prescribe available masculinities. They suggest that the role models that are available for other boys to connect with are not made available to them. It is interesting that the religious category as a gender category is a closure of gendered possibilities. As such, the institutional regulation of religious masculinities provides little discursive alterity that can be occupied outside the institutionally sanctioned and state-led gendered economy of masculinity and femininity.

Conclusion

Exploring the current conceptual manufacturing of the Muslim male student, for the Pakistani and Bangladeshi young men in this study, a central feature of their lives is schools' attempted institutional containment of them within the singular category of religion. This has major effects in limiting the range of positions that can be occupied as a young Muslim man within schools. This is informed by a wider societal 'recategorisation of various ethnic (Mirpuri, Bangladeshi, Pakistani) groups into religious (Muslim) ones' (Shain, 2011, p. 15). This chapter has suggested that marginalisation is located within local (regional) postcolonial urban spaces, marked by fracturing classes, fragmenting genders, plural sexualities and new ethnicities, that in turn are embedded within a 'bigger picture' of globally inflected socio-economic austerity, increasing inequalities, the diversity and/or fragmentation of racial politics and accompanying processes of re-racialisation.

British public institutions, such as schooling, continue to operate within a US-led race relations epistemology. In response, postcolonial analysis illustrates the limitations of the institutional production of the category of Muslim young men, which assumes that 'problem' diasporian communities are homogenous entities, marked by ethnic boundedness, fixity and social separation, which has historically and currently continues to provide a highly reductive explanatory framework in making sense of Pakistani and Bangladeshi students' experience of schooling (Mac an Ghaill, 1994; Shain, 2003; Mirza, 2009).

References

Alvesson, M. and Skoldberg, K. (2000) *Reflexive Methodology: New Vistas for Qualitative Research*. London: Sage.

Ansari, H. (2004) *'The Infidel Within': Muslims in Britain since 1800*. London: C. Hurst and Co.

Appadurai, A. (1991) 'Global ethnoscapes: Notes and queries for a transnational anthropology', in R. G. Fox (ed.) *Recapturing Anthropology: Working in the Present*. Santa Fe, CA: School of American Research.

Bhattacharya, G. (2008) 'State racism and Muslim men as a racialised threat', in G. Bhattacharya *Dangerous Brown Men: Exploiting Sex, Violence and Feminism in the War on Terror*. London: Zed.

Brah, A. (1996) *Cartographies of Diaspora: Contesting Identities*. London: Routledge.

Connell, (2005) *Masculinities*. Berkeley: University of California Press (2nd edition).

Davies, B. and Bansel, P. (2007) 'Neoliberalism and education', *International Journal of Qualitative Studies in Education* 23(3): 247–259.

Gilroy, P. (2004) *After Empire: Melancholia or Convivial Culture*. London: Routledge.

Hall, S. (1992) 'The question of cultural identity', in S. Hall, D. Held and T. McGrew (eds) *Modernity and Its Futures*. Cambridge: Polity/The Open University Press.

Hall, S. (1996) 'Politics of Identity', in T. Ranger, Y. Samad and O. Stuart (eds) *Culture, Identity and Politics*. Aldershot: Alvebury, pp. 129–135.

Harvey, D. (2003) *The New Imperialism*. Oxford: Oxford University Press.

Haywood, C. and M. Mac an Ghaill (2003) *Men and Masculinities: Theory, Research and Social Practice*, Open University Press, Buckingham.

Haywood, C. and M. Mac an Ghaill (2012) 'What's next for masculinity?' Reflexive directions for theory and research on masculinity and education', *Gender and Education* 24(6): 577–592.

Hesse, B. (2000) 'Introduction', in B. Hesse (ed.) *Un/settled Multiculturalisms: Diasporas, entanglements, transruptions*. London: Zed Books.

Hopkins, P. E. (2006) 'Youthful Muslim masculinities: gender and generational relations', *Transactions of the Institute of British Geographers* 31(3): 337–352.

Jamal, A. (2008) 'Civil Liberties and the Otherization of Arab and Muslim Americans', in A. Jamal and N. Naber (eds) *Race and Arab Americans Before and After 9/11: From Invisible Citizens to Visible Subjects*, Syracuse, NY: Syracuse University Press.

Kalra, V. S. (2009) 'Between emasculation and hypermasculinity: Theorizing British South Asian masculinities', *South Asian Popular Culture* 7(2): 113–125.

Lawrence, E. (1982) 'In the abundance of water the fool is thirsty: sociology and black pathology', in the Centre for Contemporary Cultural Studies, *The Empire Strikes Back: Race and Racism in 70s Britain*. London: Hutchinson.

Mac an Ghaill, M. (1990) *Young Gifted and Black: Teacher-Student Relations in the Schooling of Black Youth*. Milton Keynes: Open University Press.

Mac an Ghaill, M. (1994) *The Making of Men: Masculinities, Sexualities and Schooling*. Buckingham: Open University Press.

Mac an Ghaill, and Haywood, C. (2005) *Young Bangladeshi People's Experience of Transition to Adulthood*. York: Joseph Rowntree Foundation.

Miah, S. (2015) *Muslims, Schooling and the Question of Self-Segregation*. Basingstoke: Palgrave Macmillan.

Mirza, H. S. (1992) *Young, Female and Black*. London: Routledge.

Mirza, H. (2009) 'Plotting a history: Black and postcolonial feminisms in "new times"', *Race Ethnicity and Education*, 12(1), pp. 1–10.

Office for National Statistics (2006) *Religion-Labour Market*. London: Office for National Statistics.

Patton, M. (1990) *Qualitative Evaluation and Research Methods*, Newbury Park: Sage.

Phillips, D. A. (2005) 'Reproducing normative and marginalized masculinities: Adolescent male popularity and the outcast', *Nursing Inquiry* 12(3): 219–230.

Phoenix, A. (2004) 'Neoliberalism and masculinity: Racialisation and the contradictions of schooling and for 11–14 year olds', *Youth and Society* 36(2): 227–246.

Popoviciu, L. and Mac an Ghaill, M. (2004) 'Racisms, ethnicities and British nation-making', in F. Devine and M. C. Walters (eds) *Social Identities in Comparative Perspective*. London: Blackwell.

Said, E. W. (1978) *Orientalism*. London: Routledge and Kegan Paul.

Said, E. W. (1993) *Culture and Imperialism*. London: Vintage.

Shabi, R. (2013) 'British Tolerance is never a given. Post-Woolwich, it must be defended', *Guardian*, Wednesday, 3 July, p. 10.

Shain, F. (2003) *The Schooling and Identity of Asian Girls*. Stoke-on-Trent: Trentham Books.

Shain, F. (2011) *The New Folk Devils: Muslim Boys and Education in England*. Stoke-on-Trent: Trentham Books.

Spivak, G. (1988) 'Can the subaltern speak?', in C. Nelson and L. Grossberg (eds) *Marxism and the Interpretation of Culture*. Urbana: University of Illinois Press.

Townsend, M. (2011) 'Poll reveals surge of sympathy for far right'. *Observer*, Sunday 27 February, p. 1.

Ussher, J. M., Sandoval, M., Perz, J., Wong, W. K. T. and Butow, P. (2013) 'The gendered construction and experience of difficulties and rewards', *Qualitative Health Research*, 23: 900–915.

Wetherell, M. (1998) 'Positioning and interpretative repertoires: conversation analysis and post-structuralism in dialogue', *Discourse and Society* 9(3): 387–412.

Young, R. (1990) *White Mythologies: Writing History and the West*. London: Routledge.

10 Marginalized Adult Ethnic Minority Men in Denmark
The Case of Aalborg East

Ann-Dorte Christensen, Jeppe Fuglsang Larsen and Sune Qvotrup Jensen

Introduction

Danish gender equality political discourses often address ethnicity, as mainstream political and mass media discourses often implicitly or explicitly assume that gender inequality is a problem that pertains primarily to ethnic minorities (Andreassen, 2005; Marselis, 2005; Siim and Stolz, 2015). When adult ethnic minority men appear in such discourses, they are thus represented as patriarchal oppressors who are, at least in part, to blame for gender inequality amongst ethnic minorities (Jørgensen and Bülow, 1999; Charsley and Liversage, 2015). The mere thought that (some) adult ethnic minority men may experience serious social problems – perhaps sometimes more severe social problems than ethnic minority women – remains unimaginable in mainstream political discourse. Mirroring this picture, gender scholars have taken a limited interest in adult ethnic minority men and their specific experiences, challenges and problems. Although gender studies have generally embraced multiculturalism and seen a turn towards an intersectional perspective, it has often taken an interest in gender and ethnicity to be synonymous with an interest in ethnic minority *women* whereas adult ethnic minority men have rarely been addressed (for a significant exception see Charsley and Liversage, 2015).[1]

However, the limited statistics about these themes show a complex picture where ethnic minority men are, in some spheres, more marginalized than women. For instance, men are over-represented in homelessness statistics, and the specific reason for this, for ethnic minorities, seems to be divorce (SFI, 2013).[2] Another area is education, where only 47 per cent of the 30-year-old male descendants of non-western ethnic minorities have completed an education beyond high school (gymnasium), whereas the percentage is 64 for women in the same category (Danmarks Statistik, 2014).[3] Consequently, the aim of this chapter is to address a blind spot concerning the specific issues of marginalization amongst adult ethnic minority men in Denmark. We analyse processes of marginalization amongst a group of ethnic minority men in a specific multi-ethnic neighbourhood: Aalborg East (which will be described below). Besides describing the men's social problems, our analysis addresses two questions: 1) What are the mechanisms of social work and social policy in the area and the surrounding municipality that contribute to the marginalization of these men? and 2) How do class and ethnicity intersect with gender and masculinity and contribute to the marginalization of these men? The chapter consists of three main sections. The first section presents the theoretical framework for analysing marginalized masculinity through four key concepts: hegemonic masculinity, intersectionality, class journey and othering. The second section accounts for the methods and data. The third section analyses three specific processes of marginalization of adult ethnic minority men in Aalborg East: i) local and contextual mechanisms on the meso level; ii) an analysis of the implications of downward class journey; and iii) the processes of othering some of these men have experienced.

Theoretical Approach and Key Concepts

Our analysis is inspired by different theoretical traditions and key concepts. The point of departure is the concept of *hegemonic masculinity*. The concept was originally coined in an attempt to analyse and conceptualize gendered hierarchies between women and men as well as amongst men (Connell, 1987, 1995; Connell and Messerschmidt, 2005; Messerschmidt, 2012). Connell and Messerschmidt (2005, p. 832) note that hegemonic masculinity '... embodied the currently most honored way of being a man, it required all other men to position themselves in relation to it, and it ideologically legitimated the global subordination of women to men'.

The concept of hegemonic masculinities was thus coined in order to understand men's power over women as well as some men's (or masculinities') power over other men (or masculinities). Both dimensions are relevant to the analysis of marginalization processes in this chapter. Connell emphasized that hegemonic masculinity was based on a hierarchic power relation between men and different masculinities. Hegemonic masculinity is thus distinguished from other masculinities in the current Western gender order: (a) subordinated masculinities, e.g. homosexuals; (b) complicit masculinities, e.g. men who gain from hegemony and obtain a patriarchal dividend even if they do not represent a hegemonic position themselves; and (c) marginalized masculinities, e.g. men who are disqualified due to their class or race/ethnic position (Connell, 1995). Connell's work is thus central for our analysis because it emphasizes differences, inequalities and hierarchies between masculinities. In order to provide an analytical grasp of how this hierarchy amongst masculinities is produced, we consider it relevant to combine Connells work with *an intersectional perspective* that offers methodological and theoretical tools suited for analysing the complexity of differences and inequalities between men.

The concept of intersectionality emphasizes the interaction between social categories such as gender, class, race/ethnicity, age and sexuality (Crenshaw, 1991). It originated in the USA where black feminists put their particular situation in relation to gender and race in focus in order to challenge white middle-class women's dominance in feminism and black men's dominance in anti-racist organizations (Collins, 1993, 1998; Crenshaw, 1989, 1991). The original American debate put relatively high emphasis on structural power relations (Collins, 1989), whereas later adaptions of the perspective have emphasized the importance of lived lives and complex identities (Phoenix, 2011). Some authors have stressed that intersectional analyses must encompass the interplay between structures and institutions at the macro level and identities and lived lives at the micro level (Christensen and Jensen, 2012b; Christensen and Siim, 2006; Jensen, 2006, 2010).

Across debates and differences, the overall aim of intersectional analysis has been to explore how people are simultaneously positioned in multiple categories, such as gender, class and race/ethnicity (Phoenix, 2011; Phoenix and Pattynama, 2006). In our view, an intersectional approach thus refers to a common analytical core, i.e. *that different social categories mutually constitute each other as overall forms of social differentiation* (Collins, 1998; de los Reyes and Mulinari, 2005; Mellström, 2003) as well as in *creating complex identities*, where different categories are always mutually constitutive (Buitelaar, 2006; Staunæs, 2003). Furthermore, Choo and Ferree have argued for a process-centred approach to intersectionality in order to grasp complexity and multifaceted analyses. They emphasize the need to focus on dynamic forces rather than categories – 'racialization more than races, economic exploitation rather than classes, gendering and gendering performances rather than genders' (Choo and Ferree, 2010, p. 134).

Intersectionality scholars would claim that other forms of social differentiation, such as class, race/ethnicity and sexuality will influence, form and shape masculinity. The meaning, experience and power relations of masculinity thus vary for different ethnic groups, according to class, age etc. The category of masculinity is thus unstable and is successively altered in processes of intersection with other categories. Likewise, masculinity can intersect with other categories in specific configurations that challenge or subvert male privilege. Complex power relations can thus not only strengthen but also weaken male privilege. Hence, it can be argued that class, race/ethnicity and sexuality can weaken or subvert the legitimacy of some men to the extent that they are unable to gain a social advantage from being a man. In other words, intersectional theory can help us grasp how being a man can be a category of disempowerment, marginalization and lack of privilege rather than a privileged position. Intersectionality theory thus provides insight into the complex processes which advance some masculinities to the top of the hierarchy and relegate others to the margin; in Connell's (1995) terms, how some masculinities become hegemonic and others come to be marginalized (Christensen and Larsen, 2008). Put differently, intersectional analysis offers tools for nuanced and multidimensional analyses of processes of marginalization.

One process, relevant for our analysis, concerns class differences and what some authors have referred to as the *class journey*, often related to migration. Originally, the concept of class journey has been related mainly to social mobility across generation where the class traveller in the transition – typically from working class to middle/upper class – encounters new cultural norms, habits and customs that appear attractive, but also unfamiliar (Gullestad, 2002; Wennerström, 2003). Analyses of class journeys have often focused on the intersection between gender and class. For instance, Norwegian studies have shown that recent generations' upward mobility has been experienced differently for women and men and that changes in gender relations are closely related to class shifts (Nielsen, 2013; Ambjörnsson, 2004).

In relation to migration, research has shown the significance of combining the class journey perspective with ethnicity and transnational migration (Gullestad, 2002, 2006). For most migrants and refugees, it is difficult to maintain their class position in new societies (Gullestad, 2002; Charsley and Liversage, 2015). Changes in class position do however form and shape how gender and ethnicity are perceived and experienced. Immigrant men might find it difficult to uphold their masculine identity if their class position is radically altered – relative to their class position in what used to be the homeland and relative to the class position of their spouses. We might thus speak of classed processes which shape, reshape and ultimately destabilize masculinity (Christensen, 2015). We see these unstable masculinity positions as key elements in understanding the complex processes of marginalization amongst adult ethnic minority men.

The formation of subordinate masculinities is, however, also the result of processes of *othering* related to racialization and ethnification. It can thus be argued that in a predominantly white society occupied with ethnic difference – such as contemporary Denmark – whiteness is central to hegemonic masculinity. In order to obtain legitimacy and symbolic power, white hegemonic masculinity is defined in a relational opposition to other masculinities. In the current Danish and Scandinavian context, these 'others' are often ethnic minority men who are socially degraded and marginalized (Gottzén and Jonsson, 2012). In a sense, ethnic minority masculinity is constructed as Danish white masculinity's 'other'. This renders the concept of *othering* – central to postcolonial theory – relevant to our analysis. The concept of othering was coined by Spivak (1985) and draws on a number of different theoretical inspirations (de Beauvoir, 1997/1949; Said, 1995/1978; for a genealogy see Jensen, 2008). The theory of identity formation inherent in the concept assumes that subordinate people are offered, and at the same time relegated to, subject positions as others in discourse. Othering thus concerns symbolic degradation as well as the processes of identity formation related to this degradation. In this chapter, we use the concept of othering to refer to discursive processes by which powerful groups define subordinate groups into existence in a reductionist way which ascribes problematic and/or inferior characteristics to these subordinate groups. Such discursive processes affirm the legitimacy and superiority of the powerful and condition identity formation amongst the marginalized and subordinated (Jensen, 2010).

The processes of marginalization and othering – the relegation to the bottom of the hierarchy of masculinities – can be said to subvert male privilege for some ethnic minority men and result in social marginality. To add to the complexity, ethnic minority men are often marginalized and othered *because* they are imagined to be too masculine, that is, they are seen as carriers of atavistic, patriarchal, non-equality-oriented forms of masculinity. In a Scandinavian context, men and masculinities that are constructed as opposed to a dominating gender equality discourse are often relegated to the position of hegemonic masculinity's other, especially if they are also working class and Muslim (Gottzén and Jonsson, 2012; Jensen, 2007).

Overall, this means the analyses of marginalization in this chapter basically draw on four interrelated key concepts. Hegemonic masculinity and intersectionality are the concepts that form the overall conceptual framework while class journey and othering are used as more middle-range and processual concepts, closely related to the questions in the empirical analysis.

Methods and Data

The data used in the chapter were primarily collected for *The INTERLOC Project* (2008–2012)[4] which investigated everyday life and social distinctions in the neighbourhood of Aalborg East, part of the Danish city Aalborg that is located in Northern Jutland. The project examined the interplay between overall social structures, discourses and policies of contemporary Danish society on the one hand and local citizenship, belonging and identities in relation to gender, class and ethnicity on the other. The bulk of the data were collected in the period 2008–2012. In 2013, additional interview data were collected focusing specifically on ethnic minority men and marginality. The INTERLOC data were collected using a mixed-methods strategy and consist of 33 semi-structured qualitative interviews; ethnographic data from 37 meetings in two local organizations (one primarily for migrant women and one for all residents); analyses of 385 texts about the area from local and national mass media; and a quantitative survey covering economic and demographic issues.

The analysis advanced in this chapter is thus based on different types of empirical data, but with a primary emphasis on interview data with adult ethnic minority men. The INTERLOC interviews and the additional interviews make up a total of 24 interviews with ethnic minority people, 13 of these being men (eight were interviewed during The INTERLOC Project, five later). The interviewed men were between 25 and 63 years of age. They were born in Somalia, Sudan, Syria, Turkey, Kurdistan, Nigeria, Lebanon and Sri Lanka. They all migrated to Denmark as adults or young adults. The interviews covered a range of themes such as everyday life and social relations in the neighbourhood, family relations, experiences of migration, current work–life status and experiences of othering and racism. Consequently, our methodology, and the analysis forwarded in the chapter, focuses primarily on *experiences of* marginalization (see the Introduction for an overview of different methodological approaches to researching marginalization). The men were interviewed either in their own homes or in more public settings – a club and a library – according to their preference. The actual atmosphere was very different from interview to interview. In most cases, the men spoke broadly about family, their homes and life in general while in other cases they were more careful, sometimes limiting the information given, especially in relation to themes such as ethnicity and racism. We consider this an example of how overall societal discourses may frame and condition interviews and fieldwork relations; in this particular case, how racist and othering discourses may frame the relation between ethnic majority interviewers and ethnic minority interviewees regarding the intentions of the interviewers (See Jensen, 2012 for an elaborated analysis). All names used in the text are pseudonyms and data that would make interviewees identifiable have been omitted.

The Neighbourhood of Aalborg East

Aalborg East is a neighbourhood in Aalborg, a Danish city with approximately 120,000 inhabitants situated in the northern part of Jutland. Aalborg East, with 10,000 inhabitants, is the most multicultural area in Aalborg. The proportion of immigrants and descendants of immigrants is 18 per cent (Skjøtt-Larsen, 2008) with considerable variation between sub-areas. The area's minority population is made up of people with Somali, Palestinian, Turkish, Kurdish as well as a broad range of other ethnic minority backgrounds. Aalborg East was built during the late 1960s and 70s. The area has a diverse environment with single-family houses, terraced housing and housing estates consisting of blocks of flats, and it is mixed in terms of owner-occupied and rented housing. The average economic income ranks third-lowest amongst Aalborg's 23 boroughs, and the rate of unemployment rate is above average for the entire Aalborg area (Skjøtt-Larsen, 2008). The neighbourhood has seen a range of social projects, including some specifically for adult ethnic minority women, but none for adult ethnic minority men (Christensen and Jensen, 2012a).

Media analysis indicates that Aalborg East is subject to territorial stigmatization (Wacquant, 2007, 2008) primarily because it is constructed as an 'immigrant ghetto' even if the ethnic minority population is relatively small compared to multi-ethnic areas in other parts of Denmark or Scandinavia. One might argue that in the *imagined geography* (Said, 1995) of Aalborg, Aalborg East is constructed as dominated by ethnic minorities and therefore problematic. Residents do, however, not seem to internalize the stigma as most are content with the area (Jensen and Christensen, 2012). Furthermore, the INTERLOC project concluded that relations between ethnic groups are peaceful, even if there is little interaction between the different ethnic groups (Christensen and Jensen, 2012a). In addition, ethnic minority interviewees reported that they experienced little or no everyday racism in the everyday life of the area.[5] However, as we shall return to later, some interviewees reported to have been subject to racism and discrimination in other contexts.

Ethnicity and Gender in Aalborg East

One empirical finding central to the analysis forwarded in this chapter is that, amongst some ethnic minority groups in Aalborg East, women seemed to be more empowered and active in the local community than men. This is especially the case for the Somalis, as Somali women have strong social networks and have been active in building strong associations in the local community, whereas many Somali men in Aalborg East are marginalized and disempowered (Christensen and Jensen, 2012a). This picture runs contrary to popular representations of ethnic minority women as disempowered, marginalized and in need of rescue from majority society. In general, we found that ethnic minority men often suffered from *labour market marginality*. This marginality was often paralleled by what one informant – a social worker – referred to as a kind of *social invisibility* in the public life of the area. We interpret this as a kind of withdrawal motivated by resignation – perhaps shame – of being unsuccessful. But Somali men were not only marginalized and invisible in public life; our data indicate that quite a few were *marginalized from their families* as well. One indication is that adult ethnic minority men in the area often found it difficult to help and guide their children, boys in particular. Another indication relates to divorce: 'It is better to get married 30 times than staying in an unhappy marriage' has become a proverbial amongst Somali women in Aalborg East (Jesuloganathan, 2010, p. 60). This is, however, not only a saying, as many Somali couples have divorced according to the wishes of the women. Contrary to popular representations of Muslim marriage, and gender relations, Somali custom contains no prohibition of divorce. The rate of men living alone is thus much higher amongst the Somalis than amongst, for instance, ethnic minority men from Turkey, Palestine or Pakistan (Mikkelsen, Fenger-Grøndahl and Tallat Shakoor, 2010). A fourth specific problem was *abuse of khat and other substances*, including alcohol (often euphemized as khat abuse since alcohol is considered taboo amongst some ethnic minority groups). Some of our informants considered khat a primary explanation of high divorce rates and social problems amongst Somali men, but it could equally well be argued that khat abuse is an indicator of larger issues of social marginality.

Based on these overall empirical findings, we will now go more in depth and thoroughly analyse three specific processes of marginalization of adult ethnic minority men in Aalborg East. First, we address some local and concrete explanations on the meso level; in the second section, we discuss the downward class journey some of these men have undertaken and the related loss of status and male identity; in the third section, we will address the experiences of othering.

Local Explanations

One cluster of explanations of the specific problems for ethnic minority men in the area relates to mechanisms of social work and social policy in the area and the surrounding municipality. Interestingly, a number of social projects have been carried out in the area related specifically to the social problems of women, whereas no social projects have to date specifically addressed adult men. One informant, Daahir, a social worker himself of Somali origin, explained that this blind spot in the social work in the area – and the overall social policy of the municipality – might be explained as an organizational mechanism. The social projects are often short term which makes it 'easier' to orient them towards women as the contact between the women and the social workers is already established. Adult ethnic minority men with social problems, on the other hand, are often invisible to social workers, because they do not engage in public trouble or petty street crime (as marginalized younger minority men would sometimes tend to do); they might gather in ethno-specific clubs in the centre of the city – clubs that social workers do not have access to or knowledge of. Furthermore, they may drift around, sleeping on one couch one night and another couch the next. This is important, because the division of labour within the social work department of the municipality is related to geography. Persons who withdraw to the private sphere and do not display visible social problems, and who furthermore drift between the sub-districts of the municipality, run a high risk of not receiving help. Not because of ill intentions, but because of lack of knowledge and because it is not clear which district and which specific social workers are responsible.

While these explanations might not be particularly gender specific, masculinity does seem to play a role for the ability of social workers to reach out to ethnic minority men in need. The aforementioned social worker explains:

> Many of them are used to being the one who takes care of everything and holds everything together, and it is hard for them to approach a stranger and say that I need you to help me with this and that.

When asked by the interviewer why men are less willing to ask for help than women, he elaborates:

> It is shameful to ask for help, especially if it is in a public place. Women do not care if there are 20 other women sitting and listening to one that tells about how you can help yourself and each other and about the problems they have.

Ethnic minority men in the area are thus often hesitant to seek help, especially in collective contexts where knowledge of their problems is likely to be spread to wider networks in the area. Although self-reliance may be a commonly shared masculine value in many cultural contexts, this hesitance may very well be related to a feeling of failing as men, which is specific to this particular group; a feeling that is reinforced by a perhaps more traditional conception of masculinity and connected to wider issues of class journey and loss of status.

Class Journey, Loss of Status and Troubled Male Identities

Migration often entails class journey. In other words, moving or fleeing from one country to another involves class mobility and most often in a downward manner. It is thus rarely possible for migrants to maintain their original class position in a new country. Such a class journey may often be more problematic for men than for women, especially if their masculine identity was hitherto invested in a high social position in the home country and/or the role as breadwinner. In our material, both male and female interviewees, representing a variety of different ethnic minority backgrounds, emphasized the specific problems related to the loss of masculinity and privilege for ethnic minority men who had been class travellers.

One example is 48-year-old Sadiq from Sudan, who had been a tourist guide in his prior country of residence, Egypt. In Denmark, he has however found himself in a state of labour market marginality. When he arrived in Denmark he wanted to study communication in order to continue to work with tourism but, as he explains, the social worker at the unemployment office regarded studying communication as 'unreasonable'. Sadiq feels he is being commanded around: 'So I can't move forward and become better at the Danish language and study communication. So [the plan to study communication] was over. She told me to [work in the food business].'

Instead of pursuing his ambition in tourism, he was told to seek work in the food business. Here he wanted to study and become a chef, but was told by a social worker to start as a dishwasher. He feels that 'the system' has pushed him around and that he is no longer in charge of his own decisions. He has tried entering different trades, but has consistently found it difficult to get jobs or internships, even in trades that were presumably characterised by a shortage of labour power. He is saddened by his current status on the margin of the labour market and attributes some of his lack of success to racism, a theme we will return to below.

Another example is Besam from Turkey. Besam, who used to be involved in politics in his home country, is currently employed as a SOSU, a low-skill job in the care sector traditionally associated with publicly employed working-class women. Besam displays a somewhat ambivalent attitude towards his current job situation. On the one hand, he is proud that he works, that he is not a burden to society and not a welfare receiver. He prides himself of his education, and considers himself a role model to ethnic minority youth. On the other hand, he considers his current job situation as a status loss, being employed in a female trade. As he explains:

> Among us…. When you say: 'I am a SOSU assistant', our peers will say: 'You wash the ass of old people.' They see it that way, as low status. When you are a man, it is different. Then it is even more a failure and loss of status, but I do not see it that way. When you are a man and choose an education that not very many men choose…. It is a loss of status or a taboo to say that you are doing a woman's job.

Besam thus experiences a status loss in relation to his current employment. Although he personally takes pride in his job, he cannot fully ignore that some might see it as doing 'women's work'. It is not considered manly work, and therefore it challenges his social identity as a man. He is, however, keen to emphasize that doing work that is traditionally associated with women is also a problem for Danish men.

The interviews indicate that some ethnic minority women are also aware of the specific problems related to status loss of ethnic minority men. This is especially the case for some of the female Somali interviewees. For instance, Aasiya – a 33-year-old Somali woman – explains the loss of status for the Somali men in the following way:

> From being a person that provides for himself, you suddenly cannot speak the language and you are on welfare support and you do not provide for your family. So you lose a big part of your identity and a big part of yourself.

Natifa, another young Somali woman, notices that women and men handle the drop in class position in different ways:

> Somalis in Denmark are 'big' men. They were educated in Somalia and were providers. In Denmark, he finds that his kids are his equals in terms of language and other things. He cannot develop with his education and his status. So he works as a cleaner, garbage man, in slaughterhouses or whatever.... It is harder for the men than for women to come to Denmark because they are used to being providers. And now the provider is the municipality of Aalborg. If the woman works for them she gets paid, and if she works for a business, she gets paid. So he does not contribute as much as he used to.

Some ethnic minority women thus seem to have a good grasp of the specific situation of the Somali men as well as the changes in the gendered power relations. This change, the shifting of the relative balance between women and men, is also addressed by Besam who explains:

> The women take more responsibility [...]. You [the man] do not have the economic ability, so you cannot play that role [as breadwinner]. You could do that in the Middle East where there was an economic identity and status. The woman was not part of the decision making. Today it is different because she also gets paid and works, and she also has a say when making decisions. She has the right to speak up.

He thus addresses the changed role of men in relation to migration to Denmark which, in his eyes, is closely connected to economic empowerment of women. From an intersectional perspective, we can thus say that the challenges to masculinity are formed and shaped by the interplay between the changed class position of the man and a transformation of wider gender relations within ethnic minority families. This creates an identity crisis. Besam elaborates:

> When you don't have a job, don't do well in society and don't get food on the table for your family it is an identity crisis. I think that goes for all men,

but among us it is more in focus and a bigger crisis than it would be if it was a Danish man.

Besam stresses that on the one hand, it is a general problem for men if they are provided for economically by women, while on the other hand this may be experienced as a more severe problem by ethnic minority men who have often been socialized to more traditional notions of masculinity and self-reliance. Another informant, 63-year-old Adib from Syria, explains what it means to ethnic minority men that women have a more predominant role in Denmark, and that the role of the man as breadwinner/dominant often cannot be upheld after the migration:

> There are many examples of it in Denmark. It is the women who take care of the family. I know men who have lived here for 18 years, if they want to buy a beer, they can't. The women or the children have to come along to translate. I know a man who has lived here for 22 years who was in an [traffic]accident and who had to call his wife.

Having to rely on a woman for linguistic assistance and for monetary support can thus be hard for men who have lived a large part of their lives in a social and geographical context permeated by different visions of gender and masculinity. This should, however, not be confused with a nostalgic longing for a return to a more patriarchal gender order. The change of gender relations in ethnic minority communities and families also entails democratization. Besam notes this: 'On the other hand, men are also undergoing change. Going in the other direction. You cannot continue thinking in the old traditional way. You have to be flexible and join in on mutual decisions.' According to Besam, the gender relations are becoming more democratized and, as he puts it, are becoming more and more like gender relations in a Danish family.

While democratization may be thought of as the positive side of the change in gender relations, the downward mobility of the men may be thought of as the negative side. These processes of marginalization are located in the interplay between the loss of status and the crisis in male identity they consequently experience. Even if downward social mobility is a common consequence of migration, this process of downward class journey is amplified by the barriers the men run into when they attempt to enter the labour market. Barriers which – according to the men – are related to ethnicity, racism and othering.

Experiences of Othering and Racism

Having a job and being able to provide for the family is, as illustrated above, linked to masculine ideals. For some men, the role as breadwinner is a key factor to perceiving oneself as a 'real man' (Bloksgaard et al., 2015) The male ethnic minority interviewees, however, report that they are met with what they perceive as racism in the labour market; racism which results in a downward class journey and prevents them from being the men they would like to be.

As described above, Sadiq is an example of a man who is on the margin of the labour market. He has tried entering different trades but has not been able to find a job or an internship. In his opinion, there can be only one explanation for the many rejections – his skin colour. One example is that he was promised a job interview at a supermarket and later found out the job was given to another person from a town far away. Another example is from a bakery in Aalborg: 'The owner is also a teacher at the technical school, so I went over there and asked: 'Do you need help here?' They said 'no'. After a week one of my Danish friends was hired there.' According to Sadiq, the only reason he was not hired was because he was black. Sadiq is not the only interviewee who maintains that the labour market has a problem with racism; Mustafa from Lebanon is engaged in a local association and gives an example of ethnic minority young men who cannot find internships:

> My son heard his teacher make a call the other day. The person he called said: 'If it is a black-haired then I don't want him.' Then they [young ethnic minority men] end up on welfare support, and some of them start doing stupid things, steal and do drugs.

According to Mustafa, racism in the labour market can fuel processes of marginalization and the formation of delinquent street cultures. Mustafa believes that an explanation for the racism can be found in the negative media focus on ethnic minority men. He wants the municipality of Aalborg to promote 'positive propaganda' and create a positive image of the young men.

Adib agrees that there is a problem of negative stereotyping and blaming of immigrants and refugees:

> Denmark always talk about they do not have money and they talk about that refugees cost billions. If they have a problem in the society they talk about refugees. They mix refugees into everything. When one man makes trouble then they should only talk about that one man, not refugees in general. I am a refugee and I do not do anything. I am Danish.

In general, the interviewees feel that Danish mass media are overly critical and paint a negative picture of ethnic minority men. The focus of more local media was also criticized by some interviewees. The social worker from Aalborg East, Daahir, reports an episode were a local news station described episodes of fighting and unrest in Aalborg East as caused by 'young Somali men from Aalborg East'. According to the social worker the young men were, however, from different parts of Aalborg and the group of men consisted of Somalis, Danish and Arabic men. The media in this case can be seen as producing an image of ethnic minority men as problematic and violent, i.e. contributing to processes of othering. This may fuel processes of labour market marginalization and cause everyday racism. According to Besam, it is inevitable – given the sociopolitical context – that ethnic minority men will meet ethnic Danes who consider them strangers and out of place in Denmark because of their hair colour and accent: 'You will always experience that there are Danes that will not consider you as Danish and say that you are not Danish because you have dark hair and speak a little different. You will always experience that.' This creates a feeling of not being welcome and as being seen as someone who does not fit in. Sadiq has experienced everyday racism and reports an incident at a bar in Aalborg. Here he was accused of theft because the doorman, according to him, was jealous because Sadiq was sitting in the bar with an ethnic Danish girl. This theme – the white male's fear of the imagined erotic power of ethnic minority men – is also addressed by Besam: 'When we are here some Danes just think that we are coming to take the jobs and screw their girls.' Besam thus addresses the sexualization of the ethnic/racial other inherent in Western conceptions of both the orient and Africa (Mercer and Julien, 1988; Said, 1995).

The experiences of othering addressed by our interviewees do not only have consequences for the 'objective' social status of the men. They also have wider affective consequences. Sadiq explains that when he is met with what he perceives as racism, he takes it especially hard because his situation as a refugee makes him vulnerable:

> When we flee from our home country we are very sensitive. If something happens [actions that can be perceived as racist] we think that is the way he sees society [that the person has a racist understanding of society]. Because we have fled [...]. When you get hit just a little bit, then you feel very bad.

Sadiq has contemplated going back to Sudan, but the war there makes it impossible and keeps him in Denmark. The experiences that he has had with racism in the labour market and in everyday life have, however, caused him to resign and avoid 'mixed contacts' (Goffman, 1963). He no longer tries to make friends with Danes or to interact with Danes in public life or in sports associations, as he used to. He has pulled back from the 'Danish part' of society and now only interacts with people from his home country and refugees. Sadiq might be an extreme case as his decision to avoid mixed contacts is far from general in our empirical material, but his and the other examples show that labour market racism, everyday racism and media othering is indeed experienced by the interviewees, even if they don't experience it as part of their specific everyday life in Aalborg East.

We cannot, on the basis of our data, say anything about whether the racist treatment is gender specific, as this would have required the employment of different methodologies. We can however say this: When racism and othering block labour market opportunities for men who used to have a high or recognized social position in their home countries, or who have a large part of the masculine identity invested in their role as a breadwinner, the result may be gender-specific concrete social problems. From an intersectional perspective, it may thus be argued that processes related to class as well as ethnicity shape and reshape the masculine spaces these men are able to take up, resulting ultimately in the production of marginalized masculinities.

Concluding Discussion

In the analysis above, we have described problems of social marginality and troubled male identities which we encountered while investigating issues of gender and ethnicity in the Danish neighbourhood, Aalborg East. We have shown that adult ethnic minority men in the area sometimes experience gender-specific problems of marginality: labour market marginality, marginality within the family, social invisibility in the neighbourhood and substance abuse. Furthermore, we have offered an analysis of how these problems may be explained on two levels: (1) One level pertains to mechanisms of social work and social policy in the neighbourhood and the surrounding municipality that contribute to the marginalization of these men; and, (2) On another level, we have argued that these men often experience a downward class journey, inherent in migration, as worse than women, especially if they had a high and recognised class position in what used to be the home country or have invested a large part of their male identity in the role as a breadwinner. Moreover, we have shown that the men often experience othering and racism, and that this racism may block labour market opportunities – thereby making it difficult or impossible for the men to uphold the social position they used to hold in the countries they fled or migrated from. Hence, racism may make class journey – that is the loss of prior social status – more dramatic. The combined result of class journey and experiences of othering and racism may thus be concrete social problems as well as marginalized male identities. In other words, intersectional changes related to class and ethnicity drastically change the dynamics of gender relegating these men to a space of marginalized masculinity.

Some of our empirical material concerns Somali men. These may represent an extreme case. Somalis in Denmark are thus a heterogeneous group, but some Somali men in Denmark used to take up positions in the power elite of the Somali government prior to the civil war and/or have European university educations. For such men, being relegated to the margins of Danish society and to unemployment or low-paid niches of the labour market – to be degraded and disqualified as *marginalized masculinities*, to use Connell's terminology – may provide a painful challenge to male identity. Hence, it is possible that Somali men represent an extreme case that may serve to highlight specific problems that other ethnic minority men may also experience, albeit to a lesser degree. On the other hand, it is possible that men from different ethnic minority groups experience qualitatively different problems. Kurds, for instance, often come to Denmark as unskilled migrant workers and may not share the same experience of downward class mobility as some Somali men.

We have focused mainly on the situation and the hardship of ethnic minority men. However, our analysis is also indirectly related to the question of empowerment of ethnic minority women. Here, let us be clear: Our argument is *not* that it is problematic that some ethnic minority women become relatively empowered – economically and otherwise – even if this alters the balance of gender relations in relative disfavour of men. Our argument should then not be conflated with patriarchal nostalgia on behalf of ethnic minority men. In fact, our informants did not seem to wish for that, at least not in an unambiguous way: While a few male informants seemed to strive to uphold some kind of male dominance at least within the family, others accepted or even embraced the democratization of gender relations.

In this chapter, we have combined an intersectional approach with the concept of hegemonic masculinity, emphasizing especially the complexities and the dynamic forces in adult migrant men's troubled identities. Our main argument has been that the marginalized position of these men is not related to one single category but instead reflects the tension between the multiple and intersecting categories: gender/masculinity, class and race. The intersectional analysis has shown that the downward class journey as well as the processes of othering are basically intertwined, inseparable and that they are central to understanding processes of marginalization. In other words, you cannot understand the meaning of the changing class positions without race and gender/masculinity; just as you cannot understand the processes of othering and racism without class and gender/masculinity. At the same time, the analysis has shown that the intersecting processes of marginalization are located in different spheres of these men's everyday lives: the labour market; the family (as provider and husband); and in the general public where the processes of racism and othering are reinforcing the reproduction of troubled and marginalized masculinities for adult ethnic minority men living in Denmark.

Notes

1 Admittedly, a wide range of social research that addresses specific, often younger, subgroups of ethnic minority men *does* exist. As an example, criminological and sociological empirical research has to some extent focused on street cultures, subcultures and 'gangs' amongst marginalized, sometimes delinquent, *young* ethnic minority men (Hjarnø, 1998; Mørck, 1999; Andersen *et al.*, 2001; Røgilds, 2002, 2004; Hviid, 2007; Jensen, 2007, 2010, 2011; Klinker and Bilde, 2009; Bengtsson, 2012; Kalkan, 2014). This literature does, however, not focus on the adult men, the fathers and grandfathers, the non-criminal non-delinquent adult men, and it has only rarely had an explicit focus on gender and masculinity.
2 Divorce is a main reason for homelessness for 28 per cent of ethnic minorities, whereas it is only listed as a main reason by 15 per cent of homeless with an ethnic Danish background (SFI, 2013, 120).
3 Ethnic Danish women also have a higher education level compared to ethnic Danish men, but the difference is significantly smaller for Danes (Danmarks Statistik, 2014, 58).
4 See www.interloc.aau.dk
5 During interviews, we actively prompted for experiences of racism in the everyday life of the area. Somewhat to our surprise, however, interviewees consistently answered that this was a very little or non-existing problem (Christensen and Jensen, 2012a).

References

Ambjörnsson, R. (1996) *Mit förnamn är Ronny*. Stockholm: Bonnier.
Andersen, M. A., Christensen, S., Minke, L. K. and Mørck, R. (2001) Rodet ungdom – unge rødder, *Social Kritik* 77: 18–47.
Andreassen, R. (2005) *The Mass Media's Construction of Gender, Race, Sexuality and Nationality*. Doctoral dissertation. Canada: University of Toronto.
Bengtsson, T. T. (2012) Learning to become a 'gangster'? *Journal of Youth Studies* 15 (6): 677–692.
Bloksgaard, L., Christensen, A.-D., Jensen, S. Q., Hansen, C. D., Kyed, M. and Nielsen, K. J. (2015) Masculinity ideals in a contemporary Danish context, *NORA – Nordic Journal of Feminist and Gender Research* 23 (3): 152–169.
Buitelaar, M. (2006) I am the ultimate challenge, *European Journal of Women's Studies* (13): 259–296.
Charsley, K. and Liversage. A. (2015) Silenced husbands: Muslim marriage migration and masculinity, *Men and Masculinities* 18 (4): 489–508.
Christensen, A.-D. (2015) When the Strangers Take Root – Ambivalent Feelings of Belonging and Identity. In S. T. Faber and H. P. Nielsen (eds) *Remapping Gender, Place and Mobility: Global Confluences and Local Particularities in Nordic Peripheries*, pp. 93–108. Farnham, UK: Ashgate Publishing.
Christensen, A.-D. and Jensen, S. Q. (2012a) *Stemmer fra en bydel – Etnicitet, køn og klasse i Aalborg Øst*. Aalborg: Aalborg Universitetsforlag.
Christensen, A.-D. and Jensen, A. Q. (2012b) Doing intersectional analysis: methodological implications for qualitative research, *NORA: Nordic Journal for Feminist and Gender Research* 20 (2): 109–125.
Christensen, A.-D. and Larsen, J. E. (2008) Gender, class, and family: Men and gender equality in a Danish context, *Social Politics* (15): 53–78.
Christensen, A.-D. and Siim, B. (2006) Fra køn til intersektionalitet – intersektionalitet i en dansk/nordisk kontekst. *Kvinder, Køn og Forskning* 15 (2/3): 32–42.
Choo, H. Y. and Feree, M. M. (2010) Practicing intersectionality in sociological research: A critical analysis of inclusions, interactions, and institutions in the study of inequalities, *Sociological Theory* (28): 129–149.
Collins, P. H. (1989) The social construction of black feminist thought, *Signs* (14): 745–773.
Collins, P. H. (1993) Toward a new vision: Race, class and gender as categories of analysis and connection, *Race, Sex and Class* (1): 25–46.
Collins, P. H. (1998) It's all in the family: Intersections of gender, race and nation, *Hypatia* (13): 62–82.
Connell, R. (1987) *Gender and Power*. Sydney: Allen and Unwin.
Connell, R. (1995) *Masculinities*. Cambridge: Polity.
Connell, R. and Messerschmidt, J. W. (2005) Hegemonic masculinity: Rethinking the concept, *Gender and Society* (19): 829–859.
Crenshaw, K. W. (1989) Demarginalizing the intersection of race and sex: A black feminist critique of antidiscrimination doctrine, feminist theory and antiracist politics, *The University of Chicago Legal Forum* (140): 139–167.
Crenshaw, K. W. (1991) Mapping the margins – Intersectionality, identity politics and violence against women of color, *Stanford Law Review* (43): 1241–1299.
Danmarks Statistik (2014) *Indvandrere i Danmark*. Copenhagen.
de Beauvoir, S. (1997) *The Second Sex*. London: Vintage [first published in French in 1949].

de los Reyes, P. and Mulinari, D. (2005) *Intersektionalitet* [Intersectionality]. Malmö: Liber.

Demetriou, D. Z. (2001) Connell's concept of hegemonic masculinity: A critique, *Theory and Society* (30): 337–361.

Goffman, E. (1963) *Stigma – Notes on the Management of Spoiled Identity.* Harmondsworth: Penguin Books.

Gottzén, L. and Jonsson, R. (2012) 'Goda män och Andra män.' In L. Gottzén and R. Jonsson (eds) *Andra män. Maskulinitet, normskapande och jämställdhet*, Malmö: Gleerups. 7–25.

Gullestad, M. (2002) *Det norske sett med nye øyne. Kritisk analyse av norsk innvandringsdebatt.* Oslo: University Press.

Gullestad, M. (2006) *Plausible Prejudice: Everyday Practices and Social Images of Nation, Culture and Race*. Oslo: Universitetsforlaget.

Hjarnø, L. (1998) *'Rødderne' fra Blågårds Plads*. Esbjerg: Sydjysk Universitetsforlag.

Hviid, K. (2007) *'No life'*. PhD diss. Aalborg: Aalborg University.

Jensen, S. Q. (2011) 'Othering', identity formation and agency, *Qualitative Studies* 2 (2): 63–78.

Jensen, S. Q. (2006) Hvordan analysere sociale differentieringer? *Kvinder, Køn og Forskning* 15 (2/3): 70–79.

Jensen, S. Q. (2008) *Andenhed, hybriditet og agens: Ph.d. forelæsning, Aalborg Universitet, 28. November 2007*. Aalborg Universitet: Institut for Historie, Internationale Studier og Samfundsforhold.

Jensen, S. Q. (2007) *Fremmed, farlig og fræk: Unge mænd og etnisk/racial andenhed – mellem modstand og stilisering*. Unpublished PhD diss. Aalborg: Aalborg Univeristy.

Jensen, S. Q. (2010) Masculinity at the margins – othering, marginality and resistance among young marginalized ethnic minority men, *NORMA* 5 (1): 7–26.

Jensen, S. Q. (2012) 'So, it is about how negative it is?!' Understanding researcher/ researched interactions as relations between intersectional social positions, *Qualitative Studies* 3 (2): 115–132.

Jensen, S. Q. and Christensen, A.-D. (2012) Territorial stigmatization and local belonging – study of the Danish neighbourhood Aalborg East, *CITY* 15 (1–2): 74–92.

Jesuloganathan, T. M. (2010) *'Hellere gift 30 gange end at leve i et ulykkeligt ægteskab' – Et kvalitativt studie af en skilsmisses betydning for førstegeneration somaliske kvinder i Danmark.* Thesis. Aalborg University.

Jørgensen, R. E. and Bülow. V. S. (1999) Ali og de fyrretyve k(r)oner: en analyse af Ekstra Bladets kampagne De fremmede. In P. Hervik (ed.) *Den generende forskellighed*. Copenhagen: Hans Reitzels Forlag.

Kalkan, H. (2014) *Gadeliv blandt unge mænd fra Nørrebro*. Statens Byggeforskningsinstitut. Aalborg: Aalborg Univeristy.

Klinker, S. and Bilde, M.H. (2009) Gadens Koder i A-town – status og respekt blandt etniske minoritetsfyre. *Dansk Sociologi* (4): 37–56.

Lister, R. (2004) *Poverty*. Cambridge: Polity Press

Marselis, R. (2005) Majoritetskvinden som grænsemarkør: Om perkerpiger og konvertitter i mediebilledet. In H. B. and A. S. Sørensen, A. Klim and U. Mellström (eds) *Kultur på kryds og tværs*.

Mellström, U. (2003) *Masculinity, Power and Technology: A Malaysian Ethnography*. Aldershot: Ashgate.

Mercer, K. and Julien, I. (1988) Race, sexual politics and black masculinity: A dossier. In R. Chapman and J. Rutherford (eds) *Male Order: Unwrapping Masculinity*. London: Lawrence & Wishart.

Messerschmidt, J. W. (2012) Engendering gendered knowledge: Assessing academic appropriation of hegemonic masculinity, *Men and Masculinities* (15): 56–76.

Mikkelsen, F., Fenger-Grøndahl, M. and Shakoor, T. (2010) *I Danmark er jeg født ... Etniske minoritetsunge i bevægelse*. Copenhagen: Frydenlund.

Mørck, Y. (1999) 'Faktisk er Blågårds Plads utrolig smuk' – hårde drenge på Nørrebro. *Social Kritik* (65/66): 45–58.

Nielsen, H. B. (2013) Gender on class journeys. In C. Maxwell and P. Aggleton (eds) *Privilege, Agency and Affect*. London: Palgrave.

Phoenix, A. (2011) Psychosocial intersections: Contextualising the accounts of adults who grew up in visibly ethnically different households. In H. Lutz, M.-T. H. Vivar and L. Supik (eds) *Framing Intersectionality: Debates on a Multi-Faceted Concept in Gender Studies*, pp. 137–152. Farnham: Ashgate.

Phoenix, A. and Pattynama. P. (2006) Editorial: Intersectionality, *European Journal of Women's Studies* (13): 187–192.

Røgilds, F. (2002) Bander i Blokland. *Social Kritik* (81): 24–40.

Røgilds, F. (2004) *De Udsatte – bander, kulturmøder, socialpædagogik*. Copenhagen: Politisk Revy.

Said, E. (1995) *Orientalism*. London: Penguin Books [first published in 1978].

SFI, Det Nationale Forskningscenter for Velfærd (2013) *Hjemløshed i Danmark*. Copenhagen.

Skjøtt-Larsen, J. (2008) Aalborg Øst – En social og symbolsk profil. *Sociologisk Arbejdspapir* (24).

Spivak, G. C. (1985) The Rani of Sirmur: An essay in reading the archives, *History and Theory* 24 (3): 247–272.

Staunæs, D. (2003) Where have all the subjects gone? Bringing together the concepts of intersectionality and subjectification, *NORA: Nordic Journal of Feminist and Gender Research* (11): 101–110.

Siim, B. and Stolz, P. (2015) Particularities of the Nordic: Challenges to equality politics in a globalized world. In S. T. Faber and H. P. Nielsen (eds) *Remapping Gender, Place and Mobility: Global Confluences and Local Particularities in Nordic Peripheries*, pp. 19–34. Farnham, UK: Ashgate Publishing.

Wacquant, L. J. D. (2007) Territorial stigmatization in the age of advanced marginality, *Thesis Eleven* (91): 66–77.

Wacquant, L. J. D. (2008) *Urban Outcasts – A Comparative Sociology of Advanced Marginality*. Cambridge: Polity.

Wennerström, U.-B. (2003) *Den kvinnliga klassresan*. Göteborg Studies in Sociology no. 19. Göteborg: University of Gothenburg.

Conclusion

Thomas Johansson and Chris Haywood

In a famous speech in the 1970s, Swedish Prime Minister Olof Palme addressed the topic of the emancipation of men. In this speech, he made an important point regarding the way to reach gender equality in society. He stated: 'We have talked long enough about the emancipation of women, of the problem of women's role in society. But in order that women shall also be emancipated from their antiquated role the men must also be emancipated.' This might today seem like a somewhat naïve analysis, suggesting as Palme does later in the speech that such an 'emancipation of men and women would imply considerable advantages from all points of view'. Nevertheless, since the 1970s there have been repeated political attempts in Sweden and the Nordic countries to involve men in the work on gender equality. We can also see similar attempts at a European level. For example, the results of these attempts vary between different countries. In certain parts of Eastern Europe, for example, gender equality is still regarded as a question for women, and not for men (Hearn and Pringle, 2006; EIGE, 2012). Although there is strong support for the notion, often accompanied by an image of a slow but steady process towards gender equality in European countries, this process is uneven and not always easy to interpret. Many of the developments are contradictory and context-dependent. There is also massive critique of the notion of 'gender-equal paradises' in the Nordic countries (Haavind and Magnusson, 2005), while in certain areas, such as family politics and political representation, there has been considerable progress in countries across Europe (Holter, 2007). In other areas, such as violence and media representations, there are reasons to be doubtful regarding a linear process towards gender equality. Furthermore, we are beginning to be confronted with a situation where men from some of the most deprived urban districts and local regions are becoming less integrated in society, resulting in a state of permanent marginalisation. In this collection, the empirically informed paradoxical and contradictory picture of gender equality in northern Europe and across the world, raises several questions regarding the uneven and complex experience and understanding of men and marginalization.

From Marginal Man to Multiple Marginalities

In addressing these questions, one of the main aims of this collection – against the background of recent developments in research on masculinity and gender – was to explore key factors in the relationship between men, masculinity and processes of marginalization. As indicated in the introduction, there remains a contradictory picture of men being both privileged and marginalized. At one moment, men precipitate and reproduce gender inequality through the articulation of patriarchal processes. For example, across Europe, women's wages continue to be around 16 per cent lower than that of men, one in three women report physical or sexual abuse and women experience higher levels of poverty (FRA, 2014; Lancker *et al.*, 2015). We have seen how the concept of hegemonic masculinity has been useful in explaining dominant structures of power and violence (Connell, 1995; Hearn, 1998; Kimmel, 1996/2006, 2005).

At a different moment, the traditional resources through which men have traditionally made their masculinities, appear to be changing with the collapse of industrial manufacturing work, the fragmentation of family networks and the reconfiguration of cultural ideals of manhood. The theme of this book – *marginalized masculinities* – generates a number of emotive representations of boys and younger and older men. Marginality can become conflated with social problems through the circulation of images of drunk and poor men, sitting on the street begging for money, or maybe immigrant men having problems being accepted and invited into the new society; men in the margins are often poor, disadvantaged, troubled and at risk. Although, in a number of chapters in this collection we can see evidence of these kinds of marginality, one of the underlying principles of this collection has been to problematize such representations and attempt to understand what marginality and masculinity mean.

The concept of *the marginal man* was coined in 1928 by American sociologist Robert Ezra Park. The notion of the marginal man grew out of a historical situation with mass immigration to the US. This was a time of rapid urbanization, immigration, ghettoization and great poverty. People were struggling to make a living, and the cities became melting pots, where in- and out-groups were continuously constructed and reconstructed. In an influential article by Park, marginal man is described as a:

> … cultural hybrid, a man living and sharing intimately in the cultural life and traditions of two distinct peoples; never quite willing to break, even if he were permitted to do so, with his past and his traditions, and not quite accepted, because of racial prejudice, in the new society in which he now sought to find a place. He was a man on the margin of two cultures and two societies, which never completely interpenetrated and fused.
> (Park, 1928, p. 892)

This is a powerful description and analysis of the preconditions for modern man. He is captured in between two cultures, and his identity is characterized by hybridity, ambivalence and homelessness. Marginality is thus not defined as a stable and homogenous position, but rather as a relational and changeable movement in time and space. Marginal man is always defined as 'marginal' in relation to the structural preconditions forming his subject position. In the 1974 classical work *The Homeless Mind. Modernization and Consciousness*, Peter Berger, Birgitte Kellner and Hansfried Kellner describe modern identity as peculiarly open, differentiated, reflective and individuated. Their conclusion is that: 'modern man has suffered from a deepening condition of "homelessness"' (ibid., p. 82). Following this image of modern man, we end up in an overall analysis of marginality as a fundamental existential experience of the modern man.

The apparent 'crisis of masculinity' that is implicit within Park's analysis has a long past in social history (Bailey, 1988) and has been used as an explanation for a wide range of social, economic and cultural issues. Within such a crisis there tends to be an emerging sense of a transition in which the old cultural stories of gender identity formation, which are caught up in a redrawing of the boundaries – geographical, socio-symbolic and psychic, no longer make common sense (Mac an Ghaill and Haywood, 2007). For example, contemporary media scripts suggest that women are now the new 'modernity winners' with more access to opportunities within the labour markets, education and health care. Recent studies report girls increasing achievement at school and a corresponding underachievement of boys that has in many ways drawn attention away from the real difficulties that young women face when leaving compulsory education. For example, young women are less likely to leave school and gain direct employment. Furthermore, those young women who achieve lower educational attainment at school are less likely to achieve paid employment than young men (Fuller and Unwin, 2013). Alongside this, men are also negotiating and making their identities within new social and economic contexts (Mac an Ghaill and Haywood, 2007). Once leaving post-compulsory schooling, traditional jobs once associated with respectable masculinities are becoming less available which often results in young people either taking up generally low-paid, temporary service work – characterized by a 'learning to serve' (McDowell, 2000) – or becoming workless. It is important to challenge discourses of crisis as they tend to characterize change through Hegelian notions of opposites, rather than accommodating differences within the configurations of inflection, intersection and simultaneity.

In his seminal 2008 work *Urban Outcasts*, Loïc Wacquant focuses on what he calls *advanced marginality*. This ideal-typical concept offers us a baseline for identifying central aspects of contemporary marginality. Advanced marginality is characterized by a neo-liberal regime creating an insecure and precarious situation for people living in certain urban areas:

> Rather than being disseminated throughout working-class areas, advanced marginality tends to be concentrated in isolated and bounded territories increasingly perceived by both outsiders and insiders as social purgatories,

leprous Badlands at the heart of the postindustrial metropolis where only the refuse of society would agree to dwell.

(Ibid, p. 237)

Wacquant uses the concept of territorial stigmatization to capture a new regime of marginality fuelled by neo-liberal transformations of society, resulting in increasing economic differences and stigmatized areas bereft of collective identities, social justice and fair living conditions. Wacquant points to a location of being neither an outsider nor an insider. In this collection, there are examples of the impact of social change creating a liminal positionality for different groups of men. For example, in Lin's chapter, there are examples of men having to renegotiate their masculinities due to the changes in their migratory status. Moving from rural to urban locations appears to impact negatively on young single men. The normative expectation to have a family and children entailed migrating men to explain and justify their masculine status. In this sense, although not wholly causative, economic change fractures older traditions and prompts men to reconfigure their masculine identities. A similar understanding can be found in Håkansson's chapter, where labour market segmentation is producing gendered identities and shaping the nature of gendered norms. For Håkansson, who maps trends in the workforce, the changing status of occupations themselves may be impacting on how marginalization and gender is configured. As indicated at various moments throughout this collection, we have sought to distance ourselves from a 'marginal man' that is an embodied type, but rather consider marginality and masculinity as part of social, economic and cultural configurations.

However, a number of the chapters presented in this collection suggest that it is not self-evident how the reconfiguration of socio-economic structures impacts on men's subjectivities. Morten Kyed in Chapter 5, for example, explores how men in occupations traditionally held by women masculinize themselves through notions of emotional competence and proficiency. More specifically, Kyed argues that we need to understand the impact of social and economic change and the impact of marginalization at the local level through communities of practice. Thus, it is argued that while such changes may be reinscribing inequalities, they may also be recreating new social and cultural positions and diverging subjectivities. It could be argued that rather than reinforce structured inequalities '… economic and cultural transformations associated with post-modern styles of creative, economic and cultural production and consumption' are in themselves undermining traditional hierarchies of class, gender and ethnicity and as a result, creating '… new venues for emancipatory politics' (Povlika, 2000, p. 226). In Chapter 9, Mac an Ghaill and Haywood highlighted that social and cultural changes are shaping how ethnicity is being configured, moving from categories of national heritage to that of religion. The implication is that masculinity and marginality are not always attached to particular social or cultural economic positions. Furthermore, in Chapter 8, Andreasson and Johansson point out we need to begin to refocus and explore other forms of marginality such as those within subcultures where men embody and express a dangerous, but also a powerful and influential form of hard-core masculinity. In other words, men's bodies that are marginalized and socially stigmatized, may also be those bodies that are desirable. One of the results of the discussions in these chapters is that we need to challenge the conceptual integrity of masculinity and marginalization.

This challenging can be seen within the chapter by Hellman and Odenbring who utilized Ratele's concept of marginality within marginalization and in so doing, opens up not only the possibility of different registers of marginality, but also different ways of understanding masculinity. This is also something mirrored by Christensen, Larsen and Jensen in the final chapter of the collection. They explore how ethnicity and gender in the context of migration interplay to produce new forms of marginality. The implication of this is that the concept of masculinity can, in the process of application, marginalize certain forms of subjectivity in order to be cohered through a model of identity. This means that, in the process of applying masculinity, we are in the process applying a normative judgement about who meets or matches that judgement. This is clearly seen in Sørensen's chapter, as a conceptual space is opened up enabling an understanding of marginality to emerge that is not easily understood through gender categories. A similar theme can be found in Gaini's discussion in Chapter 3 on the changing nature of masculinity in Greenland. He suggests that, as a nation on the European rim, its indigenous people's experience of postcolonialism and their construction of gender identities are closely aligned. The danger, as indicated by Herz in Chapter 2, is that masculinity, understood through the lens of marginality, becomes a static category both as something desirable but also at risk. In short, the use of masculinity as a concept produces 'risky bodies' rather than young people who may be subject to risk. What is 'marginal' or marginalized is always defined relationally, that is, marginality is not a personality trait, inherited social position or stable identity, but always a malleable and changing subject position, defined in relation to a changing socio-cultural landscape.

Conclusion

To sum up, we have suggested that we need to track how marginality can be understood as part of boys' and men's broader reflexive projects where '… the transition from "solid" to "liquid" modernity has challenged individuals to find alternative ways to organize their lives, for social forms no longer have enough time to solidify and cannot serve as frames of reference for human actions' (Eadeeva and Mochizuki, 2010, p. 250). In this collection, we have done this by focusing on different forms of marginality and/or marginalized masculinities. It has broadly focused on three different 'fields' in society: Crisis, Risk and Socialization; Transformations of Work and Unemployment; and Marginalization, Bodies and Identity. By zooming in on marginality and masculinity in each subfield, we get a closer picture of what men in precarious positions in different countries, social contexts and situations experience. As a result, the collection has also engaged with the theoretical and conceptual developments in the field of marginality and masculinity. In so doing, this collection has identified how academic knowledge operates in regulative ways, endorsing and delegitimizing particular ideas, understandings and meanings. In other words, approaches to masculinity and marginality actively shape and operate as powerful mechanisms to exclude alternative legitimate understandings in the process of knowledge production. The contributors to the collection have been mindful of Farmer *et al.*'s (2003, p. 359) call for a: 'refusal to succumb to intellectual or political stagnation'. As a result, it is hoped that this collection provides a number of areas for further exploration that entails undertaking research and asking questions that move beyond what we know, towards discovering what we are able to know.

References

Bailey, B. (1988) From Front Porch to Back Seat: Courtship in Twentieth-Century America. Baltimore, MD: Johns Hopkins University Press.
Becker, H. S. (1963) Outsiders. Studies in the Sociology of Deviance. New York: The Free Press.
Berger, P., Berger, B. and Kellner, H. (1974) The Homeless Mind. Modernization and Consciousness. New York: Vintage Books.
Connell, R. W. (1995) Masculinities. Cambridge: Polity Press.
Eadeeva, Z. and Mochizuki, Y. (2010) Higher education for today and tomorrow: University appraisal for diversity, innovation and change towards sustainable development, Sustainability Science 5(2): 249–256.
EIGE/European Institute for Gender Equality (2012) The involvement of men in gender equality initiatives in the European Union. Luxembourg: Publication office of the European Union.
Farmer, B., Martin, F. and Yue, A. (2003) High anxiety: cultural studies and its uses, Continuum: Journal of Media and Cultural Studies 17(4): 357–362.
Fuller, A. and Unwin, L. (2013) Gender Segregation, Apprenticeship, and the Raising of the Participation Age in England: Are Young Women at a Disadvantage? Centre for Learning and Life Chances in Knowledge Economies and Societies at: www.llakes.org.
FRA/European Union Agency for Fundamental Rights (2014) Violence against Women: An EU-wide Survey. Luxembourg: Publications Office of the European Union.
Haavind, H. and Magnusson, E. (2005) The Nordic countries – welfare paradises for women and children? Feminism and Psychology, 15(2): 227–235.
Hearn, J. (1998) The Violences of Men: How Men Talk about and How Agencies Respond to Men's Violence to Women. London: Sage.
Hearn, J. and Pringle, K. (2006) European Perspectives on Men and Masculinities. National and Transnational Approaches. London: Palgrave Macmillan.
Holter, Ø. G. (2007) Men's Work and Family Reconciliation in Europe, Men and Masculinities 9: 425–456.
Kimmel, M. S. (1996/2006) Manhood in America. New York: Oxford University Press.
Kimmel, M. S. (2005) The History of Men. Essays on the History of American and British Masculinities. New York: State University of New York Press.
Lancker, V. W., Corluy, V., Horemans, J., Marchal, S., Vinck-Herman, J., Perrons, D. and Stratigaki, M. (2015) Main Causes of Female Poverty. European Union: Brussels.

Mac an Ghaill, M. and Haywood, C. (2007) Gender, Culture and Society. London: Macmillan.

McDowell, L. (2000) Learning to Serve? Employment aspirations and attitudes of young working-class men in an era of labour market restructuring. Gender, Place and Culture. A Journal of Feminist Geography 7(4): 389–416.

Park, R. E. (1928) Human migration and the marginal man, American Journal of Sociology 33(6): 881–893.

Povlika, L. (2000) Postmodern aging and the loss of meaning, Journal of Aging and Identity 5(4): 225–235.

Wacquant, L. (2008) Urban Outcasts. A Comparative Sociology of Advanced Marginality. Cambridge: Polity Press.

Index

9/11 164

Aalborg 170–83
adult-centric 9
advanced marginality 190–1
aesthetic labour 84
aestheticized youth culture 118
Africa 8–9, 182
African villagers 51
age 4, 25, 40, 53, 55, 68, 74–5, 89, 91, 171–2, 174
aggression 28, 141
agricultural work 104–9
agriculture 5, 104, 109
alterity 7, 118, 129, 141, 167
ambivalence 27, 45, 141, 190
ambulance 14, 84, 86–7, 91; *see also* service; work
androgyny 84, 90, 98
anti-feminism 2
anti-liberalism 164
anti-racist organisations 160, 171
anti-social behaviour 41, 46, 141
apathetic 1
Arab Bedouins 56
Arctic Canada 60
Arctic cityscape 52
atavistic 173
Athens 9
athleticism 139
austerity 160, 164, 167
Australia 3, 8, 36, 39, 89
authority 5, 6, 158

back stage region 88, 95
Bangladeshi 16, 158, 159–60, 167
banking 5
belonging 53, 84, 158, 163, 174
Benshi 14, 109, 111

'Big Man Bias, The' 21
bilingual pupils 62
binary model 7
biological: man, sex 25, 35, 40
Birmingham 159, 161
black men 161, 171
blaming men 181
blue-collar workers 58, 60
bodies: super 148
body ideals: work 140–1, 152
bodybuilder 15, 147, 148, 151
bodybuilding 7, 139, 141, 145–8, 152
Bourdieu 62, 93, 106, 113
boy 'real' 21–7, 30–1
boyhood 12
boyness: problematic 12, 21, 26, 30–1
boys 2, 4, 12–13, 15, 21–31, 34–7, 40–1, 43–5, 53–5, 60–3, 65, 117–19, 121–30, 132–8, 149, 157, 160–2, 166–7, 176, 189, 190, 192; at risk 13, 28, 34–6, 40–5; bad 160–2; bodies 15, 23–5, 30–1, 129, 167; marginalized 12–15, 21, 27, 31, 35, 44–5, 62, 65, 117–18, 133, 135, 192; typical 12, 22–3, 25, 27, 30–1, 37; young 4, 15, 24–5, 27, 34–6, 117–19, 121–36
breadwinner 45, 54, 71–2, 149–50, 179, 180, 182–3
Bronx 56
business: executive 8, 55, 60, 109, 178–9
Butler 23, 120, 123, 134

Canada 39, 40, 60
capital: flows 10, 52–8, 60, 64, 83, 93, 97, 105–6, 122, 162
capitalism: global 8, 83, 85, 96, 98
car 5, 53, 63–4; production 5, 7, 67, 70, 96, 126, 146, 158, 167, 182, 193; car production 5

Index

care 11, 14, 22, 36, 41, 44, 55, 64, 70, 74–5, 77, 79–80, 85, 90–1, 97, 178, 180
career 54, 72, 124, 148–9
categories 2, 15, 21, 16, 37, 65, 121, 157, 159, 165, 166–7, 171–2, 184, 191; of difference 157, 159, 171–2, 184, 191; of religion 16, 165–7
chi ku 110–11
child 4, 9, 21–2, 24–5, 27, 28, 30–1, 34–5, 40, 58, 64, 108, 111–12, 150–1
child care 22, 150
childhood: education 12, 21–3, 26, 30–1, 53
China 14, 39, 103–7, 110–13
citations 120, 123
citizenship 174
civilised 62, 105; civility 62, 105
class 1, 2, 6, 8, 12, 14, 16, 22, 24–5, 27–31, 53, 55, 58–60, 67–8, 70–2, 79–80, 83–6, 97, 105–8, 111–13, 117, 119, 120–1, 124–5, 127–35, 148, 157, 159, 162–3, 167, 171, 173–4, 176–80, 182–4, 190–1; analysis 16, 113, 106, 157, 171–2, 174, 183–4; journey 16, 171–4, 176–7, 180, 183–4; position 28, 83, 97, 104, 107, 158, 171–3, 177, 179, 183–4; -related barriers 135, 180
classmates 127
clinical diagnosis 122
coal mining 5
collective 10, 22, 29, 60–1, 86, 88, 163, 165, 177, 191; ethnography 22; values 61
colonial 10, 55–7, 59, 112, 163
colonialism 58, 162
commitment 2, 8, 91, 109, 159
communities 4, 11, 51–2, 55, 60–1, 80, 88, 119, 140, 141–2, 146, 164, 167, 180, 191; of relief 88; of practice 146, 191; competence 88, 191
community 13, 15, 36, 56, 60, 85, 94–6, 119, 139–40, 141–51, 159, 161–4, 175–6; local 96, 175–6
competent child 21–2, 27–31
competitive society 15, 117, 136
compulsory heterosexuality 4
conflict 8, 9, 21, 31, 135, 141
conscience 130–1
consent 11, 52
constructions of masculinity 35, 135, 139, 149
consumption 8, 191
control 5, 6, 12, 28, 27, 29–31, 38, 45, 87, 89–90, 96, 123, 126, 131–2, 134; children: 29–31

children: controlling 29–30
corporate capitalism 8
craftsmanship 86, 91
creativity 28, 31
crime 1, 5, 36, 139, 146, 177
criminality 6
crisis 3, 12, 55, 67, 160, 180, 192; of masculinity 157, 190
critical studies of men and masculinity 3, 37, 97, 104–5
Cuba 8
cultural: discourses 13, 15, 21–2, 25, 27, 31, 35, 38, 43–5, 56, 61, 85, 97–8, 109, 151, 157–8, 160–1, 163, 166, 170, 174–5, 190; dominance 5, 26, 28, 38, 58, 157, 141, 149, 171, 184; ideals 8, 13, 15, 24, 30, 44–5, 83–4, 92–3, 97, 120–1, 140–3, 146, 150–2, 180, 189; of manhood 5, 6, 10, 15–16, 87, 146, 148–50, 189; liberation 54, 119–20, 134; norms 7, 12, 14, 21, 23–5, 28–30, 39, 42, 68, 71, 79, 80–1, 93, 104, 117, 123, 140–1, 151, 172, 191; pathology 161, 164; isolation 54, 142; privilege 4, 6, 8, 16, 53, 135, 140, 157, 172–3, 179, 189; repertoires 85, 86; strategies 110, 106, 108; symbolism 88, 97; validation 88
culture: common 15, 58, 95; shock 51, 53; street 181, 184, 189

Danish 14, 52, 53, 55–9, 61–2, 65, 86, 97, 170, 173–5, 178, 180–3; colonies 53; language 52, 53, 58, 62, 178; men 52, 58, 178; workers 57, 58, 86
de-industrialising 162
demasculinization 58
democratisation 180, 184
Denmark 3, 14, 16, 39, 52–3, 55, 57, 59, 84–6, 88, 91, 97, 117, 122, 133, 170, 173–5, 178, 179, 180–4
depression 44
de-skilled 69
detraditionalized 57
deviance 139, 193
deviant: behaviours 6
diaspora 159, 163
digital: media 141; space 8
discipline 12, 23, 26, 27, 131
discourses 13, 15, 21–2, 25, 27, 31, 35, 38, 43–5, 56, 61, 85, 97–8, 109, 151, 157–8, 160–1, 163, 166, 170, 174–5, 190; of the marginalized 21, 27, 31, 44–5, 61, 85, 97–8, 157, 158, 170; of masculinity 13,

35, 43, 44–5, 85; political 85, 157, 160, 170
discrimination 161, 165
discursive alterity 167
disempowerment 172, 176
disenchanted 1
displacement 9
disposition 84, 87–8, 119
'do-it-yourself' biography 119
dominance 5, 26, 28, 38, 58, 157, 141, 149, 171, 184
dominant 1, 3, 6, 7, 8, 11, 15, 22, 24, 36, 44, 56, 57, 62, 71, 85–6, 92, 96–8, 104, 106, 109, 111, 118, 134, 136, 140–1, 143, 145, 148–51, 160, 180, 189; cultural logic of difference 7, 104; dichotomies 11; discursive ideology 106; subject positions 11, 85, 96, 134, 140, 173
doping 15, 139, 140, 142, 146
drugs 1, 15, 139, 140–5, 150–2, 181; drug trafficking 1
drug using 15, 144, 151
dual labour market theory 72

East Berlin 56
Eastern Europe 188
eating disorders 15, 121, 133, 117
economic 3, 5, 6, 8, 9, 10, 13, 16, 29, 74, 79, 104–7, 109, 112–13, 157–8, 163–4, 167, 172, 174–5, 179, 190–1; exploitation 172; marginalisation 163; modernisation 13, 104–5, 109, 112–13, 190; prosperity 109; reforms 103–4
economy 23, 69–71, 79, 84, 98, 103, 105, 107, 110, 112, 157, 162, 167; planned 103
education system 26, 60, 120, 127
educational 5, 13, 22, 26, 31, 86, 105, 120, 125, 127, 133, 134; attainment 5; choices 125, 127; opportunity 5; performance 134
egocentric 8
Egypt 178
elderly villagers 51–2
elites 53, 59, 105, 183
emergency medical technicians (EMT) 14, 83, 84, 89, 91, 97
emotional 14, 83–9, 91–8, 108, 129, 191; alienation 83; capitalism 83, 85, 96, 98; competence 14, 84, 88–9, 98, 191; intelligence 84; make-up 84; management 87–8; reflexivity 84; skills 14, 83–6, 89, 91, 93–4, 96–7; reflexive 39, 83, 85–6, 92, 105, 106, 192

emotionality 84, 89; models of 84
emotions 21, 83–4, 87–9, 131
empire 162
employment contracts 68, 70
empowerment 105–6, 170
engineering 5, 94
English 16, 60–1, 143, 163, 164–5; nationalism 16, 163–4; working class 60, 163
epistemology 10, 68, 163, 167
Erikson: identity theory 119
erotic power 113, 182
ethnic minority men 16, 170–1, 173–4, 184; adult 16, 174, 176, 184
ethnicity 2, 5, 7, 29, 37, 57, 68, 119–21, 157–8, 161, 165, 170–5, 180–1, 183, 191–2
ethnography 15, 22, 142, 158; Feminist 22; meta 22
ethno-pharmacological 145
eunuchs 8
Europe 1, 2, 8, 65, 74, 159, 189
European Union (EU) 67, 69
European 3, 56–8, 71, 140, 163, 168, 183, 192
evidence-based practice (EBP) 34, 39, 40
expectations, social 13, 15, 38, 58, 107, 110, 140, 191

family 3, 13, 28, 29, 42, 44, 53, 54, 60–1, 64, 88–9, 95, 105–11, 113, 122–3, 125, 127, 131, 150, 159, 161, 165, 174–5, 179, 180, 183–4, 188–9, 191; studies 3, 88; values 54, 107, 113
Far Right 1
fatherhood 2, 3, 38, 45, 83, 150, 151
fathers 38, 45, 55, 60, 65, 107–8, 111–12, 166–7, 184; absent 45; bad 38; responsible 15, 150–1
fear 15, 52, 56, 62–3, 96, 117–18, 121, 123–4, 129, 133, 135–6, 158, 164–5, 182
female 2, 4, 11, 25, 26–7, 38, 54, 58, 67, 70, 72–3, 79, 87, 91, 93, 105, 109, 121, 165, 167, 178, 179; masculinities 2; work 67, 70, 79
feminine 14, 25, 27, 67, 68, 70–2, 80, 84; categorizations 27; coded service sector 67, 70–2; skills 14, 67, 72
femininities 4, 157
femininity 4, 9, 25, 86–7, 167
feminists 1, 2, 37, 171
feminization 5, 26, 106; Asian young men 16; of work 106

feminized care work 87
fight 129
filial piety 111, 113; son 111
Filipino seafarer 8
Finland 39
fishermen 59
fishing 53
fitness 139
flashback 15, 142, 143, 148, 150, 140, 144–6
flexible working 84, 180
flirting 12
folk devils 160–2
food market 53
Fordist organisation 163
Foucault 23–4, 151, 120, 126
fragmentation: society 5, 132, 167, 189; family 189
fraternity 61
freedom 13, 51, 53, 60, 105, 119, 121, 127, 142, 151
friendship 28
front-line service work 84
further education 122, 148, 159

gambling 64
gaze, the 12, 23–5, 29, 30–1
gender 1–10, 12–14, 16, 21–3, 26–31, 34–46, 52, 54, 57–8, 65, 67–72, 75, 79, 80–1, 85–7, 91, 97, 105–13, 117, 119–23, 135, 139, 140–3, 146, 157, 161, 165, 167, 170–7, 180, 182–4, 188–92; assumptions 35, 170; borders 27; coding 71–2, 80–1; didactic notions of discourses 10; egalitarian 87, 91; equal society 1, 3, 146, 188; equality 1–3, 5, 22, 25–6, 30–1, 97, 140, 143, 146, 167, 170, 174, 188; hierarchies 9, 171, 191; politics 113, 161; practice 85–6, 107, 140, 161; relations 57, 173, 176, 180, 184; roles dislocation 106; specific treatments 38, 44; stereotypes 166–7; static variable 34–5, 40
gendered 11, 14, 22–5, 27, 44–5, 72, 80, 84, 96, 98, 103, 107, 113, 123, 126, 142, 158, 161–2, 167, 171, 179, 191; boundaries 25, 123; expectations 23–4, 27; nature of research 11; scripts 96; subjectivities 107
generational specificities 110
genetic max 146–8
ghettoization 189
global: economy 103, 112; hegemonic position 8; North 8–9, 103, 159, 164; South 8, 52, 112; surveillance 158, 164; transformations 163
globalization: marginal masculinities 112–13; Western models of 113
Gothenburg 74, 77–80
grandfathers 65, 184, 108; parents 65, 184, 108
Greece 9
Greenland 10, 13, 51–65, 192
Greenlandic culture 51–2, 61–3, 65
Guangdong 103
gym 139, 143, 147–8, 151

health 5, 8, 36, 71, 130, 139, 140, 145–6, 151, 158, 190; poor access 5
hegemonic 2–4, 7–8, 13–16, 21–3, 25, 27, 35, 40, 42, 45, 58, 85, 91, 118, 139, 140–1, 144, 151, 157, 163, 171–4, 181, 189; masculine position 58, 85, 91, 173; masculinities 2, 8, 118, 157; masculinity 3–4, 6, 8, 22–3, 25, 40, 85, 118, 140–1, 171, 173–4, 184, 189
hegemonies 8, 2; marginalized 8, 21; within marginality 8, 21, 192
heteronormative cultural context 108
heteronormativity 4, 95, 108, 113
heterosexual 11, 121, 149
hierarchic power 171
high skill jobs 70, 79
high touch sector 14, 70, 72, 74–5, 79–80
high-tech jobs 70
Hijab 165
hip-hop masculinity 64
hockey 27
homophobia 4, 139
homosexual 171
homosociality 3
honour 55, 57, 61, 91
hormones 147
host country 9
hotel 5, 14, 59, 70, 72–80; industry 80; sector 72–5, 77, 79–80
household registration system 104
housework 22
housing 5, 53, 158, 175; provision 5; poor conditions 5
Hukou 104
humour 91–2
hunter 13, 51–5, 60–2, 65
hunting 51–5, 59–63
husbands 55, 60, 107
hybridity 190
hyper-masculinity 139, 141, 149, 151–2, 164

hyper-sexual black body 8
hyper-sexualized 8

ICT 70, 79
ideal pupils 21
identifications 1, 7, 8, 122–3, 128, 133, 164, 190
identities 4, 7, 13, 15, 22, 55, 59, 62, 64–5, 71, 84, 86–8, 105–6, 108, 112–13, 126, 140–1, 158, 163, 167, 172, 174, 177, 183–4, 190–2; complex 172
identity 3–4, 7, 11–13, 16, 40, 43–4, 52–4, 56, 64, 70–1, 86–7, 91, 93, 97, 104–8, 112–13, 119, 126–7, 129, 133–5, 139, 141, 143, 149, 151, 158, 160, 162–3, 165, 173, 176, 178–9, 180–3, 189–90, 192; crisis 3, 160, 179, 190, 192; formations of 86, 93, 105, 107, 113, 119, 173, 190; negotiation 13, 52, 107, 113
imagined cultures 62, 161; geography 175
immigrants 72, 80, 175, 186
imperfect self 119, 124, 128, 129
inclusion 5, 29, 31, 44, 117, 126, 129, 133, 157, 158, 163
India 8
indictable offences 36
individual reflexivity 105
individualized 15, 61, 105, 117–18, 120–1, 126, 135–6; empowerment 105; society 15, 117, 120, 135–6
industrial 14, 59, 67, 69, 70, 80, 83–4, 98, 157, 191; economy 67, 70, 84, 98; habitus 14, 67, 80, 83, 84; society 59, 83
Industry professions 69
inequalities 7, 52, 62, 79, 120, 157–8, 164, 167, 171, 191
informal workers 103
informants 29, 30, 123, 132, 176, 184
institutional monitoring 158
institutions 7, 22, 62, 122, 158, 106, 161, 163, 165–7, 172, 185
intergenerational gendered practices 108
internal migration 14, 104
internet community 15, 150–1
intersectional 1, 16, 29, 170–2, 179, 182–4; analysis 16, 172, 184; perspective; 1, 170–1, 179, 182
intersectionality 16, 171–2; theory 172
inner subjectivity 123
intimate relations 105
Inuit 13, 51–3, 55–8, 60, 65
Islam 161–2, 164, 166

job security 72
Jutland 174–5

Khat 176
kissing 25
knowledge economy 67, 79
Kurdish 175
Kurdistan 174

labour market 4, 9, 14, 61, 68–72, 74, 79–81, 88, 157, 176–8, 180–4, 190–1; exclusion 14, 68, 72, 80; marginality 176–8, 183; racism 178, 180–4; transitions 14, 67, 69–72, 79–81, 103, 190
lack of masculinity 37
laoxiang network 110
late modern society 67, 105, 112–13, 135
Latin America 8
learning disabilities 11
Levant 9
life 1, 13, 23, 29, 34, 36, 44, 51–5, 59–61, 63–5, 71, 87–8, 92, 95–7, 107–9, 111, 113, 119, 120, 122–4, 127–31, 141, 148, 150, 159, 174–6, 182, 184, 189; choices 105, 120, 123–4; histories 107, 109; phases 123
liquid modernity 192
loathing 62, 121
London 159, 164
loneliness 15, 105, 122, 133
low quality service jobs 14, 69, 70
low skill jobs 14, 67, 70, 74–5, 77, 79–80, 178
low wages 70, 72, 108
loyalty 8

MacJobs 70
McJobs 69–70
mainstream society 5, 15, 117, 129, 141, 143, 146
male 4–5, 9–12, 14, 23–6, 35–6, 38, 40, 43, 45, 53–4, 58, 60, 70–4, 84–1, 93, 95–8, 103–5, 107–8, 112, 121, 141, 158, 160, 162, 167, 170, 172–3, 176–7, 178, 180, 182–4; dominance 5, 38, 58, 184; dominated 14, 58, 60, 84, 91, 96; occupations 5, 67, 71–4, 87; marginalized 2, 9, 10, 14, 38, 45, 67, 79, 87–8, 96–8, 103, 105–7, 170, 183, 184; role models 25–6, 35, 40, 167; sexuality 38, 71, 87, 172; subjectivities 9, 11, 85, 106–7, 158; troubled 177, 183–4

Malmo 10, 74, 77–80
man 1, 3–6, 9, 13, 15, 21, 23, 252–6, 34, 40–5, 51, 54, 55, 60, 63–5, 75, 92, 98, 107, 109, 110–11, 121, 127, 129, 133, 145, 148, 150–1, 161–2, 166–7, 171–2, 178–9, 181, 189, 190–1; employable 15, 151
management techniques 83
managers 83
manhood 5–6, 10, 15–16, 53, 87, 139, 146, 148–50, 189; codifications 16; discourses 15, 151; new 87, 139, 147
manufacturing work 162, 189
marginal 3, 6, 7–8, 11, 140–1, 143–5, 157, 159, 189–91; hegemonies 8, 21; land 134; spaces 4, 163, 167
marginality 2, 7–11, 21, 111–12, 107, 158, 162, 173–4, 176–8, 183, 189–93
marginalized 2, 6, 9, 10, 14, 38, 45, 67, 79, 87–8, 96–8, 103, 105–7, 170, 183–4; men 3, 62, 103, 110, 112, 157; position 16, 35, 39, 42, 44, 86, 107, 163, 184
margins 5, 7, 139, 183, 189; of society 139, 183
marijuana 63–4
market economy 103, 105, 110
marriage 108–9, 176
masculine 8–9, 11, 15, 24–5, 27, 43–5, 58, 67–71, 79–80, 84–8, 91, 93, 96–7, 107–8, 112–13, 139, 146, 147, 149, 150–2, 160, 162, 166, 173, 177–8, 180, 182, 191; coded 67, 69, 71, 79; ideals 8, 15, 24, 44–5, 151–2, 180; identity 44, 107–8, 112, 139, 149, 173, 178, 182; risk 166; stereotype 139, 149, 160, 166; subjectivities 9, 11, 85, 107; values 107, 113, 139, 151; work 67, 68, 70–1, 80
masculinities 2, 8, 118, 157; alternative 36, 58; complicit 171; constructional 35, 136, 139, 149; conventional dominant 86, 97, 98; marginalized 1–3, 6–7, 10, 14, 23, 34, 65, 67, 80, 96, 98, 103, 151, 157, 158, 171, 182–4, 192; old 14, 80; protest 6, 141, 151–2; 'real' 13; redundant 79; respectable 190; subordinate 3, 23, 27, 118, 136, 171, 173
masculinity 1–13, 15–16, 21–7, 31, 34, 36–46, 52, 54–5, 57–8, 61, 64, 67, 71, 80, 83, 85–9, 96–7, 104–7, 110, 112, 118, 123, 135, 139, 140–1, 150–2, 158, 141–3, 146–9, 160–1, 164–7, 171–4, 177–8, 180, 183–4, 189–93; deconstructing 43; dominant 15, 36, 58, 96, 97, 118, 140–1, 148, 150; heroic saviour model of 89; idealized 15, 21, 31, 141, 143, 151; muscular 7, 15, 30, 141, 144, 146, 148, 149; Muslim 15, 16, 31, 157, 158, 160–1, 164–7, 174; native 58; outdated 139; performance orientated 148; protest 6, 141, 151–2; sexualized 25; transgressive 130, 136, 151; transnational business 8; Westernized versions of 8
materialist position 157
maturity 146
media 1, 5, 9, 56, 97, 104, 106, 140–1, 151, 157–61, 165–6, 170, 174–5, 181–2, 188, 190; discourses 157, 160–1, 170; narratives 1, 56; representations 151, 188
medical discourse 145
memory 55, 63
men 1–10, 12–13, 15–16, 22, 26–7, 30–1, 35–43, 45–6, 49, 51–62, 65–73, 75–9, 83–05, 87–8, 93, 96–8, 104–5, 107–8, 110, 112–13, 132, 139, 142, 144, 146, 149, 157–65, 167, 170–84, 188–92; emancipation of 35; ethnic minority 16, 161, 170–1, 173, 175–84; migrant 9, 58, 103–13, 183–4; narratives 14, 103, 108–9, 113, 159; needs 1, 46; new 9, 71, 97, 112; non-proper 161; power 1, 6, 27, 38–9, 42, 52, 55, 57, 59, 113, 171–2, 182, 192; 'real' 9, 23, 31, 58, 180; sensitive 10, 83, 91, 97, 113, 143, 182; subordinated 3, 23, 27, 35, 107, 171, 173; unskilled 57, 69, 61, 183; violent 6, 9, 30, 31, 36, 43, 146, 166, 181; young 3, 36, 52, 54, 56, 59, 60, 62, 65, 70–3, 75, 109, 110–11, 139, 157–67, 177, 181, 190–1
men's work 13, 170; casualization 5
mental disability 5
mental health 8
methodology 10, 68, 121, 174
middle class 8, 29, 84, 106, 112, 124, 125, 127–31, 171–2; family 29, 131; nuclear family 29
migrant workers 14, 103, 104–7, 111–13, 189
Mirpuri 167
misogyny 1
mobility 67, 110, 112, 173, 180, 183; upward 110, 173
modern 3, 51, 53–5, 57–9, 61–4, 67, 80, 105, 109, 110, 112, 126, 135, 141, 163, 165–6, 189–91; masculinity 64, 190; society 55, 59, 62, 67, 112, 119

modernity theory 119–20, 126, 134
modernization 13, 14, 52, 56, 103–5, 109–13, 190; project 56, 105, 112
moral panic 26
mortality 36, 37, 44
mother tongue 30
mothers 29–30, 38, 64, 89, 150; single 29
multicultural urban environments 54
multiculturalism 170
multi-dimensional analysis 96, 172
muscular masculinity 7, 15, 146, 148–9, 151–2
Muslim masculinity 157–8, 165
Muslim 15–16, 29–31, 157–67, 174, 176; boys 29–31, 157, 161, 166–7, 176; community 159, 163; countries 29; men 16, 157–61, 164–7

name-calling 27
national curriculum 25
national security 158
native masculinity 58
nengli 110, 113
neoliberal 105, 111–13, 146; ideology 111–13, 146; subject 104–6, 111–12, 158
neoliberalism 104, 106, 113, 119
netnography 142
New York City 56
New Zealand 39
Newcastle 159
Nigeria 174
Niqab 165
non-equality oriented forms of masculinity 174
non-normative citations 120, 123
non-proper men 111, 161
Nordic 1, 22, 59, 74, 77, 80, 119–20, 133, 142, 168; countries 74, 77, 80, 142, 188; welfare states 119, 133; youth research 119, 120
normalization 6, 28, 150, 151; families 28
normalizing gaze 23
normative 7, 14, 16, 67, 68, 71, 86, 93–4, 96, 108, 120–3, 134–5, 139, 191–2; citations 120, 123; exclusion 14, 67, 68, 71; identity 7
norms 7, 12, 14, 21, 23–5, 28–30, 39, 42, 68, 71, 79, 80–1, 93, 104, 117, 123, 140–1, 151, 172, 191; masculinity 12, 23–4, 42, 123; reciprocity 95–6
North Africa 9
North America 8, 159
Northern Jutland 174–5

Norway 3
Norwegian studies 173
nursing 73, 74, 87
nutrition 147
Nuuk 52–65

occidental 163
occupations 3, 5, 67–9, 71–4, 87, 191
official statistics 35
old masculinities 14, 80
older men 4, 5, 88, 139, 189
online communities 139–42
online forum 140–2
Orientalist discourse 161
other: racialized 160, 163, 172–3, 182
otherness 7, 14, 103, 163
others: dysfunctional 59, 104
'outcasts' 6, 140

Pakistani 8, 16, 158, 159, 160, 167
Palestinian 175
panoptic gaze 23–5
Paradigm wars 10
paramedic 87, 93, 95
parent–child relations 112, 124
partners 107, 123
patients 88, 90–4, 97
patriarchal 107, 157, 161, 167, 170–1, 173, 180, 184, 189; dividend 171; gender order 171, 180
patriarchy 18; dividend 171; fathers 167
peasant workers 104, 107
peer group 12–13, 27, 76, 167
pensioners 74
perfect normality 124, 128, 129, 133
performance enhancing drugs (PED) 139–40, 142–51
performance orientated masculinity 148
personal services 70
physical 5, 13, 26, 55, 58, 92, 95, 130, 134, 139, 147, 151, 189; appearance competence 55, 58, 130, 134, 151; disability 5
play 12, 13, 15, 21–2, 24–5, 27–8, 30–1, 63, 80, 90, 108, 110, 149–50, 164, 177, 179
playfulness 31
playground 25, 162, 165
plural sexualities 167
polar bear 51–2
political 1–2, 8, 59, 85, 146, 157, 160, 170, 188, 193; discourse 85, 157, 160, 170; executives 8
post masculinity 158

post-secondary school 74
postcolonial 37, 39, 65, 158, 163, 167
post-colonialism 163, 165, 173, 192
post-industrial 83, 84, 98; economy 84, 98; service economy 84
post-modern 191
post-structuralism 117, 126
post-structuralist 113, 120, 123, 134
poverty 5, 8–9, 57, 104, 189
power 1, 2, 5–6, 13, 23, 25, 36–9, 42, 44–6, 52, 55, 57–9, 68, 104, 106, 112–13, 120, 126–7, 147, 157, 162, 165, 171–3, 178–9, 182–3, 189; zero-sum notion of 5
preschool 12, 21–2, 24–31; classes 12, 22, 24–8, 30–1; teachers 21, 26, 28–31
primary sector 72
privileged classes 53
processes 7–8, 10, 16, 24, 96, 112, 119, 120–1, 126, 130–1, 133, 140, 151, 161, 163, 165, 167, 170–3, 176, 180–2, 184, 189
protest masculinities 6, 141, 151–2
protest masculinity 6, 141, 151–2
public 6, 14–15, 25, 30, 52, 55, 61, 97, 104, 106, 110–11, 139, 159, 161, 164, 167, 174, 176, 177, 182, 184; anxiety 104; school 55; sphere 25

Qaqortoq 64
qualitative 15, 86, 107, 112, 121, 174; interviews 121, 15, 86, 174; research 107, 112
questionnaires 134

race 2, 5, 7, 16, 157, 160, 167, 171–2, 184; relations 160
racialised other 160, 162–3, 165
racism 174, 175, 178, 180–4
radicalization 27, 166
randomised studies 39
rape 39
rapping 63
rationality 101
'real boy' 21–6, 30
'real' men 23, 25, 31
reciprocity 95, 96
redundancy 14, 67, 70, 79, 84
redundant masculinities 70, 79
reflexive modernisation 105
reflexivity 1, 2, 12, 22, 84, 105, 106
refugees 9, 173, 181–2
relationality 4, 85, 108, 173, 190
religion 16, 30, 158, 161, 165–7, 191

religious extremism 1
representations 14, 151, 165, 176, 188, 189
re-settlement 56, 63
resistance 23, 45, 60
re-socialization 132, 144
respectability 106, 108
respectable masculinities 190
responsible father 15, 112, 150–1
restaurant industry 80
retail sector 14, 70–3, 75, 79
risk 3, 12–13, 28, 34–46, 52, 54, 64, 71, 84, 86, 94–7, 120, 129, 130, 134, 139, 145–6, 149, 150, 158, 166, 177, 189, 192
rite of passage 53, 147
role models 25–6, 35, 40, 166–7; same-sex 40
rowdiness 25–6
rural 13–14, 52–3, 58, 63, 74–5, 77–80, 103–13, 191; men's narratives 14, 103, 109, 113; urban migration 14, 52, 80, 103, 104, 112–13

safety 15, 28, 86, 94–5
Scandinavian 87, 97, 119, 120, 173–4; context 87, 97, 173–4; societies 119–20
scientific knowledge 39, 83, 119, 148
secondary school 55, 58, 74, 159, 166
secondary sector 72, 75
self 4, 9, 14–15, 23, 27–8, 31, 54–6, 60, 63, 67, 68, 71, 79, 80, 88, 86, 91, 97, 104, 106, 109, 111, 113, 117, 119, 120–7, 129, 130–6, 140–1, 147, 150, 158, 165, 180, 191; aestheticsation 133; authorisation 158, 165; conflict 9, 43, 135, 141; construction 117–24, 126–8, 132–6; control 27–8, 131–4; determination 118, 136; discipline 27, 105, 120, 130–1; enterprising activities 104; exclusion 14, 67–8, 71, 80, 118; harming 15, 122, 132; identity 97, 104, 106, 113, 119; optimization 120, 131–4; promotion 121; repression 131, 134; responsibility 113; surveillance 35, 158
self-help culture 140
semi-structured interviews 55, 122, 174
sensitive men 83, 143, 182
service economy 70, 79, 84, 162
service sector 14, 67, 68, 70, 72, 74, 79–80; economy 67, 69, 70–1, 79, 162; industries 5, 70; jobs 14, 67, 69–70, 74, 79–80
service work 14, 36, 67, 84, 86, 91, 190
sex offenders 36

sexual 8, 12, 121, 148–9, 161, 171, 189; dominance 38; innuendo 12; virility 141, 148, 149
sexuality 2, 3, 7, 38, 71, 87, 105, 119–20, 165, 171–2
sexualized masculinity 25
shanghai 103
ship building 5
shopping 53
siblings 64, 127–8, 133–4
single mothers 29
sociability 88, 94, 95
social 1–3, 5–16, 22–3, 31, 34–46, 52–65, 68, 70–1, 80, 84–5, 88, 90–1, 94–6, 103–7, 110–18, 120, 122, 125, 135, 140–1, 145, 157–60, 162–7, 170–2, 174–8, 180–4, 189–92; actors 85; agricultural registrations 104; awareness 90; categories 2, 15–16, 157, 172; cohesion 96, 158; differentiation 172; exclusion 5, 14, 25, 118; inequalities 62, 157, 158; invisibility 176, 183; justice 103, 191; marginalization 5, 15, 96, 104; marginality 173, 183; mobility 110, 180; policy 170, 183; problems 35, 36, 40, 43, 45, 170, 176–7, 182–3, 189; skills 94; status of men 88, 107, 182; unrest 1, 181; vulnerability 35–6, 42–3, 118, 136; welfare 5; work 13, 34–46, 176–8, 181, 183
social power 157; additive model 157
socialization 3, 12
socio-economic changes 13, 105, 158, 191
socio-emotional 14, 83–4, 86, 88–9, 91, 93–4, 96–8; competence 14, 84, 88–9, 97–8, 191; habitus 83–4, 97–8
Somali 174–6, 179, 181, 183
Somalia 174, 179
sons 60, 61, 107–8
South Africa 8
sports 30; activities 30
Sri Lanka 174
state 3, 6, 7, 10, 15, 39, 40, 55, 59, 97, 104–5, 119, 126–7, 130, 133, 143, 146, 158, 160–1, 164–6, 178; sanctioned marginalisation 158, 167
status 5, 7, 11–12, 23, 25, 27–8, 31, 54, 62, 65, 68, 74, 88, 107, 174, 176–80, 182–3, 191; loss of 177–80
stereotype 21, 25, 30–1, 52, 62, 139, 149, 160, 162, 166–7; hunter 52, 62
steroids 144–7, 149, 150
stigmatization 94, 191
Stockholm 74, 77–80

stranger 53, 56, 57, 177, 182
stratification 83
street cultures 181, 184
structuralist theories 134
sub-cultural practices 150–1
subculture 15, 140–1, 152, 184, 192
subject 5, 9, 11, 13–15, 23, 25, 43–4, 46, 61, 85, 96, 104–6, 109–12, 120–3, 126, 129, 133–4, 140, 143–5, 158–60, 163, 173, 175, 190, 192; positions 14, 46, 85, 96, 120, 126, 129, 133, 158–9, 173; gendered 107; racialized 160, 163; sexualized 126
subjectification 8, 106, 123
subjectivities 8–9, 11, 85, 106–8, 158; emerging 108, 158
subjugation 127
subordinate masculinities 3, 6, 118, 136, 171, 173
subordinated men 3, 27
Sudan 174, 178, 182
suicide 36, 44, 51, 56, 63–4, 92
super bodies 148
surplus labour 104
survey 55, 71, 74, 122, 163, 174
Sweden 3, 14, 22, 30, 31, 35, 36, 37, 38, 39, 40, 67, 69, 70, 71, 72, 73, 74, 75, 79, 80, 86, 140, 172, 188
Swedish language 29
symbolic 5, 13–14, 57, 88, 90, 93, 96–8, 103, 108, 140, 143, 146, 165, 173, 190; boundaries 90, 93, 165, 190; otherness 14, 103
symbolic language 140, 143, 146
Syria 174, 180
systems of signification 7, 8

teachers 12, 21, 25–31, 55, 62, 162–7
terrorist 15, 160, 162, 165; recruitment 15, 160
testosterone 146, 149
therapeutic culture 83, 98
third generation 158
third industrial revolution 67
toughness 13
tourism 178
traditional 11, 13–14, 22, 27, 40, 52, 54, 60–2, 80, 86, 96, 106–11, 113, 118, 162–3, 166–7, 177, 180, 189; craftsmanship 86; family values 54, 111, 113, 119; manufacturing work 162, 198
training 84, 87, 91, 128, 144, 147, 150–1
transnational business masculinity 8
transformation of the self 104–5

transgressive masculinity 130, 136, 151
transition to adulthood 64
transnational flows 8–9
transnational marginal masculinity 8–9
trust 10, 88, 94–5
Turkey 174, 176, 187

UK 39–40, 71, 164
underemployment 163
underprivileged 16, 56, 72, 80; neighbourhood 56, 174, 175, 183
unemployable 14, 67
unemployment 2, 10, 13, 69, 72, 175, 183, 187, 192
United States 3, 36, 39
unskilled men 57, 61, 69, 183
urban 13–14, 51–61, 64, 74–5, 77–80, 103, 104–5, 107–10, 112–13, 167, 188, 190–1; China 103, 105, 107, 113; citizen 51, 53; community 13; desire 105, 110
urbanization 13, 65, 80
urbanized society 59
US military 44

verbal harassment 27
victim 38, 42, 44, 59, 136
violence 3, 4, 26, 28, 31, 36, 38, 42–5, 56, 139, 163, 188
violent extremism 164
vocational courses 124
vulnerability 35–6, 42–3, 118, 136

welfare state 39, 59, 119, 133

well-being 15, 117–19, 121–4, 133, 135; lack of 15, 117–18, 121–3, 133, 135
West 2, 5, 6, 10, 60, 61, 65, 98, 103, 105, 106, 113, 119, 163, 170–1, 182
West Midlands 60
white 2, 8, 57, 58, 70, 106, 127, 157, 161–3, 165, 167, 171, 173, 182; supremacy 58
whiteness 2, 58, 173
Willis, Paul 60
willpower 131–2
women 1, 4, 6, 8, 9, 13–14, 22–3, 30–1, 36, 38, 41–2, 45, 52, 54, 55–8, 60, 67, 68, 70, 72, 73–80, 84, 106, 110, 141, 148–9, 160, 165, 170–80, 183, 188–91; ethnic minority 170–1, 173–80, 183, 184
women's employment 14, 73, 79
working class 6, 14, 60, 67, 70–2, 79–80, 84–5, 105–8, 112, 132, 135, 157, 159, 163, 174, 178; identity 70–1, 105–6; woman 106, 178
working conditions 2, 29, 68, 70, 107–8, 112, 158, 163; poor 70, 106
workless 190
world market 59, 67, 69

youth 5, 13, 41, 55, 62, 63, 72, 80, 110, 118–19, 120–1, 123, 126–7, 130, 134–5, 159–60, 178; research 55, 110, 118–19, 120–1, 135; studies 119–21; transitions 13; workers 55

Zhejiang 103

Manufactured by Amazon.ca
Bolton, ON

37873148R00120